ELECTORAL LAWS AND THE SURVIVAL OF PRESIDENTIAL DEMOCRACIES

A Title from the Helen Kellogg Institute
for International Studies

ELECTORAL LAWS AND THE SURVIVAL OF PRESIDENTIAL DEMOCRACIES

Mark P. Jones

UNIVERSITY OF NOTRE DAME PRESS

Notre Dame   London

Library of Congress Cataloging-in-Publication-Data

Electoral laws and the survival of presidential democracies / by Mark
P. Jones.
   p.   cm.
   Includes bibliographical references and index.
   ISBN 0-268-00933-3 (hard)
   1. Presidents—Election. 2. Political parties—Law and
legislation. 3. Representative government and representation.
4. Democracy. 5. Presidents—Latin America—Election. I. Jones,
Mark P., 1967– .
K3300.E43 1995
324.6'3'098—dc20   95-9149
                                        CIP

FOR RUTH S. JONES AND E. TERRENCE JONES

Contents

Acknowledgments

The goal of this book is to make the relationship between specific electoral laws and the effective functioning and survival of presidential democracy completely transparent. Its conclusion is that presidential systems with certain electoral law characteristics provide a viable form of democratic government, and therefore a realistic democratic alternative to a parliamentary system.

Many thanks are owed to the large number of people who helped aid the progress of this project from an initial idea to a completed book. At the University of Michigan Chris Achen, Ronald Inglehart, and Daniel Levine provided crucial intellectual guidance and support. All supplied many helpful suggestions and comments along with much needed encouragement as did Scott Mainwaring. Thanks are also due to James Langford and Carole Roos at the University of Notre Dame Press for their helpful assistance in the editorial process. An intellectual debt is owed to Arend Lijphart whose work initially led me to the study of democratic institutions and electoral systems and whose assistance and encouragement have aided my development as a scholar.

During the course of my research in Argentina I accumulated numerous debts. María Teresa Pianzola and Carlos Martínez of the Legislative Reference Division of the Biblioteca del Congreso de la Nación provided helpful assistance during my research of the Argentine legislative process. Marta Valle of the Departamento de Estadísticas de la Dirección Nacional Electoral and her staff made a tremendous contribution through their aid in the compilation of the Argentine provincial electoral data set. A final debt of gratitude is owed to Enrique Zuleta Puceiro in particular as well as to the many other Argentine scholars who provided insights and assistance which aided both my research in Argentina as well as my understanding of electoral systems.

My most profound level of gratitude is reserved for my family/ colleagues: E. Terrence Jones, Ruth S. Jones, and Warren E. Miller. All read numerous drafts of this work and provided truly immeasurable assistance in the form of comments, suggestions, and moral support.

1

Introduction—Legislative Support and Presidential Systems

In recent years presidentialism has been sharply criticized by the academic community (e.g., Lamounier 1989; Lijphart 1984; Linz 1994; Valenzuela 1993) with few voices raised in its defense (e.g., Shugart and Carey 1992). Despite the generally negative opinion held by scholars toward the presidential form of democratic government, presidentialism currently enjoys widespread popularity throughout the world.[1] Extending from its traditional western hemispheric stronghold in the United States and Latin America, presidentialism is the current constitutional system of choice in many African (e.g., Namibia, Zambia, Zimbabwe) and Asian (e.g., Kyrgyzstan, Philippines, South Korea) democratizing nations.

This book has two interdependent parts. It first uses a review of the relevant literature and a multi-tiered set of empirical analyses to demonstrate the importance of a strong presidential legislative contingent for the successful functioning of democratic presidential government. It then utilizes examples and data from Latin America to examine the relationship between four key electoral rules and the relative propensity of a system to provide the president with sufficient partisan support in the legislature.

The book addresses the conditions necessary for the successful functioning and in many cases the survival of democratic presidential systems. The argument presented here is that the electoral laws employed by democratic presidential systems are intricately linked to the prosperity and often the longevity of democratic government in these systems. Presidential systems that consistently fail to provide the president with adequate legislative support are inherently unstable and ineffective. Such systems may be able to muddle along, performing at a sub-optimal level for a short period of time, but eventually the strains imposed by the continuing absence of a strong presidential legislative contingent and the resulting inability of the government to govern will take their toll.

The presidential versus parliamentary debate has focused on the flaws and failures of presidentialism, framing the debate as a choice between a presidential or parliamentary form of democratic government. Yet presidentialism remains quite popular in many nations, where the level of support for the parliamentary option is often quite low. As of January 1995 there were over thirty democratic or emerging democratic presidential systems in the world (as well as over twenty premier-presidential systems). If these systems are to maintain their democratic status into the twenty-first century they need to provide their presidents with legislative majorities or near-majorities on a relatively consistent basis. If these systems fail, they will in most cases lapse into dictatorship, not democratic parliamentary rule. The success of the current third wave of democracy is thus interlinked with the survival of the world's democratic presidential (and premier-presidential) systems. The survival of the Latin American presidential democracies is of added importance for the United States. Regional economic integration via a hemispheric free trade zone (i.e., a Free Trade Area of the Americas) will not be viable if a large number of the potential member states are not democracies.

Thus the debate in which we should be engaged is not democratic presidential versus democratic parliamentary government, but rather democratic presidential government versus dictatorship/quasi-dictatorship.[2] The protection and enhancement of democracies and emerging democracies in much of the developing world today is not greatly aided by a literature which only highlights the flaws of presidential government. What is needed instead is systematic analysis of arrangements and methods which can be utilized to increase the effectiveness and the probability of survival of democratic presidential government.

One way to enhance presidential systems is by modifying the

constitutional rules that govern power relations in the political system.[3] Another prominent way to enhance the effectiveness and stability of presidential systems is through the design of the systems' electoral laws. Such electoral engineering will not guarantee success in all cases, but it often can work. The normative position is that it is far better to enhance the democratic systems which currently exist than to critique presidentialism, praise parliamentarism, and then acquiesce to the failure of democratic presidential systems as inevitable.

Electoral laws alone do not make or break a democratic system. They do however have a significant impact on its functioning. Whether or not democracy survives in many of these nations will depend in part on the electoral laws employed. The pages that follow present evidence that certain electoral laws are more compatible with the successful functioning of democratic presidential systems than others.

PERILS OF PRESIDENTIALISM

Critics of the presidential form of government tend to highlight three flaws of presidentialism: temporal rigidity, majoritarianism, and dual democratic legitimacy (Shugart and Carey 1992).[4] These first two purported weaknesses (fixed-length presidential/legislative terms and winner-take-all executive elections) are inherent traits of presidentialism and in some respects can be considered virtues since they enhance accountability and identifiability.[5] The third criticism, dual democratic legitimacy, while theoretically a virtue, in reality represents the most serious deficiency of the presidential form of government. In presidential (as well as premier-presidential) systems dual democratic legitimacies are potentially a very serious threat to governmental effectiveness and in many instances to the survival of democracy.[6] Riggs (1988, 253) considers the problem of dual legitimacies to be "the most critical contradiction found in a presidentialist regime."

The problem of dual democratic legitimacies in presidential systems arises from the separate popular election of the presidential and legislative branches of government. While latent in all presidential

systems, it generally only represents a serious problem when different political parties control the presidency and the legislature, or
more explicitly when the president's party lacks a majority or near
majority of the seats in the legislature (i.e., divided government).[7]
The tendency of a constitutional system to provide its president
with robust partisan support in the legislature is quite important.
Many factors influence this tendency but the most prominent are
a system's electoral laws. Both indirectly through their influence
on the number of parties in the legislature and directly through
their impact on the degree of linkage between the presidential and
legislative elections, electoral laws represent the most important
determinant of the tendency of a system to supply the president
with sufficient support in the legislature.

PRESIDENTIAL LEGISLATIVE SUPPORT

Strong presidential support in the legislature is vital for the success
of democratic presidential government. While the president's position is strongest when the presidential party has an absolute majority
of the seats in the legislature, there are other levels of support
below this threshold that are compatible with successful presidential
government. Such would be the case in a situation (referred to in
the text as a near-majority) where the presidential party is both the
largest legislative party (in both chambers in bicameral systems) and
is not exceptionally far from a legislative majority (i.e., with 45%
or more of the legislative seats). In this type of situation the president
is normally able to either obtain minor party support or the support
of dissidents from the other major party or parties.

Presidential systems which regularly provide the executive with
a legislative majority or near-majority are likely to be far more
effective and long-lived than systems which generally deprive the
president of a legislative majority or near-majority (Mainwaring
1993; Sabsay 1991; Stepan and Skach 1993). Divided government
leading to consensual government is a theoretical possibility. Yet,
the reality in virtually all presidential systems has been that, to the
extent to which the president is deprived of a legislative majority
or near-majority, government is rendered less effective. In situations

of divided government, the president's ability to govern is often blocked, at times forcing the executive to utilize extra-constitutional methods to implement policies. These situations reduce the stability and effectiveness of the government, undermine the democratic system, and in places lead to the breakdown of democracy. With one exception (Chile, prior to 1973) the few examples of long-standing democratic presidential (Colombia, Costa Rica, United States, Venezuela, and prior to 1973, Uruguay) and premier-presidential (France) government have on average provided their presidents with a legislative majority or near-majority.[8]

Shugart and Carey (1992) have pointed out that legislatures are much more powerful vis-à-vis the executive in presidential systems than one would expect based on the conventional wisdom espoused by Latin Americanists of "strong presidents and weak legislatures" (e.g., Veliz 1980; Wiarda and Kline 1990). This traditional viewpoint of weak and pliant legislatures is difficult to reconcile with present-day reality in Latin America. The vitality of legislatures and their ability to check the president should be apparent to anyone familiar with recent events in nations such as Brazil, Ecuador, Uruguay, and Venezuela. Once this prominence of legislatures is realized, the issue of presidential legislative support becomes far more salient. In Chapter Two the relevance of the level of this support is demonstrated employing evidence from the theoretical literature on constitutional systems, the American literature on divided government, as well as from the case study literature on the functioning of the political systems of the nations included in this study. This overview, combined with the empirical support provided in Chapter Three, make evident the severe difficulties that divided government can generate for presidential systems, where the consequence of divided government has in many cases been the weakening or downfall of democracy (e.g., Guatemala 1993, Peru 1992) (Millett 1993).

MULTIPARTISM AND PRESIDENTIAL SYSTEMS

The number of relevant legislative parties (i.e., multipartism) is the key intervening variable through which electoral laws influence a system's tendency to provide the executive with a legislative majority (or close to it). The issue of multipartism in presidential systems is thus a fundamental concept for any discussion of the political consequences of specific electoral laws in presidential systems.

Practically all of the research on the political impact of the level of multipartism in a system has either used parliamentary systems as the unit of analysis or has failed to adequately differentiate between parliamentary systems and presidential systems (Mainwaring 1990). While it is entirely plausible that the level of multipartism is not an important determinant of governmental performance for parliamentary systems (Lijphart 1994a), nothing could be further from the truth for presidential systems. Mainwaring (1990) accurately notes that the scenario associated with a multi-party dominated legislature alongside a single popularly elected executive is quite distinct from a legislature with an identical composition within a parliamentary system.

In parliamentary systems, when no party possesses a legislative majority, parties must normally broker some type of coalition in order to govern. This institutionalized mechanism does not exist in presidential systems where, as Linz (1994) points out, the incentive toward cooperation is exactly the opposite. In a similar situation in presidential systems twin forces operate to make the formation of this kind of coalition, which is institutionally encouraged in the parliamentary systems, more difficult (the smaller the presidential legislative contingent the more difficult coalition formation becomes).[9] First, presidents have their own independent popular mandate and are likely to be reluctant to cede the degree of power necessary to an opposition party in order to entice it into a legislative coalition. This is due to their independence as nationally elected officials, which often causes presidents to overestimate their power. It is also because presidents realize that their independent mandates mean it is they who will ultimately be held responsible for the activities of the government, not their coalition partners, who can and may exit the coalition when it is politically convenient. Quite literally, the buck stops on the president's desk to an extent not shared by prime ministers in multi-party parliamentary systems.

The second obstacle to coalition formation is that the principal opposition parties (or party) recognize that the executive is on the whole the one responsible for the performance of the government. Thus they are often loathe to do anything to help the president succeed. Instead, they often adopt a policy of blind opposition with the end goal of causing the government to fail with the hope that one of their party leaders will be able to win the next presidential election (Hurtado 1989).

Mainwaring (1990, 168) states that "the combination of presidentialism and a fractionalized multi-party system seems especially inimical to stable democracy." This negative relationship is not due to the number of parties in a system, but is rather a product of the interaction between the level of multipartism in a system and the form of constitutional government employed. Alone, high levels of multipartism and presidential government are potentially quite compatible with stable and successful democracy. Combined they are potentially fatal.

Chile (1932–73) represents the only case of a multi-party system where presidential government survived for more than a quarter century. Even there, the democratic system finally collapsed due in part to the strains imposed by Chile's multi-party system. The only other examples of sustained presidential government all come from party systems which on average possess or possessed at the most two relevant political parties (Colombia, Costa Rica, United States, pre-1973 Uruguay, Venezuela, and to a lesser extent the premier-presidential French Fifth Republic where four relevant parties have normally organized into two blocs).

This leaves nations with presidential systems with two options if they desire a democratic constitutional system that will be able to provide effective stable governance and thereby have a high probability of surviving longer than a single generation. One alternative is to ensure a moderate level of multipartism, with no more than two major political parties. The chapters which follow offer some suggestions on how the electoral rules of a system can be employed to this effect. In some cases, however, the use of electoral laws will not be able to reduce or constrain the level of multipartism in a nation to the extent necessary to provide the executive with a legislative majority or near-majority on a reasonably consistent basis. In these nations the second alternative of a parliamentary system is, in all likelihood, the optimal form of democratic government, because in spite of its potential problems, multi-party parliamentary government is preferable to multi-party presidential government. This is especially so when the level of multipartism is extreme. Yet the case of Brazil is instructive. Brazil, the nation which currently has the most extreme level of multipartism in Latin America and where conditions were ripest for the adoption of a parliamentary system (Lamounier 1992), recently (1993) held a referendum on parliamentary versus presidential government.[10] This referendum demonstrated two interesting points. One, many Brazilians do not care very strongly about their form of constitutional government (25.8% of the eligible voters abstained despite mandatory voting while 19.8% of all votes cast were either null or blank). Two, those that do care (i.e., cast a valid vote) overwhelmingly prefer the presidential framework (the presidential system was preferred by 69.2% of the voters while parliamentarism was the choice of 30.8% of the voters) (FBIS-LAT, 05/03/93, 085). As Thomas Skidmore (1989, 136) aptly concludes after a review of the parliamentarist critique of presidentialism, "Notwithstanding the merits of this analysis, it appears to have few adherents in Latin America."

Electoral Engineering and the Optimal Number of Parties

Given that a multi-party system is incompatible with successful presidential government, and yet the presidential form of government remains extremely popular, particularly among emerging democracies, what is to be done? Electoral laws can be utilized to help safeguard a system with two major parties in some countries, reduce the level of multipartism in others, and, in nations that have only recently begun their democratization process, have a stronger than usual impact by helping to mold the structure of the party system for the near future.[11]

Most politicians tend to be conservative about changes which have a potentially dramatic impact on their livelihood. Unlike a radical shift from presidential to parliamentary government, which is likely to be unpopular with politicians, the modification of electoral laws is comparatively moderate.

The impact of any electoral law reform on a nation's party system is influenced by the content of the reform in question as well as by a host of important contextual factors which are beyond the scope of this study (these contextual factors are generally the principal determinants of the reform, a topic which is briefly discussed in

Appendix B). Any significant electoral law reform (e.g., from a concurrent to nonconcurrent election timing cycle) is highly likely to alter the structure of a nation's party system. The only question is how strong this impact will be. It is however clear that the employment of electoral laws to reduce the level of multipartism in a system to acceptable levels will not be effective in all cases.

Lijphart notes that there is a strong relationship between the number of salient issue dimensions in a nation and the number of relevant political parties in its party system (Lijphart 1984). He implies that a two-party system is perhaps not compatible with a system with more than one or two serious political cleavages (i.e., issue dimensions). Nonetheless, within the framework of presidential systems one's view of the optimal relationship between the number of societal cleavages and the number of political parties is not particularly relevant. Under a presidential form of government, the more fragmented the party system is along multiple cleavage lines, the more threatened is the stability of the system. In a system with multiple parties representing specific issue dimensions, one of the parties inevitably must capture the presidency. In systems where this party represents one narrow issue group, as opposed to a broadly based party common to systems with two major parties, this president will in all likelihood lack anything close to a legislative majority. This president will also often govern in a chauvinistic manner, benefiting a narrow constituency, which may result in the collapse of the democratic system (e.g., Chilean President Salvador Allende, 1970–73).

This dilemma involving the size of a nation's party system faced by presidential government applies as well to the premier-presidential systems currently in vogue. In fact, due to the increased constitutional power granted to the legislature in these latter systems, the problems associated with divided government are likely to be exacerbated in the premier-presidential systems when the legislature is not controlled by the president's party.[12]

A common critique of attempts to impose a two-party dominant system upon other nations is that while this system may function adequately in some of the Anglo-American nations, it is not correct to assume that it will be equally effective elsewhere. The country specialist may conclude that a system with only two major political parties is incompatible with the issue cleavages in a particular nation. This may very well be correct, but it also may be incorrect. A nation's party system should not be considered an ingrained national characteristic. Party systems are not frozen in time; they can and do change. One should thus not assume that just because a nation has in the past had a multi-party system, this somehow signifies that the formation of a system with two dominant parties is impossible. Likewise, the rationale that because a nation has traditionally had an essentially two-party system this will continue to be the case, regardless of changes in the electoral rules, is equally untenable. The recent transformation of the Argentine party system supports this latter point. Argentina has a tradition of two-party dominated politics dating back to the nineteenth century. Currently, however, it is experiencing the emergence of a multi-party system, in part due to a set of recent electoral law reforms.

While the optimal number of parties for a particular system or electoral systems in general can be debated, once the presidential form of government is chosen there can be no debate. High levels of multipartism most often lead to disastrous consequences. If a presidential system is in use, then a system with two major parties is desirable. Parliamentary rather than any type of presidential system (with the possible exception of a collegial presidency which is a constitutional rarity) is the only democratic constitutional arrangement that functions effectively with a multi-party system.

While many factors determine the number of political parties in a party system, electoral laws have the most prominent impact. Furthermore, unlike many of the other determinants of multipartism (e.g., cultural, historical, religious, ethnic, class) electoral laws are *comparatively* easy to change. This work demonstrates the potent effect electoral laws have both indirectly (via the intervening variable of multipartism) and directly on the tendency of a system to provide the president with a legislative majority or near-majority. This tendency is in turn a salient determinant of the effectiveness and survival of a presidential democracy.

THE POPULARITY OF ELECTORAL LAW REFORM IN LATIN AMERICA

An informed understanding of the consequences of electoral laws has become increasingly important over the last decade as nations throughout the world have been critically evaluating and in many cases changing important attributes of their electoral systems. This trend is particularly notable in the Latin American presidential systems.

Table 1.1 provides an overview of the electoral law changes which have taken place between 1990 and 1994 in the sixteen nations included in this study which are currently functioning democracies. The first three columns in the table represent significant changes in the nation's electoral rules (for a description of these changes see Appendix C). The fourth column denotes moderate changes in the electoral rules employed to elect members of the legislature.

Table 1.1
Changes in the Electoral Systems: 1990–94

COUNTRY	1 Presidential Electoral Formula	2 Election Timing Cycle	3 Legislative Election Method (Significant)*	4 Legislative Magnitude or Within PR**
Argentina	✓	✓	✓	
Bolivia	✓		✓	✓
Brazil		✓		
Chile		✓		
Colombia	✓		✓	✓
Costa Rica				
Dominican Republic				
Ecuador				
El Salvador				✓
Guatemala				✓
Honduras				
Nicaragua	✓			✓
Paraguay	✓		✓	
Peru			✓	
Uruguay				
Venezuela			✓	

* A significant change of the rules governing legislative elections is defined as a shift from one type of electoral method (e.g., PR, semi-PR) to another (e.g., a German-style mixed system, plurality), the elimination of a legislative chamber, or a massive change in effective magnitude (25 or greater).

** Changes in the effective magnitude caused by alterations of the district magnitude or vote threshold are included only if they result in an increase or decrease which is greater than three (and less than 25).

The evidence in Table 1.1 reveals that in only the past five years seven of the sixteen (44%) nations have changed either their presidential electoral formula (column one), their electoral timing cycle (column two), or both. These two electoral dimensions (as shown in the pages that follow) have a very powerful effect on the level of legislative multipartism in a nation, and both a direct and indirect impact on a system's tendency to provide the president with a strong legislative contingent. Noteworthy alterations in the rules governing the election of the legislature also occurred in six nations. When important legislative electoral rule changes are combined with the presidential electoral formula and timing cycle changes, we discover that nine of the sixteen (56%) nations have engaged in significant electoral law reform over the past five years. In addition to these important reforms, many nations have carried out modest modifications to the rules governing legislative elections (see column four).[13]

Since the return to democracy in 1983, Argentina's twenty-three provinces (the other analysis population examined in this study) have engaged in a level of electoral law reform similar to that of the Latin American nations. Thirteen of the twenty-three Argentine provinces have made significant modifications (i.e., of the type included in columns one through three in Table 1.1) to their electoral laws in the eleven years between the return to democracy in late 1983 and 1994.

DOCUMENTING THE INFLUENCE OF ELECTORAL LAWS

Electoral laws influence the extent to which dual democratic legitimacies are a problem for presidential systems; the smaller the size of the president's party in the legislature, the more intense the difficulties related to dual democratic legitimacies. Our purpose in the following chapters is to present empirical and theoretical evidence to this effect.

This study utilizes two separate populations: national level Latin American democratic systems and Argentine provincial systems. The use of these two essentially independent populations allows for the analysis of a variety of factors and conditions that would be impossible if only one of the two populations were examined. The data are first incorporated in a series of bivariate analyses which explore in detail the relationship between the electoral system dimensions and both the average level of legislative multipartism and the size of the presidential legislative contingent in a system. The relationship between legislative multipartism, which is hypothesized to act as an intervening variable between the electoral laws and the size of the executive's legislative contingent, and the size of the executive's legislative contingent is also explored. The discussion concludes with a multiple regression analysis of the independent impact of four key electoral laws on legislative multipartism.

Four electoral law dimensions have an especially strong impact on the size of the president's party in the legislature. They are (1) the electoral formula employed to select the president, (2) the timing of the presidential and legislative elections, (3) the effective magnitude of the legislative districts, and (4) the electoral formula used to allocate the legislative seats. These four electoral dimensions are crucial to providing a strong presidential legislative contingent, all through their impact on the number of legislative parties, and two (presidential electoral formula and election timing) through their effect on the degree of linkage between the presidential and legislative elections. These dimensions represent tools which can be used to safeguard and improve democratic presidential government. It is thus crucial to understand how they function.

The Presidential Electoral Formula

In presidential systems the choice of electoral formula normally has been limited to two options: the majority runoff formula or the plurality formula. In his work on majority runoff and plurality formulas Duverger (1986, 70) concluded that "the two ballot majority system tends to produce multipartism" and that "the plurality rule tends to produce a two-party system." Duverger (1986, 1954) focused primarily on the mechanical and psychological impact of electoral rules for legislative elections on the number of parties receiving votes for and represented in a legislative body. The same logic applies to the differential impact which the formula employed to select the executive can have on the composition of the legislature.

Duverger also discusses the US presidential system.

If the provision of adequate legislative support for the president is a desideratum of a constitutional system, then the plurality formula should be used to select the president in place of the majority runoff alternative. There are two reasons. The first, and most important, is that use of the plurality formula will result in a lower level of legislative multipartism and hence a greater likelihood of a legislative majority than will the majority runoff formula. Second, where presidential and legislative elections are held concurrently, the plurality method assures that the president is elected on the same day as members of the legislature, while the majority runoff system allows the possibility of the final selection process for the executive (i.e., the runoff) taking place at a separate time, reducing the degree of concurrence between the two elections.[14]

Unfortunately, despite the superiority of the plurality formula an overwhelming majority of emerging presidential systems have selected the majority runoff formula. Combining misguided logic regarding the technical merits of the plurality and majority runoff formulas with partisan political calculations, many of the world's young democratic systems have selected or are selecting an inferior method of presidential election. While this choice does not signify the demise of democratic presidential government in these nations, it is likely to make governance and the firm establishment of democracy more difficult.

Presidential and Legislative Election Timing

The electoral timing cycle employed for the presidential and legislative elections has a strong impact on the size of the executive's legislative contingent. First, where these elections are held concurrently, the restraining impact which all presidential systems have on the number of parties in the legislature is stronger, leading to a lower level of legislative multipartism than when elections for the two branches are held at separate times. Second, when the elections are held concurrently the presidential coattails effect is in force with the president's party likely to do better electorally than is the case when the presidential and legislative elections are held nonconcurrently.[15] These two factors combine to make systems which hold presidential and legislative elections concurrently far more likely to provide the president with a sufficiently large legislative contingent than those systems which hold these elections at separate times.[16]

While a concurrent timing cycle for presidential and legislative elections is the norm in Latin America, many of the Eastern European and former Soviet premier-presidential systems have implemented the potentially debilitating nonconcurrent electoral cycle. This choice will likely result in higher levels of legislative multipartism and weaker presidential legislative contingents than would be the case if a concurrent electoral cycle were utilized.

Legislative Effective Magnitude and Electoral Formula

The third and fourth prominent electoral law dimensions are interrelated, governing the size of the legislative districts (effective magnitude) and the electoral formula used to allocate legislative seats.[17] These two laws influence the number of legislative seats held by the president's party exclusively through their impact on the level of legislative multipartism. All of the systems examined here (as well as a majority of the world's other democratic presidential and premier-presidential systems) utilize proportional representation (PR) with multi-member districts to elect the members of their lower/single house (a majority of the bicameral systems also employ PR for senate elections).[18]

The use of the single-member plurality district arrangement would superficially appear to be a good method to assure low levels of legislative multipartism as well as to make a presidential legislative majority or near-majority more likely. The fact is that this arrangement possesses sufficient flaws so as to make the use of moderately sized multi-member PR districts a more attractive option. The deficiencies of the single-member plurality district are discussed more fully in Chapters Five and Eight. They include the method's highly disproportional nature, strong tendency to completely exclude minor parties, negative impact on the number two party in the system, deleterious effect on the president's relationship with members of his or her party in the legislature, as well as the dangers of partisan gerrymandering.

The effective magnitude of the districts from which the members of the legislature are elected is especially important when discussing the impact of electoral laws on the number of relevant parties in the legislature, and hence the tendency of a system to provide the president with a legislative majority or near-majority. In PR systems, as the effective magnitude of a system increases so does the level of multipartism, although at an increasingly diminishing rate.[19] To achieve a relatively low level of legislative multipartism within the framework of PR and multi-member legislative districts but at the same time assure a reasonable level of proportionality in the translation of votes into seats along with at least some minor party legislative representation (holding all other factors constant), a moderate effective magnitude is the optimal choice.[20]

When PR is employed to allocate legislative seats, the exact formula within the normal bounds of PR formulae ranging from the largest remainders Hare formula to the highest average d'Hondt formula is not that important. The differential use of the two formulas has a very marginal impact on the level of legislative multipartism in presidential systems.

SUMMARY

The success of the current third wave of democracy is interlinked with the performance and survival of the world's democratic presidential systems. If these presidential systems are to become established democracies capable of resolving their problems in an effective manner and maintaining their democratic status into the twenty-first century they need to provide their presidents with legislative majorities or near-majorities on a relatively consistent basis. The electoral laws employed by a system have a prominent effect on a system's ability to provide the president with this level of support. These laws are hence vital to the success and, in many cases, the survival of presidential democracies throughout the world. In turn, the fate of these presidential democracies will determine whether or not this current third wave of democracy continues in full force, or ebbs as many presidential systems lapse into authoritarian rule.

The book proceeds as follows. Chapter Two reviews the theoretical literature on the causes and consequences of divided government in presidential systems. Chapter Three provides a multi-tiered empirical analysis of the impact of the size of the presidential legislative contingent on the survival of democratic systems, executive-legislative conflict, and governance in Argentina in general and in an Argentine province in particular. Chapter Four identifies the systems that provide the base for the electoral law analysis portion of the study and the criteria involved in their selection. In Chapter Five the relationship between the number of political parties in an electoral system and its tendency to provide the executive with a legislative majority or near-majority is explored. Chapters Six, Seven, Eight, and Nine examine the relationship between the individual electoral law dimensions and both the number of legislative parties in a nation as well as the size of the average partisan legislative contingent provided for the executive. This analysis is conducted in a straightforward bivariate manner, with each chapter focusing on the relationship between one of the electoral law dimensions and both the level of legislative multipartism and, where applicable, the size of the presidential contingent in the legislature. Chapter Ten utilizes multiple regression analysis to explore the independent impact each of these electoral law variables has on the number of legislative parties in a system. Chapter Eleven presents a summary of the relationship between each of the electoral law dimensions and both the number of legislative parties in a system as well as the size of its presidential legislative contingent. The chapter also offers a set of suggestions regarding the role of electoral engineering in presidential systems. Finally, the chapter summarizes the general conclusions drawn from the presentation.

2

Perspectives on Divided Government: Historic, American, Comparative

The previous chapter argued that when the executive lacks a legislative majority or near-majority, the dynamics of presidential systems are quite distinct from those of parliamentary systems. Whereas the likely product of a lack of an executive legislative majority or near-majority in parliamentary systems is consensual coalition government, in presidential systems the outcome is more likely to be conflictual divided government.

OVERVIEW

The first scholars to write on the topic of divided government did so with a party government orientation, focusing primarily on the United States. Early scholars of presidential government such as Bryce (1921) and Wilson (1908) reflected the opinion of the times that divided government created gridlock and inefficiency. However, because of its rare occurrence during the period in which they wrote these scholars did not devote a great deal of energy to the topic of divided government. Scholarship on U.S. politics through the 1940s, 1950s, and 1960s by Laski (1940), Ranney (1954), and Burns (1963) reflected the existing consensus about the negative impact of divided government as well as the reality that divided government had not been very common during the first half of the twentieth century in the United States.

While divided government was not commonplace in the United States during the first half of the twentieth century, in twenty-six of the forty-four years since 1950 the president has lacked a majority in one or both chambers of Congress. This upsurge in divided government has resulted in a second genre of scholarly investigation into its causes and consequences. Whereas the historic scholars possessed a relatively homogeneous view of divided government as a negative factor caused for the most part by electoral rules, contemporary scholars writing on the U.S. political system are divided over both its causes and consequences.

A third set of scholars, who in the course of their work have examined the topic of divided government, are comparativists concerned primarily with constitutional systems and/or Latin America. From a broadly based comparative perspective Linz (1994), Mainwaring (1990), Sabsay (1991), Shugart and Carey (1992), Súarez (1982), and others argue that instances of divided government in the Latin American presidential systems (the only region with a significant number of long-standing presidential systems) are a product of the systems' electoral rules. These authors focus on two consequences of divided government, one familiar to Americanists and another not so familiar. The first consequence is the ineffective and chaotic government which echoes the critics of divided government in the United States. The second consequence is the breakdown of democracy. This latter consequence is not a topic with which scholars of divided government in the United States have had to be concerned. It is very much a reality in many other presidential systems where the level of popular support for democracy is not as entrenched, the national wealth not as great, and the historic experience of democracy not as lengthy as that in the United States.

In the pages that follow work on divided government by political scientists from Wilson to Ranney is first briefly reviewed. Second, the increased frequency of divided government in the United States is discussed, with a focus on current scholarly work on the topic. The ongoing debate over the causes of divided government is examined, with the principal findings derived from work on the United States shown to be only marginally applicable to Latin American presidential systems. Then the consequences of divided government as portrayed in the academic literature are discussed. Third, the literature of comparative scholars writing on constitutional systems in general as well as evidence accumulated by country specialists is summarized. The causes of divided government identified by these authors are first discussed, followed by an examination of two prominent consequences of divided government cited by these comparativists.

The argument of this chapter is twofold. One, a presidential legislative majority or near-majority is very important for the effective functioning and survival of presidential systems. In all presidential systems divided government results in ineffective government.[1] Outside of the United States it also can lead to the breakdown of democracy. Two, in non-U.S. systems the principal determinants of the size of the president's legislative contingent are the electoral rules employed by the system.

THE HISTORIC VIEW OF DIVIDED GOVERNMENT

The issue of divided government was not a topic of principal concern for scholars during the early to mid-twentieth century. Attentive scholars did however consider the situation of a president with a legislative majority to be the only manner in which presidential government could operate effectively and properly. For Wilson, a president with a legislative majority was a requisite for the functioning of the system: "our government is a living, organic thing, and must, like every other government, work out the close synthesis of active parts which can exist only when leadership is lodged in some one man or group of men. You cannot compound a successful government out of antagonisms" (Wilson 1908, 60). Bryce also described the detrimental impact which divided government had on governance in presidential systems:

> When President and Legislature belong to the same party, it is to him that the nation looks, for he can ask the Legislature for all that the conjuncture requires, be it statutes or grants of money. But when he and the Legislature are at odds, and the country is not evidently with the one or the other, there is nothing for it but to bear with the deadlock and await the next presidential election. (1921, 471)

Others such as Laski (1940) and Ranney (1954) also argued the importance of a legislative majority for the functioning of presidential government.

Sundquist (1988) notes that it is not surprising that most party government theorists did not spend a great deal of time on the causes and consequences of divided government, simply because of the general absence of divided government during the previous half century.

> The generation who expounded this theory [of party government] paid little attention to how the government would and should function when the president and the Senate and House majorities were not of the same party. They could in good conscience disregard this question because intervals of divided government in their experience had been infrequent and short-lived. Whenever the midterm election brought a division of the government, anyone concerned about that could take a deep breath and wait confidently for the next presidential election to put the system back into its proper alignment. (Sundquist 1988, 614)

The central theme of the literature which dominated U.S. political science for much of the twentieth century was that while divided government was a negative factor for the functioning of presidential government, it was not a serious problem due to its infrequent occurrence. Until recently, conventional wisdom remained that divided government was a negative factor, but also an aberration. However, as noted by Brady (1993) the 1988 election of President George Bush demonstrated quite clearly that in the U.S. divided government has increasingly become the norm.

THE CURRENT STUDY OF DIVIDED GOVERNMENT IN AMERICAN POLITICS

This "problem" of divided government, beginning with Sundquist's seminal article in 1988, has produced a flurry of research which has had two principal interrelated goals. One is to explain the causes of divided government. The other is to examine its consequences. The previous generation of scholars had viewed divided government, when it occurred, primarily as a by-product of the electoral system (i.e., the use of midterms). They furthermore viewed its consequences as pernicious as it reduced the effectiveness and the accountability of the democratic system.

The fact that between 1954 and 1994 the Republicans failed to gain a majority at any time in the House of Representatives, despite six presidential victories, demonstrates that the electoral cycle/midterm explanation alone is no longer adequate.[2] Furthermore, although many political scientists including Cutler (1988), Mann (1993), and Sundquist (1988) continue to accept the previous conventional wisdom of divided government as obscuring responsibility and reducing effectiveness, others such as Davidson (1991), Fiorina (1992), and Mayhew (1991) have begun to challenge these well-established tenets.

The Causes of Divided Government in the United States

Current scholarly work on the causes of divided government tends to loosely (though not exclusively) fall into two categories: the structural and the political (Jacobson 1990). Representative of the structural category are authors such as Abramowitz (1983), Brady (1988), Cutler (1988), and Sundquist (1992) who attribute divided government principally to structural factors such as incumbency, gerrymandering, ballot format, and election timing. Authors whose work attributes divided government primarily to political factors include Jacobson (1990), Petrocik (1991), and Wattenberg (1991). This latter group argues that many voters want and get different things from their president and member of Congress, and hence in the aggregate a substantial subset of voters tends to vote for Democratic members of Congress and Republican presidents. In short, divided government is the result of the preferences of voters. The Democrats' ability to present better congressional candidates than the Republicans is listed as an additional cause of divided government. There is a third group such as Burns (1993) and Mezey (1989) who cite the separation of powers as a principal cause of divided government. This explanation is macro-constitutional in nature, more in line with the presidential versus parliamentary debate than with the mainstream discussion of divided government in the U.S. Furthermore, this point is not of crucial importance for our discussion, since the separation of powers is endogenous to the study of presidential systems.

The structural explanation of divided government tends to focus on why, between 1954 and 1994, the Democratic party was able to retain control of the House despite Republican victories in a majority of the presidential contests. Based on the U.S. experience the advantages accrued to U.S. House incumbents have often been identified as a reason for continued Democratic dominance of the House. Partisan gerrymandering also has been hypothesized to have aided the Democrats in the retention of seats. Jacobson (1990) provides strong evidence (e.g., in elections for open seats, Democrats win more often than do Republicans) that continued Democratic dominance cannot be adequately explained by these or other related structural factors. In any event most of these structural explanations are intricately linked to the use of single-member plurality districts, and hence are of limited relevance for systems which employ multi-member proportional representation (PR) districts, particularly those where a closed party list is used. Thus regardless of whether or not Jacobson is correct in his critique, it is apparent that the applicability of these structural explanations to the multi-member PR systems of Latin America is generally quite low.

As an alternative to the structural model, Jacobson (1990) offers his own political explanation. Complementary explanations are also provided by Petrocik (1991) and Wattenberg (1991). The first component of this generic political explanation centers on the Democrats' ability to run better candidates than the Republicans, due in part to the professionalization of the nation's state legislatures which has weakened the ability of the Republicans to present qualified and experienced candidates (Fiorina 1992). This explanation is certainly specific to the United States, the product of the particular socioeconomic composition of the nation's party system, the weakness of party (thus making candidate experience a much more important factor), the growing degree of legislative professionalization in the states, and the use of single-member districts.

The second, and most potent portion of the political explanation, is that voters, or at least a substantial subset of them, consciously vote for divided government. In general, these voters are hypothesized to view the Presidency through a different optic than the House of

Representatives. These voters, it is argued, look to the president to provide national leadership and deal with important macro-level issues. However, they look to their member of Congress to represent their particular district's interests (Petrocik 1991). According to Petrocik (1991), the Republicans have a strong advantage on the national level issues, while the Democrats, due in part to their greater heterogeneity, are better able to respond to district interests and issues.

Assessing the U.S.-Based Explanation

I cannot resolve the debate within American politics over the causes of divided government or even provide a comprehensive review of this literature here.[3] I simply seek to demonstrate that most of the causes articulated by scholarship derived from the U.S. experience are not particularly relevant for Latin American presidential systems. Of the structural explanations (e.g., incumbency, gerrymandering, electoral laws) and political explanations (e.g., better Democratic candidates, voters choosing divided government) offered to explain the presence of divided government in the U.S. system, only the focus on electoral laws has a significant parallel in Latin America. In contrast to the unique convergence in the U.S. of single-member plurality districts and weak parties, Latin American systems have distinctly different electoral contexts. To explain divided government in Latin America, one must focus primarily on the electoral system.

Analysis of the causes of divided government in the United States is overwhelmingly focused on members of Congress as individuals who find it in their best interest to represent the interests of their district over those of their party and are able to do so due to the weak nature of the U.S. parties. Furthermore, once elected, representatives acquire impressive staffs and the advantage of being members of one of the most powerful legislative branches (vis-à-vis the executive) in the world.

Single-member districts encourage members of Congress to represent district interests. This is particularly the case when the national party has little or no control over the use of the party label in the district (as opposed, for example, to the United Kingdom where the party retains control over access to the ballot under the party symbol).

The consequence of the intersection of single-member districts and weak parties in the U.S. is twofold. First, members are institutionally encouraged to represent the particularized and district-level interests of their constituents to an extent uncommon in most other democratic systems. This factor, combined with weak parties which allow the members considerable leeway in their behavior, creates the very rare situation in which voters have the actual ability to make the divided government choice. This political situation, described by Jacobson (1990), Petrocik (1991), and Wattenberg (1991), would not be possible without an electoral/institutional system which encourages this distinction between parties in regard to issue areas and between constitutional institutions in regard to policy domains.

As Table 2.1 demonstrates, the intersection of single-member plurality districts and weak parties in presidential systems is a conjunction present almost exclusively in the United States.[4] In the Latin American systems included in this study, all systems employ multi-member districts with PR to select the members of their lower/single house.[5] When single-member districts are not employed, the structural explanation of gerrymandering begins to border on the irrelevant, since with two partial exceptions (Chile I and Chile II) the multi-member electoral districts are based on pre-existing administrative boundaries (although the method of seat allocation among districts is an important issue).[6] At the same time, in closed list PR systems (and to a lesser extent in open list PR systems) the remaining structural explanations based on the individual traits of representatives, such as candidate quality and incumbency, become much less potent. Particularly in closed list systems the focus tends to be on the party, not the individual, and thus individual member traits which are so important in the context of single-member plurality districts become much less significant.[7]

The most prominent of the politically oriented explanations is that voters (or at least some portion of them) actually want divided government. While authors such as Jacobson (1990), Petrocik (1991), and Wattenberg (1991) make a convincing case for this argument in the U.S., its applicability to the Latin American situation is doubtful. To be applicable in any Latin American presidential system, two factors must be present. First, the voters must view one

Table 2.1
Structural Variables and Congressional Representation in Lower/Single Houses

Structural Exogenous Variables			Member of Congress (MOC) Endogenous Variable
Electoral District Size/Seat Allocation Method	Degree of Party Control over Access to the Ballot	Systems in These Categories	Incentive to and Ability of MOC to Represent District over Party Interests
Single-Member/ Plurality	Low	United States	Very Strong
Multi-Member/ Open List-PR	Low	Brazil Ia, Brazil Ib, Brazil II, Chile Ia*	Strong
Multi-Member/ Closed List-PR**	Low	Colombia	Strong
Multi-Member/ Open List-PR	High	Chile Ib*, Chile II, Peru	Moderate
Multi-Member/ Closed List-PR**	Medium	Uruguay	Weak
Multi-Member/ Closed List-PR	High	Argentina I, Argentina II, Bolivia, Costa Rica, Dominican Republic, Ecuador, El Salvador, Guatemala, Honduras**, Nicaragua, Paraguay, Venezuela***	Very Weak

This table offers a rough approximation of the impact of electoral law factors on the behavior of individual members of congress. For more information on the time periods for each of these systems, see Table 4.1.

* Chile Ia represents the period 1945–58 and Chile Ib 1958–73.

** In Colombia and Uruguay the voter chooses from among a list of sub-party lists, whose votes are in turn pooled for the party in Uruguay, but normally not in Colombia. Honduras employed the Uruguayan (Lema) system for the 1985 elections only.

*** This categorization is for the Venezuelan system prior to its 1993 use of a German-style mixed system. Under this new arrangement the Venezuelan system would be classified as "Weak" in the terminology of the fourth column.

Exogenous variable combinations such as Single-Member/Plurality-strong party control over ballot access (e.g., the United Kingdom) which do not occur in the study population are not included in the table.

Sources: Carey and Shugart (1993); Ministerio del Interior de España (1992); Nohlen (1993a); Shugart and Carey (1992).

party as better at certain national level issues and another better at district level issues. Second, at least some of these voters must see one constitutional institution differentially able to deal with separate policy domains. As Jacobson explains:

> Perceived differences between the parties coincides with differences in what people expect of presidents and members of Congress, which in turn, reflect differences in the political incentives created by their respective institutional positions. Presidents are supposed to pursue broad national interests; uniquely among elected officials, they can profit politically by conferring diffuse collective benefits at the expense of concentrated particular interests. Members of Congress, in contrast, survive by looking out for the particular because that is what voters want from them. (1991, 70)

The ability and incentive of members of Congress to look out for the particular interest of their districts is, however, very contingent on the electoral framework and partisan structure of the United States. The incentive and ability to represent the particular is the product of the single-member district and weak parties (particularly in regard to control over access to the ballot). This explanation is further prefaced by a popular view that the presidency predominates on certain types of issues and the congress on others. As Table 2.1 makes evident, the incentives to and ability of congressional deputies to represent particular district interests is severely reduced in multi-member PR districts (particularly where a closed list is employed).[8] Furthermore, in most Latin American nations the legislative branch is not viewed as having an important specific policy domain in which it predominates. In general the principal "political" explanation for U.S. divided government, that it is the product of the desires of at least a subset of voters, simply does not make a great deal of sense in any Latin American nation.[9]

This analysis of the causes of divided government is embedded in the unique structural and political experience of the United States. Single-member plurality districts combined with weak parties and a relatively strong legislative branch create the situation specific conditions from which the conclusions of authors such as Brady (1988), Sundquist (1992), Jacobson (1990), and Wattenberg (1991) are derived.[10]

In contrast to the United States, most of the Latin American systems in this study (1) employ multi-member districts (most of the time with closed list PR) to elect members of their lower/ single house, (2) have in most cases political parties that are more disciplined and possess greater control over ballot access than their U.S. counterparts, and (3) have legislatures which, while by no means whatsoever mere rubber stamps, are not as influential vis-à-vis the president as is the U.S. Congress.

The previous discussion by necessity dealt in broad generalizations about the U.S. and Latin American institutional systems. Of course, U.S. parties do occasionally demonstrate some discipline, some Latin American political parties are stronger than others, many legislatures in Latin America do possess important levels of power vis-à-vis the executive, and for some Latin American members of congress providing pork for the district is very important.

The Consequences of Divided Government

Divided government is hypothesized to influence the accountability and effectiveness of the U.S. government (Thurber 1991a). Until recently conventional wisdom almost universally described this influence as negative. However, in the past five years this long-held tenet has begun to be questioned.

Most recent scholarship on divided government has tended to accept (explicitly or more often implicitly) the argument that a divided government is less accountable than a government where the president's party controls both houses of the legislature. Where the schism among scholars occurs, however, is over the significance of this lack of accountability as well as related consequences of divided government for both democracy and the functioning of government.

The pernicious effect of divided government on governance was promoted by Wilson (1908), Laski (1940), Ranney (1954), Burns (1963), and Sorauf (1968) in the past and has recently been reaffirmed by scholars such as Cutler (1988), Mann (1993), Mezey (1991), Robinson (1989), and Sundquist (1988). Others, such as Cox and Kernell (1991), Cox and McCubbins (1991), McCubbins (1991), and Stewart (1991) have marshaled strong empirical evidence that divided government has had important political and economic consequences. These consequences include an increased level of conflict between the executive and legislative branches, increased government spending, and increased budget deficits. In sum, this more traditional group presents a very forceful argument that divided government does have an impact, and that this impact is most often resoundingly negative.

Lined up against this negative view of the consequences of divided government are scholars such as Davidson (1991), Fiorina (1992), Mayhew (1991), Peterson and Greene (1994), and Thurber (1991b). Collectively they have gathered empirical evidence to make the case that divided government has not had the pernicious influences attributed to it by its detractors. These authors present an array of empirical support to suggest that policymaking and governmental effectiveness have not suffered greatly as a consequence of divided government. For example, Davidson's study of legislative activity and workload determined that the "record of the past two generations casts doubt on the assumptions that unified party control raises legislative productivity and that divided government leads to stalemate" (1991, 76), while Mayhew found that divided government had little impact on two major components of public policy: major policy changes and congressional investigations. The initial findings of these authors contradict conventional wisdom. If supported by more substantial evidence this scholarship could perhaps undermine the traditional view of divided government as detrimental for governmental effectiveness. However, as both conventional wisdom (particularly among politicians and political insiders) as well as the superior empirical evidence remain on the side of those who view the consequences of divided government as negative, this position still dominates U.S. political science.

DIVIDED GOVERNMENT IN COMPARATIVE PERSPECTIVE

Until the recent resurgence of democracy in Latin America, the issue of divided government in presidential systems received little attention from the comparative politics community. Certainly some scholars noted the severe difficulties caused by divided government for governance in Latin America (e.g., Hughes and Mijeski 1973; Súarez 1982) but they were a distinct minority. In the past fifteen years, however, presidential democracy has blossomed in Latin America and the world. Increasingly, scholars concerned with democratic systems have focused on the issue of divided government. One group of leading comparativists has focused on divided government from within the framework of the presidential versus parliamentary debate. A second group of country-oriented scholars in the course of their research on specific nations has noted the negative consequences of divided government. The problems posed by divided government for Latin American presidential systems are both similar to and distinct from those discussed by the anti-divided government school in the United States. Divided government in Latin America is hypothesized to have the same types of negative effects on governmental effectiveness and accountability. In addition it also is hypothesized to undermine the stability of democratic systems and at times lead to their collapse.

Critics of presidential government such as Lijphart (1990a), Linz (1994), and Valenzuela (1990) have highlighted the gridlock caused by divided government as one of the prime examples why presidentialism is a problematic regime type. Others such as Súarez (1982) have identified the tendency of presidential governments in Latin America to experience gridlock along with the inability of these minority governments to govern effectively. Santos (1986) has further noted that in many cases the deadlock produced by a lack of a presidential majority has resulted in the overthrow of a democratically elected government. In these latter instances either principal actors within the democratic system appealed to the military to intervene to break the executive-legislative gridlock, or the military determined on its own accord that such intervention was necessary. Even scholars more sympathetic to presidentialism (e.g., Shugart and Carey 1992) have highlighted the inherent negative consequences when the president lacks sufficient legislative support. These two camps in the presidential versus parliamentary debate share a similar opinion about the role of divided government in presidential systems. The former group finds presidentialism to be a flawed institution in general, but one which functions particularly poorly when the president lacks a legislative majority (or close to it). Shugart and Carey possess a more optimistic view of the presidential form of government, but nevertheless they predict primarily negative consequences when the president lacks a legislative majority (or close to it).

A recent work by Mainwaring (1993) incorporates much of the preceding comparative literature and discusses the problematic impact of divided government in presidential systems. Mainwaring notes that for presidents:

Congressional support is indispensable for enacting laws, and it is difficult to govern effectively without passing laws. Contrary to common belief, presidents are often weaker executives than prime ministers, not so much because they have limited prerogatives, but because of legislative/executive deadlock.... Under democratic governments, a system of checks and balances operates, but ... can paralyze executive power when the president lacks support in congress. (1993, 215)

Mainwaring goes on to state a fact often ignored by those whose experience is limited to the comparatively wealthy and stable United States: "Yet the myriad conundrums that beset most poor nations require an effective, agile executive" (1993, 215). The general conclusion is that unless the president has a legislative majority or near-majority, he or she is likely to experience serious difficulties. As was noted in the previous chapter, the formation of coalitions such as is common in many multi-party parliamentary systems is institutionally discouraged in presidential systems.[11]

Panizza (1993) also acknowledges the validity of many of the parliamentarist critiques of presidentialism. He, however, suggests that a potential solution to many of the problems noted by the parliamentarists is the consistent provision of a legislative majority for the president. Panizza stresses that this level of legislative support is perhaps a necessary ingredient for successful governance in presidential systems.

Finally, Sabsay (1991) cites the lack of sufficient presidential legislative support as a serious contributing factor to the high degree of ungovernability in a set of Latin American nations. He discusses some of the negative effects that the lack of legislative support has had in Brazil, Ecuador, and Peru. He traces the primary cause of these deficient legislative contingents to the electoral laws employed in these nations. This finding concurs with that of other scholars active in this area (e.g., Linz, Mainwaring, Shugart and Carey, Súarez, Valenzuela) who attribute the occurrence of divided government in Latin American nations almost exclusively to the electoral laws employed by these systems.

In addition to the broadly comparative literature on presidential systems, a second country-specific literature also provides numerous examples of the problems posed by divided government for governability in and the survival of democratic presidential systems. In their work on Costa Rica, Lehoucq (1992) and Mijeski (1977) have both noted the difficulties which have occurred in those instances where the president lacked a legislative majority. Hughes and Mijeski (1973) have described the problems faced by Chilean presidents prior to the 1973 coup when they did not possess sufficient backing in the legislature. D'Agostino (1992) has noted similar problems in the Dominican Republic between 1978 and 1982 when President Silvestre Antonio Guzmán's lack of a majority in the Senate resulted in considerable legislative gridlock. González and Gillespie (1994) and González (1991) have listed weak support for the president in the legislature as a partial contributing factor to President Juan María Bordaberry's 1971 *autogolpe* in Uruguay. Palmer (1990, 1980) describes Peruvian President Fernando Belaúnde Terry's lack of sufficient legislative backing combined with the obstructionist tactics of the *Unión Nacional Odriísta* (UNO) and *Partido Aprista Peruano* (PAP) as contributing to the debilitation of the Belaúnde Terry administration (1963–68) to the point that the military overthrew it in a coup in 1968. Reflecting on the demise of a second Peruvian experience with democracy a quarter century after the 1968 coup, McClintock (1994, 1993) cites severe executive-legislative conflict, the product of Peruvian President Alberto Fujimori's minuscule legislative contingent, as one of the principal impetuses of Fujimori's 1992 *autogolpe*. Millett (1993, 3) echoes the point of McClintock on Peru, and notes that a principal consequence of a divided government in many nations has been clashes between the executive and legislative branches which have "helped precipitate coups" in Guatemala, Haiti, and Peru. Millett also makes the important point that while North Americans may be familiar with the term 'gridlock', "U.S. problems in this area pale into insignificance alongside those prevailing in some Latin American nations" (1993, 3).

Additional case literature demonstrating the negative consequences of divided government in Latin America could be provided; however, the point has been sufficiently made.[12] While presidents with legislative majorities or near-majorities do not guarantee effective and accountable government, they are much more likely to provide it than are presidents whose party lacks anything approaching a majority of the seats in the legislature.

This review of the general theoretical literature on comparative constitutional systems combined with the case literature reinforces three points. First, in a democracy when a president lacks a legislative majority or near-majority, government is less accountable, less effective, and more likely to collapse than is generally the case when the president possesses a healthy level of support in the legislature. Second, the electoral rules employed by a system are the principal cause of divided government in Latin America, as well as in most presidential systems elsewhere in the world. Third, presidential partisan support in the legislature is a very real concern in Latin America.

The issues of governability, accountability, and the relationship between these factors and electoral laws are the topic of daily debates in legislatures, newspapers, and public forums throughout Latin America. Unlike the United States, significant electoral and institutional reform can and does occur in Latin America and elsewhere in the world. It is thus crucial for scholars and politicians alike to gain a better understanding of the role of electoral laws in the provision of legislative majorities and near-majorities.

The overall evidence from both the literature on American politics as well as the work of comparative scholars is clear. It points to the detrimental consequences of divided government for governmental accountability and effectiveness in democratic presidential systems as well as for the actual life span of these systems. While there is some counter-evidence which minimizes the extent of the consequences of divided government, a majority of Americanists and practically all comparativists continue to view divided government as a negative factor. The causes of divided government are a point of debate within American politics. Due to the structural context within which all U.S.-based analysis of this phenomenon has taken place, the findings of these works are generally not applicable to the Latin American presidential systems studied here. Instead, the causes of divided government in Latin American presidential systems are linked to the electoral rules and institutional structures employed in these systems. The exploration of the manner in which electoral laws influence the tendency of a system to provide the president with strong partisan support in the legislature is our principal focus.

3

Presidential Legislative Support and the Functioning of Presidential Systems

The previous chapter's review of the American, comparative, and Latin American case study literature underscored the salience of a strong presidential legislative contingent for successful democratic presidential government. This chapter complements this literature by providing a multi-tiered empirical analysis of the consequences of the size of the president's partisan contingent in the legislature for executive-legislative relations and for the general performance of presidential democracy. Three levels of analysis highlight the importance of a strong presidential legislative contingent for: (1) the longevity of democratic presidential government, (2) the degree of conflict between the executive and legislature, and (3) the functioning of democratic government in Argentina in general and in the Argentine province of Salta in particular.

Weak presidential legislative contingents do not automatically lead to a democratic system's demise. In general they do, however, have a negative impact on the functioning of a democratic system. Weak presidential support in the legislature often leads to high levels of executive-legislative conflict which reduces the effectiveness of the democratic system and its ability to deal with pressing societal problems (i.e., its ability to govern). While these negative effects do not represent a serious threat to the survival of democratic government in stable and deeply rooted democracies such as the United States, in the majority of the world's presidential democracies they can combine with other factors to produce the debilitation and/or breakdown of the democratic system.

PRESIDENTIAL LEGISLATIVE SUPPORT AND THE SURVIVAL OF PRESIDENTIAL DEMOCRACIES

As noted in Chapter Two, one point which is prominent in the comparative and case study literature, yet understandably ignored by Americanists, is the propensity in many nations for divided government to lead to the breakdown of democracy. The threat of a president either closing the congress and courts or being overthrown by a military coup is virtually nonexistent in the United States. Yet, these threats are quite palpable in many Latin American nations as recent events in Brazil (1993), Guatemala (1993), and Peru (1992) clearly indicate. This possibility of the collapse of the democratic system represents a severe consequence and cost of divided government.

Cox and Kernell (1991) examine the bargaining process which takes place between the president and the legislature during periods of divided government in the United States. As succinctly summarized by Brady (1993, 192): "In this bargaining game, three strategies are available: (1) either the President or Congress goes it alone without the other branch, (2) there is an appeal to public opinion, or (3) both branches bargain within the beltway." These three options also exist in Latin American presidential systems experiencing divided government. However, important differences exist. First, in the United States the president must only bargain with one party (fragmented as it may be on occasion) to form a coalition. In Latin America, the president often must bargain with multiple parties, which as coalition theory demonstrates (Axelrod 1970; Lijphart 1984; Riker 1962) is often much more difficult.[1] Second, in most Latin American nations two additional options could be added to Brady's summary: (4) appeal to the military or international actors (e.g., the United States), or (5) the collapse of the democratic system (Santos 1986). The appeal to the military or international actors can be made either by the president or by the legislature. Likewise this game of executive-legislative conflict can escalate to the point of severe ungovernability under which the military feels obliged to oust the democratically elected government and assume control of the nation.

Executives who lack a majority or near-majority in the legislature are common in all types of democratic systems. However, the consequences of this situation differ depending on the type of constitutional system employed. As discussed in Chapter One, parliamentary systems institutionally encourage the formation of coalition governments when no one party possesses a majority in the legislature. In terms of the survival of the democratic system, these coalition governments have proven quite resilient, although as Table 3.1 demonstrates, the fact that they are all located in the world's most developed nations should not be overlooked. While consensual government works in these developed nations, its degree of success in less developed nations with greater social and economic problems awaits more extensive empirical verification.

The generally poor performance of presidential government in terms of democratic longevity has been cited by many critics of presidentialism (Linz 1992; Riggs 1988; Súarez 1982; Valenzuela 1993). However, according to Shugart and Carey (1992) this general negative relationship between presidentialism and democracy may very well be a product of the nations which have employed presidential government. These nations are overwhelmingly located in Latin America and other regions of the developing world and the life span of their democratic systems could quite conceivably have been shortened by many factors other than their constitutional regime type. Shugart and Carey, after a review of the success of democratic systems in the past century, found "no justification for the claim of Linz and others that presidentialism is inherently more prone to crises that lead to breakdown [than parliamentarism]" (1992, 42). Hence the negative relationship cited by critics of presidentialism may very well be open to a variety of interpretations. Mainwaring (1993) provides a compromise position within this debate. He acknowledges that as an institutional framework, presidentialism is somewhat inferior to parliamentarism, but at the same time he believes that presidentialism does have some positive traits and can work.

There is one point on which both critics (e.g., Linz, Lijphart, Stepan and Skach, Súarez, Valenzuela) and supporters (e.g., Main-

Table 3.1
Stable Democracies in the World, 1945–94*

Type of Constitutional System	Size of the Executive's Average Partisan Contingent in the Legislature**	
	Executive's Party Possesses an Average of 45% or More of the Seats in the Legislature	Executive's Party Possesses an Average of Less than 45% of the Seats in the Legislature
Parliamentary	(Majoritarian Democracy)	(Consensual Democracy)
	Australia	Belgium
	Austria	Denmark
	Botswana	Germany
	Canada	Ireland
	India	Israel
	Jamaica	Italy
	Japan	Netherlands
	New Zealand	Norway
	Sri Lanka	Sweden
	Trinidad and Tobago	
	United Kingdom	
Presidential	(Majoritarian Democracy)	(Conflictual Democracy)
	Colombia	*Chile*
	Costa Rica	
	Philippines	
	United States	
	Uruguay	
	Venezuela	

* The countries are taken from Mainwaring (1993). Mainwaring defines a democracy as stable if it survived for a minimum of 25 years. Following Powell (1982) countries in Mainwaring's population which possessed less than one million inhabitants were excluded.

** For the bicameral systems where the two chambers are constitutional equals the average percentage of seats in the two chambers is used.

Countries in italics experienced a serious breakdown in the functioning of their democratic system after enjoying a minimum of 25 years of continuous democratic government.

Four systems which met the requisite of 25 years of successful democracy were excluded from the table due to their use of a regime type which is neither presidential nor parliamentary. They are: Finland, the French Fifth Republic, Lebanon, and Switzerland.

The country averages are based on the average of the contingents won in all elections in the systems in question between 1945 and 1994.

Sources: See Appendix A.

waring, Shugart and Carey) of presidentialism agree. There is consensus that presidential systems which consistently fail to provide the president with sufficient legislative support are unlikely to prosper. When an executive lacks a majority in the parliamentary systems the norm tends to be what Lijphart terms 'consensual government' (i.e., government by coalition). In presidential systems, when the executive lacks a majority (or close to it) in the legislature, the norm is conflictual government. Evidence of this conflict is presented throughout the text which follows. In general, however, there are fewer successful democratic presidential systems than parliamentary systems (see Table 3.1). This relationship may be a result of exogenous traits of the nations which have employed the two different constitutional regime types, and thus spurious.

The possibility of spuriousness is much more remote in an intra-presidential system comparison. First, in the terminology of Table 3.1, majoritarian presidential systems have been just as common as conflictual presidential systems in the history of presidential democracy in the post–World War II era.[2] Second, as a large majority of the presidential systems in this population are located in Latin America, the possibility of spuriousness caused by exogenous traits of the nations involved is greatly reduced. In regard to their success, six presidential systems which consistently provided their presidents with strong legislative support (an average of 45% or more of the seats in the legislature) have enjoyed a minimum of twenty-five years of continuous democratic government during this period.[3] Conversely, only one presidential system which provided the president with inferior legislative support (under 45%) was able to survive for more than twenty-five years. Furthermore, the only case in this category, Chile, in fact broke down due in part to the strains imposed by the executive-legislative conflict during the administration of President Salvador Allende (Valenzuela 1978). Among the successful majoritarian presidential systems, two eventually experienced breakdown. One (Uruguay) broke down in part due to the fact that President Juan María Bordaberry possessed the smallest legislative contingent ever held by an Uruguayan president (González 1991).

The preceding discussion, as well as Table 3.1, suggests that while presidentialism has not enjoyed tremendous democratic success as a regime type, presidential systems which have on average provided the executive with a legislative majority or near-majority have enjoyed a much higher degree of democratic success than those which have not. While at this point I cannot *a priori* state a causal argument that presidential systems which fail to provide the executive with a legislative majority or near-majority are less likely to survive than those which on average do, the historic evidence is impressive.[4]

EXECUTIVE-LEGISLATIVE CONFLICT: A CROSS-NATIONAL ANALYSIS

Conflict between the executive and legislature is an integral part of the checks and balances system. Critics of presidentialism have, with good reason, focused on this conflict, and the ensuing immobilism often caused by it, as one of the most potent flaws of the presidential form of government. As the previous chapter detailed, when conflict between the president and legislature occurs in Latin America, its consequences are most often not beneficial checks, but rather negative obstacles to the functioning of effective democratic government.

The literature presented in Chapter Two supports the hypothesis that the weaker the presidential support in the legislature, the higher levels of executive-legislative conflict will be. This hypothesis, however, has not been examined empirically except in a very small number of single-country case studies (e.g., Coppedge 1994; Mayhew 1991; Peterson and Greene 1994).

The best way to conduct a cross-national study of executive-legislative relations would be to utilize data covering the submission, passage, and duration of legislation in the legislative process. Unfortunately, broad cross-national analysis of these and related data is not viable for three principal reasons.[5]

First, each nation has its own legislative rules, with relevant legal instruments often defined in distinct ways across nations. These classificatory differences represent a severe impediment to any type of large-scale comparative analysis. For example, what may be a private bill, and thus listed separately from public bills in one nation, may be lumped together in a single category in others. What is a law in one nation sometimes may be considered a law and sometimes a resolution in others. A set of ten new regulations which may be included in a single bill in one nation may require ten separate bills in another. In sum, as one of the foremost experts on Latin American law in the United States has noted, the aggregate comparison of legislation across more than a few nations is extremely difficult if not impossible (Medina 1992).

Second, any measure of relations between institutions which is based only on the legislative record (or any institutional record, for that matter) provides a partial and quite possibly a misleading picture of inter-institutional interaction. This is certainly the case for any examination of executive-legislative relations. These relations involve a complex game of signaling, threats, reciprocity, and deals which do not appear in the *"Diario Oficial,"* and undermine indicators based solely on its contents. Thus measures of executive-legislative relations such as the use of vetoes by the president or the success of executive-sponsored bills may have serious validity problems. For example, assessing the success of bills submitted to congress by the executive branch is fraught with difficulties. Presidents are unlikely to submit bills to congress which they expect will be rejected, except in those cases where they want to make a political statement by forcing the opposition in the legislature to block a bill. Thus examination of executive success rates can be very misleading. High rates may be the result of true executive success in the legislature, but they also might be the result of the executive only sending noncontroversial or watered down bills to congress (i.e., anticipated reaction).

Third, there is a similar set of theoretical issues related to the relationship between strong presidential legislative support and legislative production which makes the use of laws, bills, and other types of legislation as a basis for the analysis of executive-legislative conflict problematic. Theoretically when the president has a legislative majority or near-majority, we could logically expect two types of legislative behavior. One is the passage of a large number of laws as the president utilizes strong legislative backing to the fullest. Another equally logical scenario is that very little legislation is passed as the executive either receives powers from the legislature to rule by decree in certain areas or ignores the legislature counting on the legislative contingent to prevent any negative institutional reaction.

In sum, comparison of legislative data across nations regrettably is not a fruitful analytic method for the cross-national study of executive-legislative relations. This is not to say that studies which utilize legislative data do not have merit when conducted in a longitudinal manner in a single nation or in a comparative manner in a very small number of nations by scholars with a solid understanding of the nations under study. Using this methodology Coppedge (1994) has convincingly shown the strong negative impact of a lack of a legislative majority on presidential-legislative relations in Venezuela.

The absence of suitable legislative data leaves those seeking comparative analysis of executive-legislative relations at a considerable disadvantage. One alternate solution, however, is the examination of news coverage of Latin American politics for reports on executive-legislative conflict. While not ideal, this approach does provide a method by which we can enhance our dismal understanding of the factors which influence the tenor of executive-legislative relations.

Measuring Executive-Legislative Conflict

The *Latin American Weekly Report* (LAWR), published in England on a weekly basis, is the world's foremost current events newsletter covering Latin America. The LAWR has provided continuous coverage of Latin American politics and economics since 1967. Unlike many other newsletters, the LAWR reports on all of the region's nations and is found on more U.S. library shelves than any other weekly/monthly covering Latin America. In addition, the coverage the LAWR can give to any particular country is limited and thus it filters out much of the daily media chaff so as to provide coverage of only the most important issues or events in a nation.

A content analysis of the LAWR for the period 1984–93 examines the occurrence of executive-legislative conflict in Latin American nations. The unit of analysis is the presidential year.[6] A presidential year begins on the day of the president's inauguration and ends the day prior to that date the following year. A minimalist definition of democracy was employed to determine the suitability of regimes for analysis. For more information on this definition see Chapter Four.

A decision was made to begin in 1984 due to the LAWR's change of format that year. The analysis includes only those presidential years for which a minimum of six politics articles (one for every two months) were published in the LAWR. This was done to mitigate the potential for bias related to limited national coverage. Due to this criterion the number of presidential years included dropped from a potential population of 120 to 99.[7] However, analysis of both the pre- and post-reduction populations reveals very similar results, particularly for variables related to presidential strength in the legislature. The final analysis population consists of 99 presidential years (the units of analysis) from 14 countries, with 31 presidents represented (see Table 3.2).

Table 3.2
Executive-Legislative Conflict Analysis Population

Country	Presidential Years	N
Argentina	1983–84, 84–85, 85–86, 86–87, 87–88, 88–89*, 89–90, 90–91, 91–92, 92–93	10
Bolivia	1985–86, 86–87, 87–88, 88–89, 89–90, 90–91, 91–92, 92–93	8
Brazil	1990–91, 91–92, 92–93*	3
Chile	1990–91, 91–92, 92–93	3
Colombia	1984–85, 85–86, 86–87, 87–88, 88–89, 89–90, 90–91, 91–92, 92–93	9
Costa Rica	1985–86, 89–90, 91–92	3
Ecuador	1984–85, 85–86, 86–87, 87–88, 88–89, 89–90, 90–91, 91–92, 92–93	9
El Salvador	1984–85, 85–86, 86–87, 87–88, 88–89, 89–90, 90–91, 91–92, 92–93	9
Guatemala	1986, 87, 88, 90, 91, 93*	6
Honduras	1984–85, 85–86, 86–87, 91–92, 92–93	5
Nicaragua	1984–85, 85–86, 86–87, 87–88, 88–89, 89–90, 90–91, 91–92, 92–93	9
Peru	1984–85, 85–86, 86–87, 87–88, 88–89, 89–90, 90–91, 91–92*	8
Uruguay	1985–86, 86–87, 87–88, 88–89, 89–90, 90–91, 91–92, 92–93	8
Venezuela	1984–85, 85–86, 86–87, 87–88, 88–89, 89–90, 90–91, 91–92, 92–93	9

* Presidential year terminated prematurely.

Executive-Legislative Conflict: The Dependent Variable

For each presidential year two pieces of information were collected. First, all articles which had politics as their primary or secondary theme were tallied.[8] Second, for the politics articles, a detailed summary was recorded for all those which discussed any type of executive-legislative conflict.[9] From these two computations, a third was developed which is our principal focus in the analysis: the percentage of articles in each presidential year which had politics as their primary or secondary theme that were devoted to the coverage of executive-legislative conflict.[10] This measure is taken to demonstrate the prominence of executive-legislative conflict in a nation as well as the likely salience of the topic in a nation.

A potential difficulty with measuring conflict as a percentage of all politics articles is that in some countries unique events occurred which might have led to an excessive coverage of politics by the LAWR, thereby diluting the extent of executive-legislative conflict as measured in this study. Two types of events in particular could theoretically result in a consistent increase in the number of politics articles and hence a commensurate decrease in the percentage of conflict articles: (1) a serious insurgency (i.e., Colombia, El Salvador, Guatemala, Nicaragua until 1991, and Peru) and (2) the occurrence of a presidential election during the year in question. Each of these factors was controlled for in an initial multivariate analysis using the independent variables listed in Table 3.3, and neither was found to have a significant impact on the degree of executive-legislative conflict.

Determinants of Executive-Legislative Conflict

The theoretical literature on presidential systems identifies five principal factors as having a potential impact on presidential-legislative relations. They are: the size of the presidential party in the legislature (particularly whether or not the president has a legislative majority or near-majority), the temporal status of the president (i.e., at the beginning, middle or end of his or her term), the constitutional legislative power of the president, the constitutional non-legislative power of the president, and the control the president has over presidential party legislators. These five factors along with a sixth country-specific variable are examined to gain an enhanced understanding of their impact on executive-legislative relations.

With the exception of the presidential legislative support and country-specific variables, the current academic literature fails to provide reliable indicators for these potential determinants. Thus untested measures for the four other determinants are utilized, more to provide a control for the analysis of the effect of presidential partisan support in the legislature than to test the impact of these other determinants. The pilot study nature of these measures along with a desire to maintain this study's primary focus on electoral laws limits their inclusion to our analysis here and in Chapter Four where some of the difficulties surrounding their measurement are discussed.

The partisan strength of a president in the legislature can be measured in a number of ways. In this analysis two distinct measures are employed with each included in a separate regression. This is done to demonstrate that no matter how it is measured, presidential partisan support in the legislature has a salient impact on the degree of executive-legislative conflict in a nation. As is the case for all of our legislature-related measurements, these are based on the results of the legislative election and do not account for defections or other changes in the composition of the legislature which might occur between legislative elections.

The first measure of presidential legislative support is the percentage of seats held by the president's party in the legislature (in bicameral systems the lowest percentage of the two chambers).[11] The values for this measure range from a high of 64% in Nicaragua during the years 1984–90 to a low of 0% for Brazil in 1990–91, with a mean of 43% and standard deviation of 15.[12] Analysis of the data points suggests that the relationship between this variable and the executive-legislative conflict variable is linear.

The second measure of the president's degree of support in the legislature is based on whether or not the presidential party had a majority or near-majority of the seats in the legislature. Where a president's party possessed at the minimum a near-majority (i.e., it was the largest party and possessed 45% or more of the seats) in the unicameral house or both bicameral houses, that year is coded one (59% of the presidential years). Where the president's party failed to reach this threshold the year is coded zero (41% of the presidential years).

The second prominent explanatory variable for executive-legislative conflict is temporal. Work by Bond and Fleisher (1990), Coppedge (1988), and Light (1991) suggests that presidents have increasing problems with the legislature as their term progresses due to their inability to seek reelection (lame duck status). We would thus expect that as a president progresses through his or her term, executive-legislative conflict would increase, with a positive relationship between time in office and conflict.

In our analysis population no presidents, with the exception of the two Nicaraguan presidents, could seek immediate reelection, and in fact many were prohibited from ever seeking reelection (Jones 1995).[13] The time in office of the president is measured as the percentage of the term completed as of the first day of the presidential year. Thus for presidents who have a four-year term, the percentage completed in the first year would be 0%, in the second year 25%, etc. This measure is used in place of a simple year-based calculation in order to enhance the comparability of nations in the region where presidential term lengths range from four to six years.

The third prominent variable which may exert a strong influence on the degree of executive-legislative conflict is based on the constitutional power of the president over legislation. Shugart and Carey (1992) have hypothesized that the greater the legislative power of the president, the more likely democratic instability. An extension of their theory can be offered as a constitutional-based explanation for conflict between the president and the legislature: the stronger the constitutional legislative power of the president, the greater the degree of executive-legislative conflict. Shugart and Carey were referring much more to macro-level systemic stability than the more micro-level relations between a president and congress. Nevertheless, one would expect that the legislative powers of the president would have an impact on presidential-legislative relations.

Initially, two measures of presidential power over legislation resting on differential combinations of the same components were examined. Only one was employed in the analysis presented in Table 3.3 after initial analyses revealed the two measures to be very similar in effect. Shugart and Mainwaring (1995) identify what they consider to be the president's three most important legislative powers: (1)

veto power, (2) the exclusive introduction of legislation other than the budget, (3) decree authority. For veto power they divide presidential systems between those with strong veto power (where a two-thirds majority is required in the legislature to override), weak veto power (where less than a two-thirds majority is required to override), and no veto power. In this study systems with strong veto power are coded one and those with weak or no veto power are coded zero.[14] When referring to the exclusive introduction of legislation, Shugart and Mainwaring (1995) signify that "certain important bills in addition to the budget must be initiated by the president; or congress may not increase items of expenditure in a budget proposed by the president." Systems where the president has the power of exclusive introduction are coded one and those without this power zero. Finally systems where the "president may establish new law without prior congressional authorization (not including decrees of a regulatory nature)" (i.e., the president has decree authority) (Shugart and Mainwaring 1995) are coded one and those where the president lacks this power are coded zero.

The variable, constitutional power of the president over legislation, employed in the analysis presented here is binary. For this binary variable the systems were divided into two categories. Coded one were those systems where the president had two or three of the legislative powers (i.e., at least two of the above powers were coded one). Coded zero were those systems where the president had one or none of the legislative powers. Not discussed here, although yielding results similar to those of the binary variable, was an ordinal measure of constitutional power ranging in value from three to zero based on the number of the three constitutional powers held by the president.

Shugart and Carey (1992) stress the importance of the president's non-legislative power for executive-legislative relations. They cite four important areas of non-legislative power: (1) cabinet formation, (2) cabinet dismissal, (3) dissolution of the assembly, (4) censure (i.e., the ability of the legislature to censure government ministers). All of the presidential systems in this study give the president complete control over cabinet formation and dismissal, and while two endow the president with the power of dissolution, the constraints on and implications of such an act effectively annul this power.

Only for the power of legislative censure is there any real variance among the systems. Where a legislature has this power (coded one) the president is weaker constitutionally than where the legislature lacks the power of censure (coded zero). Where the legislature has this power it may very well intrude in an area (the functioning of the president's cabinet) which executives in presidential systems tend to see as their exclusive domain. We would thus expect the presence of a legislature with censure power to have a positive relationship with executive-legislative conflict. Contrary to the other variables whose impact on presidential-legislative relations is posited to be general, this censure variable focuses on one specific aspect of these relations. Hence, it is better seen as a type of control variable than a general measure of non-legislative constitutional power. An additional word of caution regarding this variable is in order. As the indicator of executive-legislative conflict is based on press reports, and the censuring of ministers is a very public act, it is likely that this type of executive-legislative conflict is captured better by the dependent variable than other more subtle and less public forms of conflict.

In all cases these two constitution-based variables (presidential power–legislative, legislative power–censure) are identical for all presidents who governed under the same constitution. The only instances of national differences in terms of the constitutional powers of the president occur for Colombia following the 1991 constitutional reform and Nicaragua following the 1987 constitutional reform.

A fifth factor which influences executive-legislative relations is the degree of control which a president has over members of the presidential party in the legislature (Fiorina 1977; Molinelli 1991; Shugart and Mainwaring 1995). One commonly employed measure of presidential control is whether or not an open versus closed party list is used to elect members of the legislature. Shugart and Mainwaring hypothesize that presidents have greater control over their party's legislators where a closed list is used than where a open list is employed (for more information on the reasoning behind this hypothesis see Chapter Two). Systems which employ a closed party list format for the election of members of their lower/single house are coded zero. Coded one are those systems which employ an open list ballot (Brazil, Chile, Peru) or two methods similar in their hypothesized impact on presidential control: the Ley de Lemas

(Uruguay, Honduras 1985–89), and a near-SNTV (single non-transferable vote) arrangement (Colombia). Bicameral systems where the senate is not elected using a party list represent a difficulty for this variable. Of the nations included in this analysis only in Argentina and Brazil is a party list not used to elect the senators. However, in Argentina this difference in election methods is mitigated as 46 of the nation's 48 senators (44 of 46 prior to 1992) are elected indirectly by the provincial legislatures.

Finally, many scholars have noted the uniqueness of the Bolivian system in terms of the coalition-inducing effect of its method of presidential election (Gammara 1995; Valenzuela 1993). In Bolivia, if no candidate receives an absolute majority of the vote a runoff is held between the top three candidates from the first round in the Congress.[15] Since the return to democracy in 1985 all three Bolivian presidents have been elected by the Congress. According to scholars this election method leads to a more inter-dependent and compromise-oriented presidential-legislative relationship which has allowed Bolivia to avoid much of the inter-institutional conflict that has taken place in other multi-party presidential systems. Given the special place of the Bolivian model in the literature, a Bolivia dummy variable is examined, with the eight Bolivian presidential years coded one and all other presidential years coded zero. If Gammara and Valenzuela are correct, we would expect there to exist an inverse relationship between the Bolivia dummy variable and conflict.[16]

Examining the Relationships

One traditional critique of Latin American presidential systems has been that their legislatures are of little relevance, existing more as rubber stamps than countervailing powers. While this position is difficult to sustain in the face of the theoretical and case study evidence presented in Chapter Two, if it were correct there would be very little incidence of executive-legislative conflict being reported by the LAWR. This lack of conflict would also hold true regardless of such factors as presidential support in the legislature, tenure in office, constitutional power, and control over presidential party legislators. Granted, the measurement of executive-legislative conflict (particularly its severity) with systematic data is a difficult task. The data examined here however do not support the traditional position of legislative irrelevance. Severe executive-legislative conflict exists in many nations, primarily those where the presidential legislative contingent is weak. Of course, this finding should not be very surprising to anyone familiar with Latin American politics over the past decade. The ability of Latin American legislatures to block, constrain, and defeat presidents has been amply shown in a diverse range of nations such as Argentina (Raúl Alfonsín), Brazil (Fernando Collor de Mello), Ecuador (León Febres Cordero, Rodrigo Borja, Sixto Durán), Guatemala (Jorge Serrano), Peru (Alberto Fujimori), Uruguay (Luis Lacalle), and Venezuela (Carlos Andrés Pérez).

Table 3.3 displays the results of two ordinary least squares (OLS) regression analyses focused on the determinants of executive-legislative conflict for the 99 presidential years from fourteen Latin American nations. The results demonstrate the importance of the size of the presidential legislative contingent for the tenor of executive-legislative relations as well as the salience of several other factors for executive-legislative relations.[17]

Presidential Legislative Strength. In the two regressions presented in Table 3.3 presidential legislative strength (unlike the other determinants) is measured using two distinct variables. The first variable (used in Regression One) is the most refined. The percentage of seats held by the president's political party in the legislative chamber (for bicameral systems, the chamber where the percentage was the lowest) has a very strong and significant impact on the degree of executive-legislative conflict. The estimated coefficient of $-.551$ is significant at the .001 level for a two-tailed t-test. This suggests that a one percent increase in the number of seats held by the president's party reduces the level of executive-legislative conflict 0.55%.

For the variable (used in Regression Two) measuring the presence (coded one) or absence (coded zero) of a presidential majority or near-majority of the seats in the legislature (in both chambers in bicameral systems) the estimated coefficient is -11.929 and the t-ratio -4.588. Here the presence of a majority or near-majority signifies a level of conflict that is 12% lower than would be the case if the presidential party lacked a majority or near-majority in the legislature.

These results indicate that the more variance in the measure of presidential legislative strength the better its predictive ability. This

Table 3.3
*Determinants of Executive-Legislative Conflict
in Latin American Presidential Systems*

Regression One

Variables	Estimated Coefficient	T-Ratio 92 DF
Percentage of Seats	−0.551	−7.441 **
Presidential Term	−0.062	−1.898
Presidential Power-Leg	0.944	0.311
Legislative Power-Censure	7.744	3.003 *
Presidential Control	−1.561	−0.515
Bolivia Dummy	−12.865	−3.586 **
Constant	35.145	9.443 **
R-Square: .587		

Regression Two

Variables	Estimated Coefficient	T-Ratio 92 DF
Near-Majority	−11.929	−4.588 **
Presidential Term	−0.030	−2.807 *
Presidential Power-Leg	2.440	0.695
Legislative Power-Censure	10.680	3.639 **
Presidential Control	−5.760	−1.722
Bolivia Dummy	−12.040	−2.803 *
Constant	19.905	7.062 **
R-Square: .461		

** Significant at the .001 level for a two-tailed *t*-test.

* Significant at the .01 level for a two-tailed *t*-test.

suggests that while it is very useful to focus on the presence or absence of a legislative majority or near-majority, we also need to keep in mind the actual size of the presidential legislative contingent, particularly when the president lacks a majority or near-majority. Despite their differences, both measures of presidential legislative support have a very strong impact on executive-legislative conflict with coefficients in the hypothesized direction that are significant at the .001 level for a two-tailed *t*-test. Compared with the other five independent variables, each of the presidential legislative strength variables is the most prominent influencing factor on the level of executive-legislative conflict within its respective regression.

The findings provide solid empirical evidence that the size of the presidential legislative contingent has a powerful impact on the degree of conflict between the president and the legislature. Where presidents have strong contingents, conflict is minimal. Where, however, presidents have a weak legislative contingent, conflict is often rampant between the two branches.

Presidential Time in Office. The variable measuring the president's time in office was hypothesized to have a positive relationship with executive-legislative conflict, with conflict increasing as the president progresses through his or her term. The findings in Table 3.3 are surprising as they detail an impact which is robust and opposite that hypothesized in direction, and in one case statistically significant at the .01 level (Regression Two) for a two-tailed *t*-test. This finding goes against conventional wisdom (which is based mostly on conjecture, not empirical evidence). It suggests that at least in these nations presidents do not experience an increasing level of conflict with the legislature over time. Bivariate analysis provides complementary support that, in general, in these systems presidential conflict with the legislature is highest at the beginning of the presidential term and decreases as the term progresses. The bivariate correlation between the presidential time in office and conflict variables is −.199 and is significant at the .05 level for a two-tailed *t*-test.

Presidential Power–Legislative. The legislative constitutional powers held by the president have a very weak and insignificant impact on the degree of executive-legislative conflict. This may reflect the micro-level nature of the relationship examined here, whereas the theory from which this hypothesis was derived is a macro-level concept positing a strong relationship between constitutional powers and democratic stability. Alternative explanations focus on two areas. First, that due to subtle differences in the specific constitutional powers and how they interact with other institutional and partisan factors in a nation, it is difficult to adequately measure the concept of presidential legislative constitutional power in a statistical analysis. Second, in some nations presidents at times fail to comply with certain constitutional rules and regulations, particularly where the constitution is vague or ill-defined (e.g., the use of executive decrees by President Carlos Menem in Argentina [Ferreira and Goretti 1994]). Obviously, to the extent that these rules are not observed the explanatory value of any variable based on them will be reduced. Greater discussion of these two points is provided in Chapter Four.

Legislative Power–Censure. The results from both regressions show that the legislature's possession of the power to censure government ministers results in an increased level of executive-legislative conflict. This finding is quite robust and suggests, as hypothesized by Shugart and Carey (1992), that the presence of this power leads to a confused presidential-legislative relationship, which engenders conflict between the two branches.

Presidential Control Over Presidential Party Legislators. The findings revealed that this variable did not have a significant impact on conflict in either of the two equations, though in both the coefficient was negative (i.e., use of a closed list results in a higher degree of executive-legislative conflict than use of an open list/Ley de Lemas/ SNTV). This is opposite what we would expect based on the theoretical literature and in general suggests that presidential control over his or her party's legislators (as measured here) does not have a strong effect on the degree of executive-legislative conflict in a system. A difficulty is the possibility that the direction of ballot structure's impact on executive-legislative conflict is contingent on whether or not the president has a legislative majority or near-majority. A critical discussion of this variable is provided in Chapter Four.

Bolivia Dummy Variable. It was initially hypothesized that the unique attributes of the Bolivian system would reduce executive-legislative conflict. The findings for both regressions support this hypothesis being in both the hypothesized direction as well as significant at the .001 level (Regression One) and .01 level (Regression Two) for a two-tailed *t*-test. Clearly something about the Bolivian system reduces the level of executive-legislative conflict. It is quite likely that the unique Bolivian trait is its method of presidential election as suggested by Gammara (1995) and Valenzuela (1993). The Bolivian system's promotion of coalition type governments has provided each of the three presidents in the 1985–94 period with a working parliamentary majority during most of their term, despite each of their own parties' lack of anything approaching a legislative majority or near-majority. No other brokered majority coalition between a presidential party and other prominent political parties anywhere in the region has registered the type of long-term stability and success of the Bolivian coalitions.

Analysis Summary

These results provide support for the hypothesis that the level of presidential partisan support in the legislature has a notable impact on the degree of conflict between the president and legislature. This conflict has been cited by many authors (e.g., Linz 1994; Lijphart 1994b; Nino 1992; Valenzuela 1990) as a tremendous weakness of the presidential form of government, one that in some cases can contribute to the breakdown of the democratic system. Some executive-legislative conflict is an integral part of the checks and balances of presidentialism. However, as both theoretical and case study evidence suggests, in Latin America this conflict is all too often of an extreme negative type which inhibits good governance and in places leads to the weakening and/or collapse of the democratic system.

Tests also were conducted on the impact of alternative factors which have been hypothesized in the theoretical literature to have an influence on executive-legislative relations. This book does not explore these alternative factors in any greater detail for reasons discussed more fully in Chapter Four. They are included in this chapter primarily as a control, thereby allowing for an enhanced understanding of the independent impact of the size of the president's legislative contingent on the degree of executive-legislative conflict in a nation.

An Example of the Problem: Argentina

This section examines the salience of presidential legislative support in one specific nation, Argentina. A general section based on personal interviews with Argentine elites followed by a case study of an Argentine province provide a rich and detailed examination of the relevance of strong legislative support for an executive's ability to govern.

Presidential Legislative Support in Argentina

Presidential legislative majorities or near-majorities are tremendously important in Argentina. This assertion was echoed by an overwhelming majority of the more than thirty Argentine politicians, academics, and civic leaders interviewed in Argentina between February and May 1993.[18] Many of those interviewed considered strong presidential legislative support important because with it a president is able to govern, while without it there is often a tendency toward governmental paralysis and gridlock. Presidents with healthy legislative support are considered to be well positioned to implement their policies and programs. Presidents who lack such support must face an opposition which often attempts to frustrate the president's policies (e.g., blocking them in congress) for the sole purpose of damaging the political image of the president.

While many respondents in the interviews also noted the danger of tyranny which may result if the president has a legislative majority (or close to it), all but a select few felt that the problems associated with a lack of a majority—of paralysis, inefficiency, and ungovernability—outweighed any potential dangers related to presidential tyranny if the executive were to have a majority. Many interviewees, particularly the politicians, gave the sad case of *Unión Cívica Radical del Pueblo* (UCRP) President Arturo Illia (1963–66) as a poignant example of the problems associated with a lack of sufficient legislative support. Illia's UCRP controlled only a little over a third of the seats in the legislature, and his government at one point went over a year without a budget due to congressional intransigence. Both Deputy Raúl Baglini (former president of the *Unión Cívica Radical* bloc in the Chamber, and a deputy between 1983 and 1993) and Deputy Jorge Vanossi (a *Unión Cívica Radical* deputy between 1983 and 1993) expressed the sentiments of many when they listed Illia's weak legislative contingent, and the governmental chaos caused by it, as one of the principal causes of the 1966 military coup against

Illia which led to seven years of military rule (Baglini 1993; Vanossi 1993).

Moreover, many of the respondents considered healthy legislative support to be particularly important in a country such as Argentina, where the political maturity of the opposition is not as developed (in the words of the interviewees) as in countries like the United States. Prominent politicians from Argentina's three largest parties (Deputy Hugo Rodríguez Sañudo [*Partido Justicialista*], Deputy Antonio María Hernández [*Unión Cívica Radical*], and Deputy Francisco de Durañona y Vedia [*Unión del Centro Democrático*]) possessed similar opinions regarding the salience of strong presidential support in the legislature (Rodríguez Sañudo 1993; Hernández 1993; Durañona y Vedia 1993).[19] All three considered a presidential legislative majority to not only be crucial for the ability of the president to govern effectively and avoid ungovernability, but of particular importance in a country such as Argentina where when in opposition, the principal parties (i.e., the *Partido Justicialista* [PJ] during the presidency of Raúl Alfonsín [1983–89] and the *Unión Cívica Radical* [UCR] during the presidency of Carlos Menem [1989–95]) tend to lead highly disciplined and often negative campaigns to obstruct many of the president's legislative programs.

> A presidential majority is especially important in a country like Argentina, where the civic order is underdeveloped, and the opposition tends to obstruct the government without purpose. There is no sense of a loyal opposition. (Rodríguez Sañudo 1993)

> Possession of a legislative majority by the president is particularly important in a country such as Argentina where a political culture of consensus between the governing party and the opposition is not highly developed. The lack of a legislative majority in Argentina is not the same as in the United States where politicians sit down and work out differences. In Argentina the lack of a presidential majority often leads to impasse. (Hernández 1993)

> When you have a situation where the congress, due to the lack of a presidential majority, obstructs the president, you get too great a degree of ungovernability, which reduces the effectiveness of the democratic process. (Durañona y Vedia 1993)

Argentine observers stress this obstructionist role played by the opposition (which often is purely obstruction for the sake of obstructing) as a key difference between the United States and Argentina. They implicitly and explicitly stated that the methods used in the United States to achieve bipartisan consensus or to woo individual opposition members are not always as feasible in Argentina where a fiercer opposition and more disciplined parties are the general rule.

Of course, the lack of a legislative majority or near majority does not signify constant conflict over all policies. Ana María Mustapic and Matteo Goretti (1992) have demonstrated that in many policy areas the Argentine government and opposition are able to work out consensual agreements. However, on issues that are politically important, issues where consensus cannot be reached and/or which are presented close to an election, the opposition is more likely to play an obstructionist role and block presidential initiatives in Congress. Legislative intransigence may of course be principled and based on legitimate criticism of the legislation. However it is also often purely political, for the opposition obstructs the legislation in order to damage the government (i.e., the president's administration) and to prevent it from implementing its policy program. In this situation the lack of a legislative majority or near-majority is not acting as a bulwark against tyranny, but rather as a barrier against effective government.

Salta 1991–93: A Governor with Deficient Legislative Support

The provincial government of Salta Governor Roberto Ulloa during the period 1991–93 offers an example of the problems faced by an executive who lacks sufficient legislative support.[20] Field research carried out in Salta on the impact of insufficient legislative support on Ulloa's ability to govern provides an opportunity to examine in greater detail the dynamic of policymaking in an environment of presidential legislative deprivation.[21] It provides a concrete example of the consequences of situations in which the executive lacks sufficient legislative support.

The sources of Governor Ulloa's weak legislative contingent can be traced primarily to two electoral rules. One is Salta's mixed timing cycle for gubernatorial and legislative elections which results in only one-half of the members of the bicameral provincial legislature being elected at the same time as the Governor. A second is the malapportionment of the seats in both the Chamber and particularly in the Senate. The impact of these electoral laws as well as more information on their impact in Salta is analyzed in Chapters Seven and Nine.

In 1991 Roberto Ulloa of the *Partido Renovador de Salta* (PRS) was elected governor of the province of Salta. His election ended eight years of Peronist control of the executive branch of the province. However, due in large part to the province's electoral laws, Ulloa lacked the advantage of a legislative majority (1) which his Peronist counterparts had enjoyed during their tenure as governor and (2) whose *Partido Justicialista* in fact continued to possess legislative majorities in both houses of the provincial bicameral legislature.

In 1991 Salta (like the rest of Argentina) was experiencing serious economic problems. Compounding these problems were a provincial public sector which under the PJ government had grown dramatically in size, a virtually bankrupt treasury, and outstanding debts contracted by the previous administrations. Following the lead of the Menem (PJ) administration (1989–95), as well as the strongly worded advice of President Carlos Menem's economic "czar" Domingo Cavallo, Ulloa set out to rationalize the provincial government (through layoffs and privatization) as well as to tackle some of the province's most severe problems such as the reform of the provincial government's pension system (Ulloa 1993). While all of these reforms were necessary if the province was ever to emerge from its dire economic situation, in implementing them Ulloa faced a severe obstacle, the PJ.

Not only did the PJ possess a majority of seats in both houses, but it also had been the party responsible for the increased size of the public sector as well as many of the substantial outstanding loans. It was also quite bitter about being displaced from office for the first time in the democratic period (Puig 1993). This combination suggested that Ulloa might have a difficult time implementing his policy programs. To better understand how Ulloa and his *Partido Renovador de Salta* handled the twin dilemmas of desperately needing to implement serious reform, but at the same time lacking anything approaching a legislative majority or near-majority, interviews were conducted in Salta with Governor Roberto Ulloa, the provincial Minister of Government Alfredo Gustavo Puig, the president of the Senate bloc of the PRS Senator Ennio Pedro Pontussi, as well as with other PRS officials and members of the Salta business community.[22]

On October 27, 1991 Roberto Ulloa was elected governor of the province of Salta with 56.06% of the popular vote (200,446 votes), outdistancing his nearest rival, the PJ candidate with 35.80% of the vote (128,005 votes), by more than 70,000 votes (see Table 3.4). Ulloa, who had been a highly popular governor of the province during the military dictatorship (1976–83), was thus, in late 1991, in the position to implement the reforms which he felt would rescue the province from its economic crisis (Adrogué 1993). However, the PRS success at the gubernatorial level had not translated into a majority for Ulloa in the provincial bicameral legislature. Due in large part to the electoral framework of the province, Ulloa lacked a majority in either house (see Tables 3.4 and 3.5). In the 1991 elections, the PRS won 13 of the 30 Chamber seats and 2 of the 11 Senate seats, giving it a legislative contingent of 17 of 60 seats (28%) in the Chamber and 3 of 23 (13%) in the Senate. This contrasted with the PJ legislative contingent which consisted of 33

Table 3.4
1991 Salta Provincial Election Results

Party	Election for Governor		Election for Senate*			Election for Chamber**		
	Votes	Percentage	Votes	Percentage	Seats	Votes	Percentage	Seats
Partido Renovador de Salta	200446	56.06	53370	39.29	2	163834	50.41	13
Partido Justicialista	128005	35.80	61884	45.56	9	123357	37.95	17
Unión Cívica Radical	20971	5.87	18592	13.69		28033	8.63	
Fuerza Republicana	1689	0.47	826	0.61		3765	1.16	
P. Demócrata Cristiano	1350	0.38	405	0.30		1590	0.49	
Others	5071	1.42	765	0.56		4447	1.37	
Total	357532	100.00	135842	100.01	11	325026	100.01	30

* One-half of the Senate renews every two years. In 1991, 11 of the 23 departments renewed their senators.

** One-half of the Chamber renews every two years. In 1991, 30 seats from 17 of the 23 departments were renewed.

Source: Data Files of the Argentine Ministerio del Interior, Dirección Nacional Electoral, Departamento de Estadísticas.

Table 3.5
Composition of the Salta Legislature: 1991–93

Party	SENATE Composition	Percentage of Seats	CHAMBER Composition	Percentage of Seats
Partido Renovador de Salta	3	13.04	17	28.33
Partido Justicialista	18	78.26	33	55.00
Unión Cívica Radical	1	4.35	9	15.00
P. Demócrata Cristiano	1	4.35	1	1.67
Total	23	100	60	100

Source: Data Files of the Argentine Ministerio del Interior, Dirección Nacional Electoral, Departamento de Estadísticas.

of 60 seats (55%) in the Chamber and 18 of 23 (78%) in the Senate.

When Ulloa assumed office in late 1991 following eight years of Peronist rule he inherited a bloated public bureaucracy and a virtually bankrupt treasury. Between 1983 and 1991 the size of the provincial bureaucracy work force had exploded from 26,203 employees to 58,683, a 124% increase (Banco Mundial 1991, 61; *Clarín* 04/26/92, 22). As a result, when Ulloa took office, those employed in the provincial bureaucracy accounted for 20% of the economically able population in Salta (*Clarín* 02/16/92, 9). This was 10% above the national average for provincial bureaucracies and placed Salta fifth out of Argentina's twenty-three provinces in terms of the percentage of the economically able population employed in the provincial public sector.

In addition to this bloated public sector, Ulloa also found an almost empty treasury, a fact which was worsened by the presence of debt obligations contracted by the previous PJ provincial administrations (Pontussi 1993; Puig 1993). A review of the economic condition of all of the Argentine provinces carried out shortly after Ulloa had assumed office classified the situation in Salta as "very difficult," and highlighted the tremendous economic strain placed on the provincial government by its debt burdens (*Clarín* 04/26/92, 22). In principle, when loans are used wisely, debt in and of itself is not a negative thing. However, as is all too common, many of the loans contracted by the PJ administrations were not channeled into productive activities. Particularly galling was the recently constructed seven million dollar Cable Car–Gondola which runs from the city center to a hill "Cerro San Bernardo" which overlooks the city (Pontussi 1993). Senator Pontussi considered this seldom used and money losing white elephant (there is both a stairway which offers a pleasant half hour walk to the top, as well as a road which leads there) as inappropriate for a province that has such severe health, educational, and infrastructural problems (e.g., a province where, according to the World Bank, 42.4% of the households are classified as having unsatisfied basic needs) (Banco Mundial 1991, 144).

Upon assuming office, on a tack very similar to that taken by Argentine President Carlos Menem, Ulloa set out to rationalize and shrink the public sector; to privatize money-losing provincial enterprises, restructure remaining provincial activities, and lay off redundant public employees. His goal was to put the provincial house in order (Ulloa 1993; Vittar 1993). The need to reduce the size of the provincial bureaucracy can hardly be argued. It was consuming between 75% (1988 official estimate) and 90% (1991 unofficial estimate) of provincial government expenditures.[23] Since from 1988 to 1991 the public sector had continued to grow in size while provincial expenditures remained relatively constant, this 90% estimate is probably reasonably accurate. In any event, it is obvious that when a government is spending practically all of its resources on salaries, precious little remains for administration and public works, the latter of which are desperately needed in Salta. In addition, the combination of money-losing provincial enterprises as well as debt obligations made the privatization of provincial enterprises (e.g., the provincial-run energy sector and water company) an attractive method to both reduce costs and raise revenues. This method had been successfully employed by the Menem administration at the national level.

Ulloa thus prepared a policy program along the same "liberal" economic line espoused by President Menem: reduce the bloated public sector, privatize money-losing provincial enterprises, and reform those that would remain under the control of the provincial government. Ulloa had no real problem getting legislation passed that was considered not to have a great deal of political importance (Pontussi 1993; Ulloa 1993). However, policies which were considered politically/economically important were difficult if not impossible to get through the legislature (Sanz 1993; Vittar 1993). On themes related to his principal policy program, such as privatization, reducing the size of the bloated bureaucracy, and reforming the provincial pension system, Ulloa encountered steadfast resistance in the legislature.[24] Examples of this type of obstruction include the Peronist rejection of (1) Ulloa's Decree 1091, which called for the privatization of the provincial government-run energy sector, water company, and other parastatals, all of which run a large deficit which the provincial government must then cover; and (2) Decree 72, which was Ulloa's plan to reform the ridiculously inefficient provincial government pension system (Vittar 1993).

As a result of this type of legislative obstruction, the Ulloa government, after a year and a half in office, had been unable to implement the majority of the most important components of its policy program. According to Ulloa, the lack of a legislative majority had seriously hurt his ability to implement many of his most important projects: "The lack of a majority has seriously damaged my efforts to restructure the province. It has hurt my ability to implement a set of policies which I feel are very important" (Ulloa 1993). However, in part by allying with President Menem (PJ) and getting Menem's public support for a project, Ulloa has at times been able to get a modified version of some of his legislation approved (i.e., he submits a decree with his project, the PJ-dominated legislature rejects it, but then passes a law which is a modified version of the decree) (Puig 1993; Ulloa 1993). Thus the system functions to a certain extent, although Ulloa found it difficult and hoped to have a legislative majority after the October 1993 elections (Ulloa 1993).[25]

Why did the Peronist opposition make such a strong effort to obstruct Ulloa's attempts to implement a set of policies which were so obviously needed? First, after their loss the embittered and shocked PJ began a political battle with the PRS, which previously had not been a very serious political threat. The PJ blocked Ulloa's policies with the intent that his government would be ineffective (Pontussi 1993; Vittar 1993). The PJ goal was to make the PRS government appear ineffective by obstructing the functioning of government, regardless of the negative consequences this obstruction entailed for the province. Second, the provincial PJ (unlike PJ President Menem) tended not to share the liberal economic ideology of Ulloa and was against his policies of privatization and the shrinking of the public sector (Hirsch 1993). While PJ opposition to privatization can perhaps be seen as a legitimate resistance to a method of economic policy, its opposition to the interwoven theme of reducing the size of the public sector is suspect. This intransigence in all likelihood stemmed not from a principled viewpoint, but rather from a hope of saving the jobs of people (many of whom had ties to the PJ) to whom the PJ had given jobs during its administrations (Vittar 1993). The source of the PJ opposition can thus be divided into three parts: (1) a political battle with the goal of ensuring the failure of the PRS government, (2) an attempt to save the jobs of people (most of whom had been hired by the PJ) in the inefficient and bloated public sector, and (3) a goal of blocking the privatization of money-losing provincial enterprises due partly to ideological opposition to this "liberal" policy as well as to the fact that it would reduce the size 'of the public sector (i.e., source 2).

In sum, the Salta legislature operated not so much as a democratic "brake" against an executive trying to implement a tyrannical policy program, but rather as a negative barrier which obstructed a governor's attempt to implement badly needed legislation. As a result, today, Salta's economic and social crisis continues to worsen. While we cannot be sure that Ulloa's "liberal" economic polices and efforts to reduce the size of the state would have resulted in economic success, we can be sure that his inability to implement major portions of his program has at best kept the province in the same precarious socioeconomic situation it was in when he took office.

Legislative gridlock, due primarily to an obstructionist opposition, has cost Salta dearly in terms of its future prosperity as well as its present standard of living. For example, as the legislature has prevented Ulloa from shedding redundant bureaucrats and money losing provincial enterprises, there is little money remaining to spend on public works such as sanitation and water supply. At the same time, between January 1 and May 1, 1993, Salta registered over 500 cases of cholera, a disease which is at its root the product of poor sanitation and an inadequate water supply. This tragic example is only one of many problems faced by the population of Salta, problems which cannot be solved while the legislature continues to obstruct the ability of the executive to govern. In essence, Salta represents an example of the concept of "ungovernability" which often occurs when an executive does not posses adequate support in the legislature. While Ulloa's possession of a PRS legislative majority or near-majority would not lead to miracles, it certainly would be a preferable alternative to the current troubled situation in Salta.

The general information on Argentina and the Salta case study suggest that executives who lack a legislative majority or near-majority face serious obstacles as they attempt to implement their policy program. In particular the case of Salta provides a poignant example of the policy consequences of the types of electoral laws employed by a system in regard to their tendency to provide the executive with strong support in the legislature.

Based on the results of this multi-tiered empirical analysis, I can make three primary observations. At the most general level, there exists a noticeable relationship between the presence or absence of a legislative majority or near-majority on a consistent basis and continuous success with democratic government. With the exception of Chile (prior to 1973), no presidential system has managed to combine a consistent lack of a presidential majority or near-majority and long-term democratic success. Second, cross-national analysis of *Latin America Weekly Report* articles identified the existence of a strong relationship between the size of the presidential legislative contingent and executive-legislative conflict. The level of presidential support in the legislature has a strong and significant impact on the degree of executive-legislative conflict, with the greater the extent of this backing, the lesser the incidence of conflict. Additionally, in their explanatory power the two presidential legislative support variables outperformed the other potential determinants of executive-legislative conflict most common in the scholarly literature. Finally, examination of the general importance of a strong presidential legislative contingent in Argentina along with the more in-depth analysis of the province of Salta echoes the findings of case studies conducted elsewhere which stress the importance of a strong presidential contingent to governmental success.

4

The Latin American and Argentine Provincial Systems

The analysis portion of this study utilizes electoral data from two separate populations: Latin American democracies and the provinces of the nation of Argentina. The data (unless otherwise noted) are the averages for these constitutional systems since the goal of the study is to analyze the impact of institutional arrangements on representation and the party system, a task which is best accomplished by examining systems, not individual elections. Two salient criteria were involved in the selection of these systems: one restricted the analysis to Latin America and a second required a system to satisfy certain democratic criteria.

THE RELEVANCE OF LATIN AMERICA

A majority of the world's democratic presidential systems are in Latin America. Latin America is therefore an ideal laboratory in which to examine the impact of electoral laws on presidential government. Current theories of the impact of electoral laws are based primarily on developed nations and any study focusing on developed nations tends to underrepresent the presidential form of government due to its limited presence among them (e.g., Lijphart 1984; Rae 1967; Sartori 1976). However, presidential government (in addition to its dominant status in Latin America) has a significant degree of

64

popularity in many non–Latin American democratic and democratizing nations.

By focusing exclusively on Latin American nations, one is able, to an important degree, to control for such "intervening" factors as religion, colonial history, and culture. These factors are important when considering institutional arrangements that are grounded in a nation's history and societal beliefs (Wiarda 1982). By restricting the analysis to a relatively small set of nations, there is a greater opportunity to conduct an informed contextual analysis which is enhanced by a developed understanding of the culture and history of the region. This analysis thus attempts to avoid the potential pitfalls inherent in both the cross-national method of analysis (i.e., a lack of contextual understanding of the nations being analyzed and thus an omission of important details which are not readily apparent) as well as in the case study method of analysis (i.e., to overlook the systematic regularities which exist in many nations, with an overweighted focus on what is unique in one nation). Avoiding these pitfalls is particularly important in the study of the impact of electoral laws, since at one level the analysis of the general impact of electoral structures truly requires a comparative perspective. At the same time, when studying the political consequences of electoral laws, a lack of understanding of the political reality which exists in the individual systems under study can very easily lead to false assumptions and inaccurate interpretations.

DEMOCRATIC SYSTEMS

The second criterion used for selecting cases was that the nation had to be a democracy. A nation is considered democratic if its government has been elected through open and competitive elections. The merits of this institutional approach toward the classification of democratic systems have been discussed by Diamond, Linz, and Lipset (1990) as well as by Remmer (1991). Remmer succinctly summarizes the logic of this institutional approach:

> Following the conventions established in the study of Latin American politics over the course of the past two decades, democratic governance is defined here strictly in institutional terms, leaving

open to empirical investigation questions regarding the consequences of competitive institutions for popular participation in policy formation, socioeconomic equity, and other political outcomes. (1991, 796)

The ultimately arbitrary nature of the selection of particular countries is acknowledged; however a degree of arbitrariness in defining "democratic countries" is hard to avoid.

This narrow focus on open and competitive elections as the principal defining characteristic of a democracy may elicit some criticism. The subject of this work, however, is elections and their political impact. Critiques of this definition notwithstanding, the holding of fair and free elections and the degree to which the results of these elections are respected have become the most common international standards of democracy. Many who study the region might also question the strength of the relationship between elections and "real" politics in Latin America. While one can debate the relative salience of elections for Latin American politics, their unique role in the expression of mass sentiment and the legitimation of government cannot be overstated.

In a select number of nations the electoral laws which govern the conduct of elections changed during the period of analysis. Where these changes resulted in a major shift in one of the key electoral law dimensions examined in the study, the electoral system in question was divided into separate systems. Thus if a system changed the electoral formula used for executive selection, the timing cycle for executive and legislative elections, the electoral formula (from plurality to PR) used to allocate legislative seats, the effective magnitude (in extreme cases), or the number of legislative chambers; a new analytic system was created.[1] This classification method is very similar to that employed by Lijphart (1994a) in his analysis of electoral systems in twenty-seven democracies.

THE POPULATION

Table 4.1 lists the Latin American systems employed in the data analysis along with the time period for which elections were included.[2] Table 4.2 shows the same information for the Argentine systems for the post-1983 era. Unless stated otherwise the provincial systems marked with an asterisk in Table 4.2, which provide an absolute majority (of varying sizes) of the lower/single house legislative seats to the plurality vote winner, are excluded from the analysis.[3] The 1973 Argentine population (not shown in a table) includes all of the same provinces listed in Table 4.2, with the exception of the twenty-third province, Tierra del Fuego, which only recently (1990) achieved provincial status.[4] There are twenty national systems and nineteen provincial systems (post-1983 era) which will be focused on in the chapters that follow.[5]

Table 4.1
Latin American Democratic Systems

System	Time Period
Argentina I	1973–1976
Argentina II	1983–1995
Bolivia	1985–1997
Brazil Ia	1945–1954
Brazil Ib	1954–1964
Brazil II	1989–1994
Chile I	1945–1973
Chile II	1989–1997
Colombia	1974–1991
Costa Rica	1953–1998
Dominican Republic	1978–1994
Ecuador	1978–1996
El Salvador	1984–1997
Guatemala	1985–1995
Honduras	1981–1997
Nicaragua	1984–1996
Paraguay	1993–1998
Peru	1980–1992
Uruguay*	1942–1994
Venezuela	1959–1998

* The Uruguayan data exclude the elections of 1954, 1958, and 1962 when a collegial executive was employed, along with the years 1973–84 during which time the nation was governed by a military dictatorship.

Table 4.2
Argentine Provincial Systems

System	Time Period
Buenos Aires	1983–1995
Catamarca I*	1983–1991
Catamarca II	1991–1995
Cordoba*	1983–1995
Corrientes	1983–1995
Chaco	1983–1995
Chubut*	1983–1995
Entre Rios*	1983–1995
Formosa	1983–1995
Jujuy	1983–1995
La Pampa	1983–1995
La Rioja	1983–1995
Mendoza	1983–1995
Misiones	1983–1995
Neuquen*	1983–1995
Rio Negro	1983–1995
Salta	1983–1995
San Juan I	1983–1987
San Juan II	1987–1995
San Luis I	1983–1987
San Luis II	1987–1995
Santa Cruz	1983–1995
Santa Fe*	1983–1995
Santiago del Estero I*	1983–1987
Santiago del Estero II*	1987–1995
Tierra del Fuego	1991–1995
Tucuman I	1983–1991
Tucuman II	1991–1995

* An asterisk indicates that the system provides the plurality winner in the lower/single house election with an absolute majority of the legislative seats.

Note: For analysis not involving the issue of bicameralism, San Luis is treated as a single system.

THE ARGENTINE PROVINCES

The Argentine provinces represent an ideal population in which to examine the political impact of electoral laws. Argentina is a federal republic with a constitution which in many aspects is quite similar to that of the United States in terms of its distribution of power between the national government and the constituent units of the federation. All twenty-three provinces employ a presidential form of government, electing a governor for a four-year term.[6] Each province possesses its own constitution and distinct electoral laws. Argentine provincial governors are not as independent politically and economically as their counterparts in the U.S. states, due primarily to greater central government control over tax revenue and the presidential power of provincial intervention in extraordinary situations. Nevertheless, after the Brazilian state governors, Argentine governors are the most powerful non-national elected officials in all of Latin America. Argentina provides two sets of provincial electoral systems, a set which has been in place since the return to democracy in 1983 and a set from the 1973–76 democratic interlude. While the former population tends to receive the majority of the focus in this work, the latter set also is employed where appropriate.

These provincial electoral systems do not operate in a vacuum. Far from being the autonomous units that national electoral systems are, these systems are influenced by the Argentine national electoral system. This influence occurs in two principal ways.

First, there is a powerful incentive for the provincial systems to mirror the national system in regard to the number of parties which operate in the provincial elections. In Argentina there are two relevant national parties, the *Unión Cívica Radical* (UCR) and the *Partido Justicialista* (PJ). Due to the predominance of these two parties at the presidential and congressional (national) level, there is a strong tendency for them to also be the dominant two parties locally. Thus there is pressure from outside the individual provincial electoral system pushing it toward a two-party dominated system, regardless of the electoral laws employed at the provincial level.

At the same time, in provinces where relevant parties other than the two principal parties operate (these additional parties in most cases are active in only a single province), there is a tendency for the number three party, when it is one of the two prominent national parties, to continue to compete in provincial elections, independent of the province's electoral laws. This continued competition stems largely out of a desire to continue to compete for votes in the province in the national lower house and presidential elections. This outside force has the opposite effect of pulling a select number of provinces toward a multi-party system. In 1994 in seven of Argentina's twenty-three provinces a provincial party ranked as one of the two largest political parties in the provincial legislature, displacing either the PJ or UCR. Thus at least in these (as well as other) provinces the domination of the PJ and UCR at the national level has not been transposed to the provincial level.

The contagion effect from the national system does prevent the examination of the Argentine provinces as completely autonomous systems. However, the presence of a diverse population of electoral systems within one nation allows for the examination of the independent impact of electoral laws, holding a multitude of exogenous variables constant, to an extent that is impossible in cross-national analyses of electoral systems.

FRAMEWORK OF ANALYSIS

The analysis section examines the impact of a set of key electoral laws on the number of political parties in an electoral system and on the size of the president's political party in the legislature. The number of parties in the legislature is considered to be a crucial intervening variable between many of the electoral law variables and the size of the executive's legislative contingent.

The discussion begins with the relationship between the number of parties and contingent size. Then, five key electoral law and constitutional structure dimensions are examined. The first one discussed is the electoral formula employed to elect the executive, with the key distinction being between those systems which employ the plurality electoral formula and those that use a majority runoff formula. The second dimension is the election timing cycle for executive and legislative elections, with the systems divided primarily between those which hold these elections concurrently and those which hold them nonconcurrently. The third and fourth dimensions are the effective magnitude of the electoral districts used to select the legislators and the electoral formula employed to allocate the legislative seats. The principal area of interest revolves around the impact of varying levels of effective magnitude in systems which utilize a proportional representation (PR) formula to allocate legislative seats. The fifth and final dimension is the number of chambers in the legislature (either unicameral or bicameral). Following this straightforward bivariate examination the analysis concludes with an examination of the independent impact of the first four dimensions on the key intervening variable of legislative multipartism.

RELEVANT OMISSIONS

The objective of this analysis is not to explain the overall power of presidents. Rather it is primarily concerned with the manner in which electoral laws influence the tendency of a system to provide the executive with a legislative majority or near-majority. It focuses specifically on the role played by electoral laws on the assumption that these laws have a significant impact on the nature of politics in a nation through their ability to influence the distribution of governmental power.

There are, however, two important issues related to the topic of presidential legislative support which nonetheless merit a brief discussion. These issues were referred to in Chapter Three in the analysis of the determinants of presidential-legislative conflict. They concern: (1) the constitutional distribution of power between the executive and the legislature, and (2) the degree of presidential control over deputies of his or her party in the legislature.

Shugart and Carey (1992) have demonstrated that a wide variation both in the level of presidential power vis-à-vis the legislature as well as vis-à-vis members of the president's own party exists among Latin American constitutional systems. Obviously the distribution of constitutional power in a system along with the extent of the executive's control over deputies of his or her party is important to any discussion of the salience of a legislative majority or near-majority. For example, the lack of a legislative majority or near-majority is perhaps more important to a president whose ministers are subject to legislative censure (e.g., Ecuador) than it is to one whose cabinet is completely independent from the legislature (e.g., El Salvador). Likewise, a legislative majority for a president who is the unquestioned leader of his or her party and has the ability to impose severe sanctions on deputies who defy him or her (e.g.,

Argentina) is of greater value than a legislative majority for a president who has very little control over members of his or her party in the legislature (e.g., Brazil).

Presidential Constitutional Power

Shugart and Carey (1992) classify constitutional systems based on the degree of constitutional power granted to the president vis-à-vis the legislature. Using ordinal scales they rate each constitutional system in terms of the president's legislative and non-legislative powers. Shugart and Carey find that for the systems included in this study, the presidential power scores on these two indices vary considerably. However, the true extent of these differences is currently very difficult to measure. The Shugart and Carey (1992) book represents the only comparative effort to empirically study the constitutional distribution of power in presidential systems. While providing a strong discussion of the distribution of constitutional power, this very important work has two weaknesses. One, to construct their measures of presidential constitutional power, the authors use ordinal classifications for different categories which are treated as equivalent and then summed to create an index. While a useful first step, these ordinal classifications cannot be treated as additive interval data because they are based on the questionable logic that each constitutional factor is of equivalent importance in regard to its impact on presidential power.[7] Efforts to devise an alternative measure of presidential power using legislative and decree output also have been found wanting because each constitutional system tends to have a distinctive method of implementing decrees and laws.[8]

Two, the Shugart and Carey classification is based strictly on the written constitution of a nation which is not always followed to the letter in many Latin American countries.[9] This is particularly the case in systems that place limits on the president's power to an extent uncommon in the neighboring presidential systems. For example, according to Shugart and Carey, under the 1979 Constitution the Peruvian president was institutionally (vis-à-vis the legislature) one of the weakest executives of the systems included in this study. However, due to the efforts of the Peruvian presidents, the system evolved to a level of presidential power in relations with the legislature comparable to that of other Latin American nations where the president is granted a level of constitutional power much greater than that prescribed in the Peruvian document (Sabsay 1991; Torres y Torres Lara 1992). The inability to document empirically the fit between the written constitution and political reality weakens this measure of executive power based on formal constitutional provisions.

Partisan Control

The lack of an adequate framework to compare the level of centralization and discipline of political parties both across and within nations is a significant problem for the comparative study of democracies. As Lijphart (1994a) has noted, the salience of the findings of research on electoral systems is conditioned by the degree of party centralization and discipline. The control which a president has over his or her party's deputies in the legislature is a product both of a system's laws governing political parties, campaign finance, and electoral procedures as well as internal party-specific rules. As such, the level of presidential control is likely to vary both across nations and within nations across parties. The measurement of executive control over the legislative party in a comparative manner is a difficult task which as of today no one has been able to accomplish for the party systems of Latin America (or for all intents and purposes those elsewhere).[10] While we do have some descriptive evidence that for example executive control over members of his or her party in the legislature is weaker in some nations (e.g., Ecuador and Brazil [Conaghan 1994; Mainwaring 1992, 1991]) than others (e.g., Argentina and Venezuela [Molinelli 1993, 1992; Kornblith and Levine 1993]), we lack the measures and rigorous comparative analysis necessary to adequately measure the degree of presidential control over his or her legislative party.

While constitutional power and party centralization and discipline are central to a comprehensive understanding of executive effectiveness, our basic tenet remains unchanged. Regardless of the degree of executive constitutional and intra-party power, a president with a legislative majority or near-majority will be more effective than one without such legislative support. The differences imposed by these two important structures, both across and within systems, are merely a matter of degree.

The data analysis in this study incorporates two separate primary populations. One population is twenty Latin American democratic systems. The second is nineteen Argentine provincial systems. The end goal of the study is to demonstrate the salience of electoral laws for the functioning of government in a democratic presidential system. While no one factor determines whether a democratic system succeeds or fails, the electoral laws employed by a system do have a salient impact, and unlike many other important factors such as a nation's culture and level of economic development, electoral laws are relatively easy to change.

5

Legislative Multipartism and Presidential Legislative Support

The political consequences of the number of political parties in a party system have been a subject of considerable debate among scholars. Mayer (1980) and Taylor and Herman (1971) point to the advantages of cabinet stability provided by systems with low levels of multipartism and Powell (1982) has cited the greater accountability of governments in two-party systems. Haggard and Kaufman (1994) posit that high levels of multipartism have negative consequences for the construction of a stable and coherent economic policy. Geddes (1994) has noted that systems with two principal parties are more conducive to the achievement of consensus among politicians to initiate and later deepen crucial structural reforms. Others such as Lijphart (1994a, 1984) tend to be less sanguine about the superior traits of the two-party dominant systems over their multi-party counterparts.[1] Lijphart has identified flaws in the method by which scholars such as Mayer and Taylor and Herman have measured stability, noting that cabinet stability is a very poor indicator of regime stability (e.g., in Italy cabinets can fall without causing any major political crisis). Lijphart also has detected what he considers to be an overweighted focus by bipartite system proponents on multi-party systems which failed (e.g., the French Fourth Republic and the German Weimar Republic) and a lack of consideration of some of the successful multi-party systems (e.g., the Netherlands and Sweden). Lijphart also questions many of the assumptions of the pro two-party school such as the system's greater level of accountability and tendency to lead to moderation in policymaking. There is, however, little debate among scholars that multi-party systems allow for a greater level of minor party representation and are more proportional than their two-party dominated counterparts.

LEGISLATIVE MULTIPARTISM AND PRESIDENTIAL SYSTEMS

Chapter One examined the distinctly different scenarios associated with a legislature where the executive lacks a majority or near-majority in parliamentary and presidential systems. The political impact of high levels of multipartism in parliamentary systems can be debated, but its impact in presidential systems cannot. High levels of multipartism are incompatible with successful presidential government.

Juan Linz (1992), a strong advocate of parliamentary government, has identified the strong relationship between high levels of multipartism and ineffective and unsuccessful presidential government. The lesson Linz draws from this reality is that except for the small number of presidential systems with low levels of multipartism (i.e., Argentina, Colombia, Costa Rica, Venezuela; and in the past Uruguay), presidential government is likely to lead to ineffective and perhaps short-lived democratic government.[2] His solution to the dismal prospects faced by multi-party presidential systems is that they should adopt a form of parliamentary government. He rejects the possibility of using electoral engineering to reduce the number of parties in a system and highlights specific instances where this engineering already has been tried and failed (i.e., General Augusto Pinochet's two-party design for Chile, and Brazil under the military dictatorship [1964–85]), or that where it has worked (South Korea, 1988–) it is likely to lead to an opposition which feels shut out and alienated from democracy due to the dominant status of the largest political party.

Linz's argument against electoral engineering has several flaws. First, many of the party systems in Latin America which he cites as multi-party systems have this high level of multipartism due primarily to their electoral laws and not so much the consequence of a set of natural fissures in the polity. For example, in 1990 four parties of the ideological right and three of the center-right competed in the Guatemalan presidential and/or legislative elections. The presence of this large number of parties representing the right half of the political spectrum is more the consequence of Guatemala's multipartism-encouraging electoral laws than it is the product of a massive set of sociological divisions within the conservative political community.[3] Second, the case of Chile II (1989–), while still too early to make any firm conclusions, does suggest that the system's two-party–encouraging law (two-member legislative districts for both houses of the bicameral legislature) has led to the formation of two relevant coalitions of parties which demonstrates partial success for this example of engineering.[4] Third, while the Brazilian military's attempt to create a two-party system failed, the principal source of the current extremely high levels of multipartism in Brazil lies with its electoral laws (e.g., its majority runoff presidential formula, nonconcurrent timing cycle [reformed in 1994], and high legislative effective magnitude) (Mainwaring 1991, 1990; Power 1991). It would be difficult to design a presidential electoral system which encourages multipartism as much as that of Brazil II.

Finally, Linz uses the case of South Korea as his example of successful electoral engineering in which (due in large part to the system's use of the plurality formula to select the president) the then-ruling Democratic Justice Party (DJP), the Reunification Democratic Party (RDP), and the New Democratic Republican Party merged in 1990 to form the Democratic Liberal Party (DLP). Confronted with an engineered two-party dominant system in which one of the two parties (the DLP) was at the time predominant, Linz states that it is "questionable if a system in which one of the two parties would enjoy a large majority and be quite assured of gaining the presidency leaving the opposition minority PPD (Party for Peace and Democracy) . . . with little chance of sharing power or alternation, will assure stability" (1992, 72). Linz contrasts the situation of South Korea when the DJP and RDP ran separately in the 1987 presidential race and together won 64.6% of the vote with that of the United States, Costa Rica, and Venezuela where the president's party on average has held 45.8% (United States), 49.6% (Costa Rica) and 45.4% (Venezuela) of the lower house seats (these percentages are the ones employed by Linz). He implies that, contrary to the situation of these latter three countries where no party is completely dominant, in South Korea the mega-DLP would dominate, leading to the exclusion of the PPD. It is probably a little early to proclaim DLP omnipotence. First, in 1953 in the first post-revolution election in Costa Rica the *Partido Liberación Nacional* (PLN) won 64.7% of the presidential vote and 66.7% of the seats in the unicameral legislature while in Venezuela in the 1958 election (the first after the fall of the Pérez Jiménez dictatorship) *Acción Democrática* (AD) won 49.1% of the presidential vote, 54.9% of the seats in the Chamber, and 62.8% of the seats in the Senate.[5] Thus even two of Linz's exemplary competitive two-party dominant cases did not start out that way. In the aftermath of these initiating elections, the Costa Rican and Venezuelan party systems were more similar to the 1990 party system of South Korea than to their own respective present day party systems. However, the electoral laws of these systems progressively helped encourage the growth of a competitive two-party dominant system. Second, the results of the 1992 South Korean presidential election suggest that the single dominant party system feared by Linz has not crystallized, with the DLP winning the presidential race with only 41.96% of the vote against 33.82% for the principal opposition (Keesing's 1992, 39234).[6]

PRESIDENTIAL SYSTEMS AND PROPORTIONAL REPRESENTATION

In presidential systems, high levels of multipartism reduce the size of the president's legislative contingent and hence increase the likelihood that the president will lack a legislative majority or near-majority. Where the president lacks this level of legislative support, effective governance will be more difficult, creating a greater opportunity for the emergence of ungovernability, the negative impact of which is felt throughout the nation. Thus while the number of parties is perhaps not of supreme concern to scholars whose principal area of interest lies with parliamentary democracy, for students of presidential government, the number of parties in a system is crucial. The higher the level of multipartism in a system, the more likely is the type of ineffective and unstable presidential government which critics of presidentialism such as Linz (1994) and Valenzuela (1990) often cite to exemplify the perils of presidentialism. Conversely, where this level of multipartism is limited, presidential majorities and near-majorities are more probable and hence presidential government is likely to be more effective and prosperous.

Finally, as the data which follow show, the level of multipartism necessary to achieve an executive majority or near-majority most of the time does allow for some minor party representation. This representation, while not large, does accomplish at least four important tasks. First, it provides descriptive representation for a limited number of minor parties. Second, it provides these same groups with a "bully pulpit" from which they can make public the needs and positions of their party and constituency. Third, these parties can utilize their official congressional status to call for government investigations and for related purposes. Fourth, in those cases where the president's party is short of an absolute majority these minor parties can achieve some benefits in exchange for their support in the legislature for the governing party's proposals.

All of the lower/single houses in this study (with one very minor exception) utilize PR to allocate their legislative seats. Single-member plurality districts (SMPDs) are probably not a viable alternative option for elections in Latin America (nor perhaps elsewhere) for the lower/single house.[7] This is due primarily to their highly disproportional nature, the inherent dilemmas and wide potential for abuse involved in the creation of single-member legislative districts, and their potentially deleterious impact on the relations between the president and the congressional members of the presidential party.

Disproportionality in the translation of votes into legislative seats is evident in all electoral systems. It is, however, most severe in the single-member plurality systems (disproportionality is both mechanical and psychological in nature, with only the former subject to measurement in the calculation of the translation of votes into seats). The disproportional nature of the single-member plurality arrangement is evidenced both by its tendency to marginalize the number two party in the system in terms of the proportion of seats it receives relative to that of the number one party as well as by the propensity of the arrangement to exclude most if not all minor parties.

A second and equally problematic effect of the use of single-member plurality districts is related to the method of electoral district creation.[8] Some of the most virulent partisan conflicts in the United States (where partisan sentiment is abnormally tepid) occur over redistricting, and adding this issue to the already volatile partisan situation in most Latin American nations would be tantamount to dousing smoldering embers with gasoline.[9] The ability to severely manipulate the redistricting process is exemplified by the Peronist orchestrated gerrymandering for the 1951 Chamber election in Argentina where using single-member plurality districts (appropriately gerrymandered) the Peronists won 133 (95.7%) of the 139 SMPD seats in the Chamber of Deputies with only 62.7% of the vote.[10] Conversely the principal opposition *Unión Cívica Radical* (UCR) won only 6 (4.3%) SMPD seats in 1951 with 33.1% of the vote (Dirección Nacional Electoral 1994). Given this potential for abuse, the use of single-member plurality districts is likely to exacerbate the "winner-take-all" nature of presidential systems by denying the principal opposition a significant presence in the legislature. Such was the case following the 1951 elections in Argentina where the UCR was practically non-existent in the official organs of government. Not surprisingly the UCR was a strong supporter of the 1955 military coup which overthrew President Juan Perón (Rock 1987).[11]

Finally, the use of single-member plurality districts increases the tendency of members of congress from the president's party to represent the interests of their district at the expense of those of the president/party. This is particularly the case in systems where there is a weak level of party control over the members of congress (e.g., weak control over access to the ballot using the party symbol). Thus while single-member plurality districts may provide a higher average of seats for the presidential party than some of the PR alternatives, this benefit is counteracted by their debilitating impact on the degree of control which a president has over his or her legislative bloc in the congress.[12]

Later in the chapter I will demonstrate that it is possible to have a limited degree of proportional representation while at the same time consistently providing the executive with the legislative majority (or near majority) needed to govern effectively. In a sense presidential government combined with PR (with electoral laws that encourage moderate levels of multipartism) represents the ideal type of presidentialism. It tends to provide stability and effectiveness through its ability to supply the president with a strong legislative contingent while at the same time allowing for a greater level of minor party representation than a system that utilizes single-member plurality districts (e.g., the United States).

LEGISLATIVE MULTIPARTISM

Legislative multipartism is calculated utilizing a measure based on the percentage of legislative seats won by the various parties in the lower/single house (and where relevant, senate) elections (i.e., Laakso and Taagepera's measure of the "effective number of parties" in a party system [1979, 3–27]).[13] Legislative multipartism is used instead of the most prominent alternative, electoral multipartism, for the lower house (and senate), for two reasons.[14] First, it better reflects party representation at the governmental level, and hence the existence of relevant parties (although at the cost of overlooking the presence of very minor parties). Second, it allows for the inclusion of six systems which could not be analyzed (in whole or in part) if electoral multipartism were employed.[15] In any event, analysis of the available data revealed electoral and legislative multipartism to be highly correlated (.93 for 17 systems), with legislative multipartism consistently lower than electoral multipartism for all systems. Theoretically, where legislative multipartism is high, a presidential legislative majority or near-majority is less likely. Conversely where it is low, a presidential legislative majority or near-majority is more likely.[16]

In order to construct this measure of legislative multipartism, a definition of a legislative political party is required. The definition used here is based on the legislative election. Candidates who are elected on the same party ticket or run under the same party label are considered to be members of the same political party. For example, despite their factionalism, the Uruguayan *Colorado*, *Blanco*, and *Frente Amplio* parties are all treated as single parties. In the case of coalitions of parties running under the same ticket, these groups are treated as a single party. In instances of coalitions among parties in isolated cases, the legislators elected are treated as members of the dominant coalition partner. The classification procedure does, however, also take into account the issues and arrangements surrounding these coalitions. The resolution process for the more controversial classifications is described in Appendix E.

The values for the multipartism variable for the national systems have a reasonably continuous distribution, with a mean of 3.39 effective parties and a standard deviation of 1.59. Values for this variable range from a low of 1.99 (which is the value for Chile II and corresponds to slightly less than two effective parties) to a high of 7.46 (which is the value for Brazil II and corresponds to roughly seven and one-half effective parties). Legislative multipartism for the Argentine provincial systems ranges from a low of 1.30 for La Rioja and San Juan I to a high of 3.12 for San Juan II.[17] The mean level of multipartism for these systems is 2.27, with a standard deviation of 0.43.

EXECUTIVE LEGISLATIVE CONTINGENT

The average percentage of seats held by the executive's party in the legislature (i.e., the executive legislative contingent) is the preferred measure of executive legislative strength. It is less arbitrary than the principal alternative measure of simply whether or not the president had a majority or near-majority and provides an interval measure of the degree of executive partisan support in the legislature. A system's score for its average executive legislative contingent is the sum of the averages of the size of the contingents held by the system's executives during their terms in office. In most cases the lower/single legislative house contingent is used due to its presence in all systems. However, in specific portions of the analysis where its inclusion is considered beneficial, a separate analysis of the average size of the executive's senate contingent is also utilized. The partisan affiliation of these legislators is based on the most recent legislative election and does not take into account events such as partisan defections, mergers, and new party formation. This decision rule is preferable for reasons of methodological accuracy and because this work holds constant factors such as the laws governing the functioning of political parties and party cohesiveness and discipline. Matters such as defection and new party formation are intricately linked to the rules governing the functioning of political parties and their level of internal discipline.

For the national systems the mean size of the average presidential lower/single house contingent is 42.64% of the legislative seats with a standard deviation of 12.69. The average size of these contingents ranges from a high of 59.49% for Nicaragua to a low of 6.36% for Brazil II. For the Argentine provincial systems (1983–95) the mean size of the governor's legislative contingent is 54.80% of the lower/single house seats and the standard deviation 11.97. La Rioja provides the largest average contingent (88.31%) while Chaco (44.28%) provides the smallest average lower/single house contingent.

LEGISLATIVE MULTIPARTISM AND THE EXECUTIVE LEGISLATIVE CONTINGENT

Figures 5.1 and 5.2 demonstrate graphically the very strong relationship between lower house multipartism and the size of the lower house executive legislative contingent. The correlation between these two variables for the national systems is −.941, while for the Argentine provincial systems (excluding those provinces which provide an absolute majority to the plurality winner in the lower house) the correlation is −.887.[18] Clearly, as the level of multipartism increases, the size of the executive's legislative contingent decreases. On each of the two figures, movement from the left toward the right on the legislative multipartism scale results in a progressively decreasing executive legislative contingent.

Earlier it was noted that presidential systems with legislatures elected using PR (but with a low level of multipartism) represent the ideal form of presidential government. They combine a strong tendency to provide the executive with a legislative majority or near-majority with at least some minor party representation. Table 5.1 shows a representative legislative composition for the three systems which have experienced more than a dozen years of continuous democratic government that on average provide their president with the largest legislative contingents. These representative samples of

Figure 5.1
The Relationship between Legislative Multipartism and the Size of the President's Legislative Contingent in 19 Latin American Systems

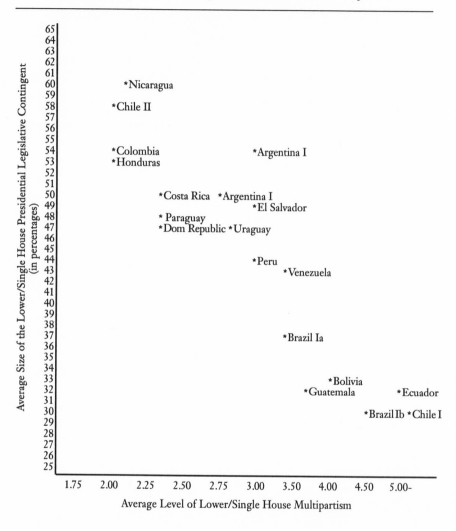

Note: Brazil II has a level of multipartism of 7.46 and an average presidential contingent of 6.36. In order to provide a better graphic presentation of the other systems it was excluded from the figure. If included it would, however, conform to the above distribution, located in the extreme lower right portion of a quadrant of the figure not shown.

Source: See Appendix A.

Figure 5.2
The Relationship between Legislative Multipartism and the Size of the Governor's Legislative Contingent in 18 Argentine Provincial Systems

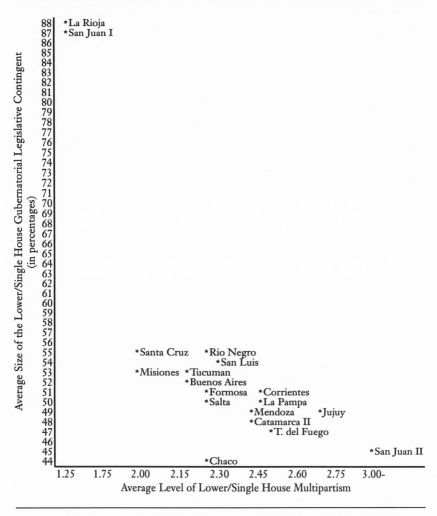

Note: These data are for the 1983–95 period only. Systems which provide the plurality winner in the lower house with an absolute majority of the seats are excluded. Finally, two separate systems were employed for the province of San Juan due to that province's switch from single-member plurality districts to a mixed districting system after the 1983 election.

Sources: Data files of the Argentine Ministerio del Interior, Dirección Nacional Electoral, Departamento de Estadísticas.

Table 5.1
A Representative Composition of the Lower/Single House in Three Systems

Country and Time Period	Political Party	Distribution of Lower/Single House Seats	Percentage
COLOMBIA 1978–82			
	Partido Liberal Colombiano	111	55.78
	Partido Conservador Colombiano	83	41.71
	Unión Nacional de Oposición	4	2.01
	Frente por la Unidad del Pueblo	1	0.50
	Total	199	100.00
COSTA RICA 1986–90			
	Partido Liberación Nacional	29	50.88
	Partido Unidad Social Cristiana	25	43.86
	Alianza Popular	1	1.75
	Pueblo Unido	1	1.75
	Unión Agrícola Cartaginesa	1	1.75
	Total	57	99.99
HONDURAS 1989–93			
	Partido Nacional de Honduras	71	55.47
	Partido Liberal de Honduras	55	42.97
	Partido de Inovación y Unidad	2	1.56
	Total	128	100.00

Sources: See Appendix A.

the legislative composition of three lower/single houses (Colombia 1978–82, Costa Rica 1986–90, Honduras 1989–93) reveal the normal functioning of these systems where the president receives a legislative majority and at the same time minor parties receive representation in the legislature.

In Colombia during the period 1978–82 the *Partido Liberal* of President Julio César Turbay held an absolute majority in the Lower House, followed by the *Partido Conservador*, with the system providing some representation for two left wing parties (*Unión Nacional de Oposición* and *Frente por la Unidad del Pueblo*). In Costa Rica (1986–90) the Partido Liberación Nacional of president Oscar Arias held an absolute majority of the seats in the Costa Rican Legislative Assembly where (in addition to the sizable contingent of the *Partido Unidad Social Cristiana*) representatives from two left wing parties (*Pueblo Unido* and *Alianza Popular*) and one regional party (*Unión Agrícola Cartaginesa*) also possessed seats. The Honduran system (1989–93) provided president Rafael Callejas' *Partido Nacional* with an absolute majority of the seats in the Chamber and, in addition to the well-represented *Partido Liberal*, at the same time allowed for the representation of a small reformist party (*Partido de Inovación y Unidad*). In each of these systems the combination of presidentialism and proportional representation proved to neither deprive presidents of legislative majorities, nor to exclude minor political parties from at least partial representation. These ideal compositions are not a chance result. They are very much a product of the electoral laws employed in these three systems (i.e., a combination of at least three of the following: plurality presidential electoral formula, concurrent timing of presidential and legislative elections, a moderate effective magnitude, proportional representation). These laws will be identified and examined in detail in upcoming chapters.

The level of multipartism in a legislature has a very strong impact on the size of the executive's legislative contingent. The size of this contingent tends to be a crucial determinant of the degree of effectiveness and in places longevity of presidential government in a system. Thus the level of legislative multipartism is a crucial intervening variable for the understanding of the influence of electoral laws on the functioning of presidential government. In the sections that follow, the impact of a set of salient electoral laws on both legislative multipartism and the size of the executive's legislative contingent will be examined. The systemic effect of these electoral rules is quite strong and demonstrates the crucial role which electoral laws play in the functioning of democratic systems.

6

The Executive Electoral Formula

The electoral formula used to select the executive in presidential systems is strongly related to a system's tendency to provide the executive with a legislative majority or near-majority. The electoral formula's primary impact is indirect, operating through the intervening variable of legislative multipartism. Its other, secondary impact, is direct, but occurs only under certain electoral conditions.

METHODS OF EXECUTIVE SELECTION

A populace can select its executive in presidential systems in many ways. These popular elections can either be direct (in which voters directly choose a candidate) or indirect (in which the citizenry selects electors who in turn choose the executive). All of the Latin American systems examined in this study directly elect their executive with the exception of Argentina II, a few of the Argentine provinces, and to a certain extent Bolivia and Chile I.[1] Two separate methods of selection are employed by the systems which directly elect their executive: the plurality and majority runoff formulas.[2] Under the plurality formula the candidate who receives a relative majority of the popular vote in the first and only round of popular elections becomes the executive.[3] In majority runoff systems a candidate who receives an absolute majority of the valid popular vote (over 50%) in the first round of elections becomes president. If, however, no candidate receives an absolute majority of the vote, then a runoff is held between the top two challengers from the first round with the second round winner becoming president.[4] A third formula which is a variant of the majority formula is the majority congressional system used by Bolivia and Chile I. Under this formula if no candidate receives an absolute majority in the first round of elections, then the executive is chosen in a joint session of the bicameral legislature from among the top two (Chile I) or three (Bolivia) candidates from the first round. Theoretically, the Bolivian and Chilean I majority congressional systems are considered to be similar in their functioning to the majority runoff systems, particularly in regard to their direct effect on legislative multipartism and indirect and direct effect on the size of the president's legislative contingent. Like the majority runoff systems the Bolivian and Chilean I systems require that for a candidate to be elected in the first round he or she has to receive a majority of the popular vote, thus encouraging multiple first round competitors in the same manner as the runoff systems as well as reducing the degree of concurrency between the presidential and legislative elections. Also similar to the runoff systems, a choice is made in the second round among the top finishers (two in all of the runoff systems and Chile and three in Bolivia). In the data analysis (where appropriate) Bolivia and Chile I will be included along with the majority runoff systems in a "majority" formula category.

Tables 6.1 and 6.2 detail the distribution of the different formulae in the national electoral systems included in the study as well as in the Argentine provinces. While traditionally the plurality formula has been the favored method of executive selection in Latin America, in recent years the majority runoff formula has grown in popularity. Of the thirteen instances in which the Latin American nations in this study have rewritten their constitutions (or at least the portion of the constitution related to the selection of the president) in the past two decades, in seven (Brazil, Chile, Colombia, Ecuador, El Salvador, Guatemala, and Peru) the majority runoff system was chosen while in only three (Honduras, Nicaragua, and Paraguay) was the plurality system selected.[5] This popularity has also extended to the Argentine provinces where two (Corrientes and Tierra del Fuego) have recently adopted the majority runoff formula. The popularity of the majority runoff system can be attributed to a number of factors (e.g., a desire to avoid precariously low presidential electoral mandates and partisan political strategy) which are discussed more fully in Appendices F and B respectively.

One prominent effect of the use of the majority runoff formula is a reduced likelihood of presidential party majorities and near-majorities in the legislature. Electoral formula influences the size of the president's party contingent in the legislature in both an indirect and in places a direct manner. It influences the size of the president's legislative bloc (and hence the probability of a legislative majority or near-majority) indirectly through its effect on the number of legislative parties which in Chapter Five was shown to be the most salient determinant of the size of the president's legislative contingent. It directly affects the size of the president's party in systems with concurrent presidential and legislative elections since the runoff provision of the majority runoff systems increases the probability that the president's party will not be the one which won the most seats in the legislative election.[6]

Table 6.1
Electoral Formula and Legislative Multipartisam
in 20 National Electoral Systems

Legislative Multipartism	Electoral Formula Employed to Select the Executive			
	Plurality	Electoral College	Majority Runoff	Majority Congress
1.99–2.25	Colombia Honduras Nicaragua		Chile II	
2.26–2.50	Costa Rica Dom Republic Paraguay			
2.51–3.50	Brazil Ia Uruguay Venezuela	Argentina II	Argentina I El Salvador Peru	
3.51–5.00	Brazil Ib		Guatemala	Bolivia
5.01–			Brazil II Ecuador	Chile I

Sources: See Appendix A.

Table 6.2
Electoral Formula and Multipartism in the Argentine Provinces:
1973 and 1983*

Effective Chamber Multipartism	Distribution of the Electoral Formulae Employed to Select the Governor (in percentages)		
	Plurality**	Electoral College	Majority Runoff
1.25–1.75	11	0	9
1.76–2.00	47	0	23
2.01–2.25	26	33	9
2.26–2.50	0	33	18
2.51–3.00	16	33	32
3.01–4.00	0	0	5
4.01–	0	0	5
Total Percentage	100	99	101
Number of Cases	19	3	22

* The plurality and electoral college formula provinces are from the 1983 election and the majority runoff formula provinces are from the 1973 election.

** Included in the plurality column are seven provinces which, using a single district for the lower / single house election, give an absolute majority of the seats to the plurality winner.

Source: Data Files of the Argentine Ministerio del Interior, Dirección Nacional Electoral, Departamento de Estadísticas.

THE INDIRECT EFFECT: ELECTORAL FORMULA AND LEGISLATIVE MULTIPARTISM

The distinction between the plurality and majority formulas has been a relatively understudied aspect of electoral systems (Riker 1986). Work in this area by Duverger, most rational choice theorists, and to a lesser extent Riker does however provide support for the hypothesis that whereas plurality elections tend to result in two-party systems, majority runoff elections tend to lead to multi-party systems (Shugart 1988). Furthermore, Riker's corollaries to Duverger's Law do not seem to apply to Latin American presidential elections (Riker 1986). First, the election is a national one and thus Riker's corollary involving parties which are third nationally but one of the top two locally is not relevant.[7] Second, the presence of a Condorcet winner at the presidential level in Latin American systems is doubtful, given the fact that the executive office has been occupied by more than one party in all of the systems included in the study during the period of analysis.[8] This reality is inconsistent with the hypothesis of a Condorcet winner in any of the systems in the study. If any nation approached this status it would have been Chile in the 1960s with the potential of the Christian Democrats becoming a Condorcet party between the left and right. This of course did not occur, as Socialist Salvador Allende's election as president in 1970 demonstrates.

The formula used to elect the president is hypothesized to have a strong impact on the number of parties in a nation's legislature. This strong impact is considered to be the product of an interaction between the rational actions of individuals who do not want to waste their votes in plurality elections (with this factor indirectly influencing their vote choice in legislative elections, in part by limiting the voters' realistic alternatives in the voting booth) and the rational actions of party leaders who in plurality presidential electoral systems tend to coalesce into larger parties than is the case in majority presidential systems since the principal electoral prize, the presidency, goes to the plurality winner. Thus, given the regular occurrence of presidential elections (in the absence of a Condorcet winner) there is less incentive in plurality (as opposed to majority) systems for most politicians to form alternative parties whose probability of capturing the presidency is quite low.

This dynamic has been identified by Shugart and Carey as being linked to strategic decisions of political elites in response to the electoral formula used to select the executive. In plurality systems there exists a tendency among party elites to both "form a broad coalition behind the front-runner" as well as when in opposition "to coalesce behind one principal challenger" (Shugart and Carey 1992, 209). This contrasts with the majority runoff systems which "actually discourage the coalescence of opposing forces," with political elites making the decision to run their own presidential candidates with the goal of either finishing in the top two in the first round or else demonstrating an electoral following that can be delivered in the runoff election to one of the top two finishers in exchange for selective benefits in the future (Shugart and Carey 1992, 210). Strategic bargaining occurs among relevant political actors in all of the Latin American presidential elections. When this bargaining occurs, however, depends to a great extent on the electoral formula employed. In plurality systems it takes place prior to the election, whereas in majority systems it occurs after the first round of elections (Shugart and Carey 1992). Consolidation prior to the election as occurs in the former system should result in a lower level of presidential, and indirectly legislative, multipartism than should the post-first round bargaining which occurs under the majority framework.

The nineteen Latin American national systems examined are almost evenly split between those which utilize a plurality selection process to select their executive (ten) and those that employ a majority system to select their executive (nine).[9] Due to the assumed differential psychological impact of plurality versus majority systems on both rational voters and rational party leaders, we would expect plurality presidential elections to be dominated by two parties, with the first round of the majority system elections involving strong competition among multiple parties. This premise is confirmed by an initial analysis of data for presidential elections corresponding to the legislative elections included in the study.[10] Presidential elections in the plurality systems tend to be dominated by two parties, with the top two parties in the plurality systems averaging 83.79% of the vote, as opposed to the majority systems where the top two parties average only 65.24% of the vote in the first round.[11] This relationship is illustrated graphically in Table 6.3 with the plurality systems concentrated in the upper ranges and the majority systems falling (although with less regularity) at the lower end of the scale.

Tables 6.1 and 6.2 graphically illustrate the relationship between electoral formula and legislative multipartism in the national electoral systems and the Argentine provincial electoral systems.[12] For the national systems, the bivariate correlation between the electoral formula used to elect the president (with plurality systems scored a zero and those with a majority formula a one, excluding Argentina II) and lower house legislative multipartism is .440, a relationship which is significant at the .05 level for a one-tailed t-test. This strong relationship is demonstrated in Table 6.1 with the plurality formula systems concentrating in the upper portion of the table and the majority runoff and majority congressional systems tending to occupy the lower section of the table. The two principal outliers

Table 6.3

*Percentage of the Valid Popular Vote Received by the Two Leading Parties
in First Round Presidential Elections for 19 Plurality
and Majority Latin American Systems*

	Percentage of the Vote Received by the Two Leading Parties in the First Round of Elections				
Presidential Election Formula	85–100	75–84.5	65–74.5	55–64.5	40–54.5
Plurality	Colombia Costa Rica Honduras Nicaragua	Brazil Ia Dom Republic Paraguay Uruguay Venezuela	Brazil Ib		
Majority		Chile II El Salvador	Argentina I Chile I Peru	Bolivia	Brazil II Ecuador Guatemala

Sources: See Appendix A.

(Brazil Ib and Chile II) are explained by other factors, such as the employment of nonconcurrent timing in Brazil Ib and the use of a very low (2.00) effective magnitude for legislative elections in Chile II. Overall the formulae follow the hypothesized distribution. Majority systems tend to have a high level of legislative multipartism, averaging a little more than four effective parties (4.16 for the majority systems and 3.99 for the majority runoff systems alone). The plurality formula systems have a much lower level of legislative multipartism averaging more than one party less (2.78) than the majority systems.

Table 6.2 which details the relationship between executive election formula and lower house multipartism for the Argentine provinces tends to parallel Table 6.1. Among the Argentine provinces electoral formula is significantly correlated with legislative multipartism (a correlation of .313 which is significant at the .05 level for a one-tailed t-test).[13] While not quite as strong as the relationship for the national systems, the Argentine cases still demonstrate the general trend with plurality systems tending to concentrate at the upper end of the scale while the majority runoff systems (with some exceptions) tend to concentrate more in the middle of the scale. Noteworthy is both the average level of multipartism of the two different formulae (2.14 for the plurality systems versus 2.40 for the majority runoff systems) as well as the presence of over four-fifths of the plurality systems against nearly three-fifths of the majority runoff systems among the group of systems with 2.50 or fewer effective parties.

Overall the bivariate statistics along with the graphic demonstration of the tables for both the national and Argentine provincial systems show that electoral formula does have a strong impact on multipartism. The data clearly demonstrate that Latin American systems which employ a plurality formula to elect their president have presidential elections which correspond much more closely to those of a two-party dominant system than do those systems which utilize a majority framework and thus tend to have a larger number of parties effectively competing in presidential elections. The choice between a plurality and majority executive election formula has a strong impact on the level of legislative multipartism, which in turn influences the size of the executive's legislative contingent. Plurality systems clearly possess lower levels of legislative multipartism than do majority systems and hence larger presidential legislative contingents than their majority counterparts. This strong relationship, combined with the previous demonstration of the salient impact of legislative multipartism on the size of the presidential legislative contingent, confirms the important indirect impact which the electoral formula used to elect the executive has on the provision of adequate support for the president in the legislature.

THE DIRECT EFFECT: ELECTORAL FORMULA AND LEGISLATIVE SUPPORT

In systems where executive and legislative elections are held concurrently, the influence of the executive selection process on the legislative election is quite strong. The focus of the campaign revolves around the presidential candidate, and hence the fate of most candidates for legislative office is strongly tied to that of their presidential candidate. This is particularly the case for "relevant" political parties. Given the prominence of the presidential race along with the links of the legislative election to it (a few systems such as Bolivia, Honduras, Uruguay, the Dominican Republic [for most of its elections], and Guatemala [for a quarter of the legislative seats] go as far as to employ a single fused ballot for the election of the president and members of the legislature), it is normal in concurrent systems for the party of the winner of the first or only round of the presidential contest to also win the largest partisan contingent in the legislature. In 86% of the elections in the fifteen national systems which hold their presidential and legislative elections concurrently, the party of the first round plurality winner in the presidential contest also won a plurality of the seats in the legislature.[14]

Unlike under the plurality formula where the president is always selected in a single round of elections, the majority systems with concurrent executive and legislative elections, of which there are six in this population, select their executive on a separate day from the legislature when no candidate achieves an absolute majority of the vote in the first round. While often the winner of this second round is the candidate who won the relative majority in the first round, in three of the twelve elections which have occurred in the five majority runoff systems the candidate who eventually became president was the one who finished second in the first round and, as one would hypothesize, had a legislative contingent which was smaller than that of his opponent in the runoff.[15]

The use of the majority runoff formula encourages fragmented party systems, which in turn tend to result in moderate to small legislative contingents for all presidential parties. In each of the three cases in the majority runoff systems where the second place finisher in the first round won the runoff election, this winner was faced with the dismal prospects of not only having a small legislative contingent due to the use of a majority runoff system (which on the whole provides contingents which are much smaller than those of its plurality counterpart), but with a contingent that was small even by majority runoff standards due to the fact that his political party had come in second (or even third) in the legislative balloting.

This situation is further exacerbated by the majority runoff system's (and this is a feature not shared by the majority congressional systems) encouragement of and accessibility to candidates without strong traditional party ties (e.g., political outsiders like Alberto Fujimori in Peru and Jorge Serrano in Guatemala). The first round of majority runoff elections normally has several relevant presidential candidates. As a result of the majority runoff formula's permissive nature, the vote in this first round often tends to be highly dispersed among multiple candidates. This dispersion opens up a potential route (not present in plurality systems) to the presidency for political outsiders whose strategy is to finish second (but force a runoff) in the first round and then win against their more established competitor (who is often hampered by his or her identification with one specific party or coalition) in the runoff (Shugart and Carey 1992). These "outsider" candidates by their very nature as "outsiders" tend to have political parties which are often unable to fully capitalize in the legislative contest on their presidential candidate's success. This failure can be attributed to a combination of some or all of the following factors: a lack of a strong established party network or organization in some or all parts of the country (often "outsider" candidates do quite well in the capital while failing to win many seats in rural areas where party organization is more important), a low level of voter identification with or knowledge of the political party as an organization, and weak or unknown candidates on the party's legislative ticket.[16] These "outsider" parties thus often fail to translate the president's strong finish in the first round into a comparable success in the legislative contest.[17]

Finally, both Juan Linz (1992) and Daniel Sabsay (1991) have identified the tendency of majority runoff elections to exacerbate the political divisions of a country and polarize both the populace and the parties during the runoff election. Since the candidate who won the relative majority in the first round is in all likelihood a member of the party which won a plurality of the legislative seats, this polarization will mean that there is a strong chance that after the runoff the winning candidate (when this candidate is the second place finisher in the first round) will face the undesirable situation of having the largest parliamentary bloc as a hostile opposition. This opposition party will tend to see itself as the frontrunner for the next presidential election (due to its status as the nation's plurality party). It will therefore have little incentive to refrain from obstructing the policy program of the president and his or her party which is likely to be its most prominent rival in the next presidential election.

Excluding the majority congressional system of Bolivia, of the twelve presidential elections which have taken place in the majority runoff-concurrent systems: two were won in the first round, seven were won in the second round by the plurality winner of the first round, and three were won in the runoff by the candidate who finished second in the first round.[18] In these latter three cases, the runoff provision exacerbated the majority system's already strong tendency to provide the executive with a small legislative contingent. These "second" place winners received ridiculously small legislative contingents (averaging 15.33% of the seats in the lower/single house) leaving the executive in a highly precarious situation vis-à-vis the legislature (see Table 6.4 for electoral data for the three cases).[19] It is further noteworthy that two of these presidents (Fujimori in Peru successfully and Serrano in Guatemala unsuccessfully) eventually staged an *autogolpe* and closed the congress, in part due to their inability to govern utilizing democratic mechanisms because of difficulties in passing legislation through congress (Millett 1993). The third case, that of León Febres Cordero in Ecuador, resulted not in a presidential assault on the democratic system, but instead in gridlock and chaos, exemplified by a non-binding resolution passed by the Ecuadoran Congress which called for the resignation of President Febres Cordero (Schodt 1989).[20]

The minuscule legislative contingents of Febres Cordero (*Partido Social Cristiano*: PSC), Serrano (*Movimiento de Acción Solidario*: MAS) and Fujimori (CAMBIO 90) were primarily the result of the combination of two (Febres Cordero) and three (Serrano and Fujimori) factors indirectly and directly related to the three systems' use of the majority runoff formula.

First, due in part to their use of the majority formula these systems have a high level of multipartism which results in average presidential legislative contingents which are smaller than those of their plurality counterparts and in most cases less than a majority or near-majority of the legislative seats. For example, in these three noted elections, even if the plurality winner from the first round had won the runoff election (Rodrigo Borja [*Izquierda Democrática*: ID] in Ecuador, Jorge Carpio [*Unión del Centro Nacional*: UCN] in Guatemala, and Mario Vargas Llosa [*Frente Democrático*: FREDEMO] in Peru), the

Table 6.4
National Election Results for Ecuador 1984, Guatemala 1990/91, and Peru 1990

| Country | Political Parties* | Percentage of the Vote Won in the Presidential Elections** | | Lower House Seats Won in the Election*** | Percentage of Lower House Seats Won |
		First Round	Second Round		
ECUADOR					
1984	ID	28.73	48.46	24	33.80
	PSC	**27.20**	**51.54**	**9**	**12.68**
	CFP	13.52		7	9.86
	MPD	7.33		3	4.23
	FRA	6.78		6	8.45
	PD	6.64		6	8.45
	DP	4.70		3	4.23
	FADI	4.26		2	2.82
	Others	0.84		11	15.49
	Total	100.00	100.00	71	100.00
GUATEMALA					
1990/91	UCN	25.75	31.92	41	35.35
	MAS	**24.17**	**68.08**	**18**	**15.52**
	DCG	17.52		28	24.14
	PAN	17.32		12	10.35
	MLN-FAN	4.76		4	3.45
	Others	10.48		13	11.21
	Total	100.00	100.00	116	100.02
PERU					
1990	FREDEMO	32.62	37.50	63	35.00
	CAMBIO 90	**29.09**	**62.50**	**32**	**17.78**
	PAP	22.64		53	29.44
	IU	8.24		15	8.33
	IS	4.81		4	2.22
	Others	2.60		13	7.22
	Total	100.00	100.00	180	99.99

* The political parties of Presidents Febres Cordero (Ecuador: PSC), Serrano (Guatemala: MAS), and Fujimori (Peru: CAMBIO 90) are in bold.

** Parties which received less than 4% of the vote in the first round of the presidential election are included in the "Others" category.

*** The elections for the lower house occurred concurrently with the first round of the presidential elections.

Sources: See Appendix A.

average size of their legislative contingent (each of their parties was the plurality winner in the legislative contest) in the lower/single house would still have been a mere 34.72% of the seats (for Guatemala and Peru only this average would have been 35.18%).

Second, due to the runoff provision of the majority runoff formula, there exists the possibility (which was actualized in these three cases) of the candidate who came in second in the first round winning the runoff, resulting in an even smaller legislative contingent for the president in almost all cases. This second direct consequence of the use of the majority runoff formula can be (and was in Guatemala and Peru) exacerbated by the tendency of the majority runoff system to encourage "outsiders" to run for the presidency. In Guatemala and Peru the immature parties of these "outsider" candidates were unable to completely translate their presidential candidate's number two finish into a comparable success at the legislative level. Each party in fact ended up placing third behind their nation's best organized party, the *Democracia Cristiana Guatemalteca* (DCG) in Guatemala and the *Partido Aprista Peruano* (PAP) in Peru, each of which came in second in the legislative contest, although third in the presidential race. If these two parties which came in second in their respective legislative contests had won the presidency then their president's legislative contingent would have averaged 26.79% of the seats in the lower house. This is over 10% higher than the actual average percentage of seats held by Fujimori's and Serrano's legislative blocs (16.65%).

In Ecuador where the second place finisher won, yet was a member of an established party that finished second in the legislative seat balloting, one can contrast the difference between the size of the legislative contingent (i.e., the percentage of legislative seats) of the plurality winner in the first round and that of Febres Cordero (33.80% versus 12.68%). For Guatemala and Peru, there exists a three-point comparison of legislative contingents: that won by the parties of the plurality winners in the first round of the presidential contest (35.18%), that won by the parties of the second place finishers in the legislative contest (i.e., what the party of the second place presidential candidate in the first round might have won had the candidate been from an established party, and not an "outsider" candidate with a corresponding weak political party) (26.79%), and the percentage actually won by the parties of the first round runner up "outsiders" (i.e., of Fujimori and Serrano) (16.65%).

Majority systems tend to indirectly reduce the size of the president's legislative contingent by increasing the level of multipartism in the system. This "Achilles' heel" of majority systems is exacerbated (especially in the runoff systems) when the presidential elections are held concurrently with those of the legislature.[21] These concurrent elections, combined with the use of a majority framework, can set off a combination of factors which act to severely reduce the size of an executive's legislative contingent. Three cases (Febres Cordero, Fujimori, and Serrano) were discussed where these factors combined to create very difficult situations for the executive. As has already been suggested, a legislative majority or near-majority is very important for a president, and legislative contingents as low as the ones in these three cases create an extremely difficult situation. Patching together a coalition to pass legislation is quite difficult when you possess less than 20% of the seats in the legislature. It is not a coincidence that the only two "reversions" to authoritarian rule (temporary in the case of Guatemala) in Latin America against the recent wave of democratization have occurred in Guatemala and Peru, and are in essence the response of a president to the difficult situation imposed on him by the lack of sufficient partisan support in the legislature.[22] Multiple regression coefficients and levels of significance aside, the majority runoff formula in these cases is in part responsible for the decay of democratic government in Guatemala and its demise in Peru. This represents a conditioned, yet direct impact which electoral formula has on the size of presidential legislative contingents and the functioning of a nation's democratic system.

This chapter has highlighted many of the negative consequences of the use of the majority runoff formula for the functioning of democratic presidential systems. Proponents of the majority runoff formula often claim that the formula has two beneficial effects: (1) the provision of strong presidential electoral mandates, and (2) the prevention of the election of presidents with weak popular mandates. An empirical test provided in Appendix F reveals that there is little support for the premise that the majority runoff formula provides popular mandates that are superior to those supplied by the plurality formula. The results do however reveal that unsurprisingly, the majority runoff formula does do a good job of protecting against the election of presidents with a dangerously low (i.e., below 40%) percentage of the popular vote.

There are two important ways in which the electoral formula utilized by a system to select its executive affects the size of the executive's legislative contingent in that system. Electoral formula indirectly affects legislative multipartism which in turn influences the size of the executive's legislative contingent. Where presidential and legislative elections are held concurrently, electoral formula directly affects the size of the presidential legislative contingent by providing for (majority systems) or not providing for (plurality systems) a second round of elections when no candidate achieves an absolute majority in the first round. Where this second round exists, there is the possibility (not present in the plurality systems) that the candidate who is eventually elected president will not be the one who finished first in the initial round of voting. When this occurs the president is most often left with a legislative contingent that is smaller than the already marginal one common under majority systems with concurrent presidential and legislative elections. As the cases of Fujimori and Serrano demonstrate, the consequences of this situation can be disastrous for democracy.

7

The Timing of Executive and Legislative Elections

The timing of presidential and legislative elections is of double importance to the provision of presidential legislative majorities and near-majorities. The degree of temporal concurrence between the elections for these two branches influences the number of parties in a legislature (and hence indirectly the likelihood of a presidential majority or close to it). The timing of these elections directly affects the legislative partisan composition primarily through the presence or absence of presidential coattails bringing into office a legislature whose members (when the elections are concurrent) are more likely to be of the president's party then is the case when the legislative elections are held separately from the executive contest (i.e., nonconcurrently).

METHODS OF ELECTION TIMING

The timing of presidential and legislative elections can be concurrent (where the executive and legislative elections are held on the same day), nonconcurrent (where the executive and legislative elections occur on separate dates), or "mixed" (where legislative elections are held both concurrently and nonconcurrently with the executive contest).[1] As Table 7.1 details, concurrent election timing is by far the most popular method among these Latin American national systems, with fifteen of the systems following the concurrent method and only four employing nonconcurrent elections.[2] While the mixed type of elections (where both concurrent and nonconcurrent election timing is employed) is in the minority among the national systems, it is the preferred timing method of a majority of the Argentine provincial systems.[3]

Shugart and Carey (1992) have classified nonconcurrent elections into three categories, to which I add a fourth. First are honeymoon elections, which occur within one year after the presidential inauguration. Second are counter-honeymoon elections, which take place

Table 7.1

*The Timing of Presidential and Legislative Elections in 21 Electoral Systems**

Concurrent Election Systems	Nonconcurrent Election Systems	Mixed Timing Election Systems
Argentina I	Brazil Ib	Argentina II
Bolivia	Brazil II**	Ecuador II
Brazil Ia	Chile I	
Chile II**	El Salvador**	
Colombia***		
Costa Rica		
Dominican Republic		
Ecuador I		
Guatemala		
Honduras		
Nicaragua		
Paraguay		
Peru		
Uruguay		
Venezuela		

* The timing given is for the lower/single house of the legislature.

** In 1994 Brazil II switched to a concurrent timing cycle. In 1994 Chile II switched to a nonconcurrent cycle. The Salvadoran system has legislative elections every three years and presidential elections every five years. Every fifth legislative election is concurrent with the presidential election. The first of these concurrent elections took place in 1994, the next will occur in 2009.

*** Colombian legislative elections occurred an average of three months prior to the elections for president and are thus neither fully concurrent or nonconcurrent. The Colombian arrangement is however considered to be near-concurrent and therefore will be included with the concurrent systems in most of the analysis. In 1974 the Colombian presidential and legislative elections took place on the same day.

within a year prior to the first or only round of the presidential election. Third are midterm elections (a category that is extended to comprise all elections which occur beyond the honeymoon phase during the executive's term). To these three categories I add a fourth, counter-midterm elections, which are merely all legislative elections which occur prior to the counter-honeymoon period, yet are for a legislature with which the executive must interact during his or her term in office.

All of the nonconcurrent systems examined have different term lengths for their executives and legislatures. In these cases, where at least one of the term lengths in each system is a prime number, it is inevitable that each of these systems will experience each of these types of elections (as well as in some cases the occasional legislative election concurrent with that of the executive). This mixture, however, is not inevitable, since a system could conceivably give the two offices the same term length and merely schedule their respective elections at different times. The analysis of the methods of nonconcurrent timing focuses on the impact of a particular election as it affects a specific executive. In nonconcurrent systems elections are two-sided. For example, a honeymoon election for one president also very well can be a counter-midterm election for the next president. This effect is very much a product of the term lengths used for the different constitutional branches as well as the electoral cycle employed. This analysis treats each legislative election's relationship with an executive as a separate event. While the potential dual impact of these legislative elections is not explicitly examined, this effect can easily be inferred from the conclusions presented.

THE INDIRECT EFFECT: TIMING AND LEGISLATIVE MULTIPARTISM

There is strong theoretical support for the hypothesis that in presidential-PR systems the timing of presidential and legislative elections has a significant impact on the level of multipartism in the latter elections (Shugart and Carey 1992). Concurrent systems should be expected to have lower levels of multipartism than is the case when the two elections are held at different times and the restraining impact of the executive selection process is much weaker. Since the level of multipartism in a system strongly influences the size of the president's legislative contingent, the timing of presidential and legislative elections indirectly affects that system's tendency to provide the president with a legislative majority or near-majority.

The link between presidential and legislative elections which exists in all presidential systems is stronger when these executive elections are held at the same time as the legislative elections than when the elections for these two branches are held at separate times. Presidential elections help reduce the field of effective parties (even under the majority runoff and majority congressional frameworks) at both the elite (i.e., in regard to the number of relevant political parties competing) and mass (i.e., in regard to support at the polls by focusing voter attention on the dominant executive race) levels.

An analysis of the relationship between election timing (with concurrent systems scored a zero and nonconcurrent systems a one) and lower house legislative multipartism for the national systems reveals a bivariate correlation of .633, a relationship which is significant at the .01 level for a one-tailed t-test.[4] This strong relationship between timing and legislative multipartism for the national systems is, however, not evident in the Argentine provinces. Among these provincial systems the difference in regard to election timing is between provinces which renew their legislature completely at the time of the gubernatorial election and those which renew one-half of their legislature every two years (where one-half of the legislature is elected concurrently with the executive and the other half two years before/after the gubernatorial election). With the systems which have complete renovation of the legislature scored a zero and the systems with partial renovation scored a one, the bivariate correlation between timing and legislative multipartism is an insignificant −.046, and not even in the hypothesized direction. This null result is supported by the finding that for those eleven systems which utilized partial renovation throughout the 1983–95 period, the average level of legislative multipartism for the concurrent elections (2.13) is scarcely distinguishable from that of the midterm elections (2.18). This finding would suggest that in these hybrid systems, the executive contest is able to continue to exert a strong impact on the party system, with minor parties unable to capitalize on the absence of the executive contest to achieve success in the midterm elections. It would appear that the logic of the system continues to revolve around the executive contest every four years, with the midterm elections operating within this dynamic and not conducted on their own terms as suggested by Shugart and Carey (1992).

In sum, the data for the national and Argentine provincial systems reveal two important findings regarding the relationship between election timing and legislative multipartism. First, there does exist a strong difference between concurrent and nonconcurrent elections, with the latter method resulting in much higher levels of multipartism than the former. Second, data from the Argentine provinces demonstrate that this distinction is not evident in systems where one-half of the deputies are elected concurrently with the executive and one-half are elected separately during a midterm election.

THE DIRECT EFFECT:
TIMING AND LEGISLATIVE SUPPORT

The direct effect of election timing on the size of the president's legislative contingent results primarily from the well-known coattails effect (Campbell 1991; Jacobson 1990). The presidential election is considered the most prominent/important in the nation. It has a contagious effect on all elections for lower elective offices such as the legislature. This effect is present in all presidential systems regardless of their timing method. It is, however, at its peak of strength in elections where the presidential and legislative contests are held concurrently. When presidential and legislative elections are held at the same time, the greater visibility of the presidential candidates often leads members of the electorate to vote for members of the president's party in the congressional contest as a by-product of their support for the presidential candidate. Thus presidents are hypothesized to be more likely to obtain a legislative majority or near-majority when the presidential and legislative elections are held concurrently than is the case when the elections are held at separate times (i.e., nonconcurrently).

Combined with this sense of presidential preeminence in the

electoral process is the desire by most voters, particularly in concurrent elections, to be consistent with their vote choice (i.e., to not vote for the presidential candidate of one party and then a congressional list of another). Ticket splitting in the United States is partially explained by the hypothesis that, due to the unique structural and partisan context of the U.S., at least a subset of voters consciously opts for divided government (Jacobson 1990). This logic does not appear to apply to the Latin American cases.[5] Finally, elections held during the president's term are often used as referenda on his or her performance in office. While the use of these elections as referenda could have either a beneficial or pernicious effect on the size of the president's legislative contingent, evidence from the United States (Campbell 1991, 1985; Kernell 1977) shows that in general these midterm elections have resulted in a reduction in the size of the president's legislative contingent.

Given the strong theoretical logic regarding both the direct and indirect impact of election timing on the size of the presidential legislative contingent, the strong bivariate correlation which exists between timing, with concurrent systems scored a zero and nonconcurrent systems a one, and the size of this contingent (–.581, which is significant at the .01 level for a one-tailed t-test) is not surprising. The average size of the president's lower/single house legislative contingent for the concurrent systems is 46.05% of the seats, nearly double the nonconcurrent systems' average of 28.11%. It is quite clear that concurrent systems are much more likely to provide an executive with strong legislative support than are the nonconcurrent systems. Therefore, if the goal of a system is to provide a legislative majority or near-majority, the use of a nonconcurrent electoral cycle is ill-advised. As Table 7.2 indicates, only three of the ten presidencies in the nonconcurrent systems had a majority or near-majority in the lower/single house during even a portion of their tenure in office (Eduardo Frei in Chile, 1965–69; José Napoleón Duarte in El Salvador, 1985–88; and Alfredo Cristiani in El Salvador, 1989–94).[6] However, within these nonconcurrent systems, the timing of the legislative election in relation to the executive contest does appear to make a difference in regard to the level of presidential legislative support. This impact of timing is mostly direct (i.e., influencing the strength of presidential coattails) and less indirect through its impact on the level of legislative multipartism.

Table 7.2
Nonconcurrent Elections in Chile I, Brazil Ib, El Salvador, and Brazil II *

Country and Presidential Election Term	(percentage of seats won by president's [of term] party listed below			
	Counter-Midterm or Earlier Elections	Counter-Honeymoon Elections	Honeymoon Elections	Midterm or Later Elections
Chile I: 1946–52		20		22
Chile I: 1952–58	19		29	15
Chile I: 1958–64		35		31
Chile I: 1964–70	16		56	33
Chile I: 1970–76		37		37
Chile I: Averages	**18**	**31**	**43**	**28**
Brazil Ib: 1955–60		35		36
Brazil Ib: 1960–65	22			23
Brazil Ib: Averages	**22**	**35**		**30**
El Salvador: 1984–89	40		55	37
El Salvador: 1989–94		52		46
El Salvador: Averages	**40**	**52**	**55**	**42**
Brazil II: 1990–95	**0**		**8**	

* The elections examined are for the lower/single house only.

Note: The Chilean data include formal coalitions of parties which combined to support the president. For more information see Appendix E. The seats held by the president's political party are based on the number won by the party in the most recent lower/single house election. The constitutional terms of Presidents Salvador Allende (Chile, 1970–76) and Fernando Collor (Brazil, 1990–95) ended prematurely in 1973 and 1992 respectively.

Sources: See Appendix A.

When discussing the relationship between nonconcurrent elections and the size of a president's legislative contingent, two factors are of preeminent importance: temporality and proximity. First, all things being equal, the president's party is much more likely to achieve a greater level of support if the legislative elections are held after he or she becomes president rather than before. Second, the presidential party should do better the closer elections are to the presidential election, particularly within the honeymoon and counter-honeymoon periods. Based on these criteria, the optimal election for legislative majority seeking presidents in nonconcurrent systems is the honeymoon election.[7] At this point they are in office, and yet the euphoria of their recent presidential victory is still in the air. It is not surprising that two of the three lower/single house legislative majorities/near-majorities provided by nonconcurrent systems have come as the result of honeymoon elections: El Salvador (1985–88) and Chile (1965–69).

The next most desirable election cycle from the point of view of the executive is a toss up between counter-honeymoon and midterm elections. The advantage of the counter-honeymoon election is that if the presidential race is already highly developed at the time of the legislative election then the electorate is influenced in this election by its prospective vote choice in the upcoming presidential race. This was the case in El Salvador for the 1988 legislative election where the race for the 1989 presidential election was already known to be a contest between the *Alianza Republicana Nacional* (ARENA) and the *Partido Demócrata Cristiano* (PDC). Even if one does not accept that people vote in these legislative elections based on their future presidential vote choice, it is plausible that their partisan choice will not change a great deal in the period of a year and thus that their presidential vote will be similar to their legislative vote. However, counter-honeymoon cycles can pose a serious problem which manifests itself particularly in majority runoff systems. Majority runoff systems tend to encourage political outsiders to run for the presidency. As these candidates are often political unknowns until perhaps three to six months prior to the presidential contest (e.g., Alberto Fujimori in Peru and Fernando Collor in Brazil), the success of their party in the counter-honeymoon elections is likely to be anemic. This can lead to a highly negative situation where presidents take office with minuscule or even nonexistent partisan legislative contingents.

On equal status with these counter-honeymoon elections are the midterm elections. The success of the president in these contests depends a great deal on the conduct of his or her administration, since midterm elections often act as referenda on the performance of the administration. Therefore, the impact of these elections on the size of the president's legislative contingent varies, although the data at hand place it slightly weaker than that of the counter-honeymoon elections.

From the standpoint of an executive, the least desirable of the nonconcurrent elections are the counter-midterm elections. These elections leave the president with an inheritance of a legislative contingent that in extreme cases was elected three years before the president.[8] The data for the counter-midterm elections demonstrate the quite predictable impact of these elections on the size of the presidential legislative contingents (see Table 7.2). For the four systems in Table 7.2, the average size of the legislative contingent inherited from the counter-midterm election by the executive upon his assumption of office was 20% of the lower house seats. The size of the senate contingents inherited by the presidents for Brazil Ib (32%), Brazil II (0%), and Chile I (21%) was an average of 18% of the seats. The impact of these counter-midterm elections on newer or less well-established parties is particularly strong, since over a year or two prior to the presidential contest, the support for these parties in the legislative contest is likely to be quite mild. No case better illustrates this danger than that of Brazil where Fernando Collor (previously the governor of a small state) came out of nowhere in the six months prior to the 1989 presidential election to win the presidency. Unfortunately for Collor his party had not even existed at the time of the previous legislative election in 1986.[9] Collor's lack of any semblance of a viable legislative contingent made it difficult to implement his new sweeping economic restructuring program through the normal legislative process due to the necessity of brokering together a legislative coalition from an inordinate number of parties (Economist Intelligence Unit 1991; Power 1991).

No strong relationship was found between the differential use of completely concurrent elections (coded zero) as opposed to the use of partial renovation by midterms (coded one), and the size of a governor's legislative contingent for the Argentine provincial systems. The bivariate correlation between the two variables was a mere .011. Furthermore, data in Table 7.3 clearly demonstrate that the impact of the timing of the elections within the partial renovation systems is minor. For the eleven Argentine systems which have continuously employed partial renovation during the 1983–95 period, the difference in both seats and votes won by the governor's party in concurrent and midterm elections is quite small. In regard to seats won the difference is minuscule, with the governor's party winning an average of 56% of the lower house seats in the concurrent elections and 55% of the seats in the midterm elections. Similarly,

Table 7.3

*Percentage of Seats and Votes Won in the 11 Argentine Provincial Partial
Renovation Systems by the Governor's Political Party in the Lower
or Single House Elections, 1983–93*

	Election Years: 1983–93					
	Governor Elected 1983	1985	Governor Elected 1987	1989	Governor Elected 1991	1993
Percentage of Seats Won in the Election	56.47	52.52	56.26	57.45	56.13	54.96
Percentage of Votes Won in the Election	47.67	44.97	48.41	49.23	50.20	48.39

Note: Four of the elections included (in addition to those of 1983) were complete renovations of the legislature; this, however, does not affect this portion of the analysis. The same eleven systems were used throughout the period in order to hold constant as many factors as possible. In each system one-half of the lower / single house was renewed (with the exception mentioned above) in each election.

Source: Data Files of the Argentine Ministerio del Interior, Dirección Nacional Electoral, Departamento de Estadísticas.

while there also exists a slight difference in regard to the percentage of the vote won by the governor's party in the concurrent (49%) and midterm (48%) legislative elections, it is minor.

These generally null findings tend to hold true, although to a lesser extent, for the two national systems which employ a type of mixed electoral cycle, Argentina II and Ecuador II. In Argentina II, as in the provinces with partial renovation, one-half of the Chamber is renewed every two years. Unlike the provincial executives who have four-year terms (and thus one concurrent and one midterm election during their tenure in office), the Argentine president has a six-year term and thus experiences one concurrent election and two midterms during his or her stay in office.[10] The findings from the brief Argentine national experience show that the midterm elections have on average been only somewhat worse for the president than have the general elections (i.e., the average percentage of seats won in the two concurrent elections is 52% and in the four midterm elections 48%), with this latter average lowered significantly by the dismal showing of President Raúl Alfonsín's UCR in his second (1987) midterm (winning only 41% of the Chamber seats being contested).

Beginning with the Febres Cordero administration (1984-88) Ecuador has renewed all of its district level deputies every two years while renewing its twelve national district deputies every four years concurrently with the presidential election. During this period the president's party has achieved an average victory of 25% of the district level seats in the three concurrent elections and of 14% of the seats in the three midterm elections. Whereas a difference of means test found the difference between the percentage of seats won in the concurrent and midterm elections by the president's party in Argentina II not to be significant at the .05 level for a one-tailed *t*-test, for Ecuador this difference was significant at the .05 level.

Based on the findings above, are we to conclude that the use of a combination of midterm and concurrent elections has at best a minor impact on the size of an executive's legislative contingent? In general, yes. It appears that at least for the Argentine provinces, the use of partial midterm elections has no significant net impact on the size of an executive's legislative contingent. However, these midterm elections do in one specific situation have a strong negative impact on the size of an executive's legislative contingent. In the Argentine provincial systems every four years a new executive is chosen. Thus in 1987 and 1991 every province elected a new governor. In the concurrent provincial systems the entire legislature was renewed at the same time that the new governor was elected. However, in the provinces which employ partial renovation of the legislature, only one-half of the legislature was renewed. Unlike the case of the concurrent systems, in the partial renovation systems the governors had to spend the first half of their administration with a legislature, one-half of which had been elected two years prior to their election to office.[11]

As we have already seen, in the aggregate midterm elections have little impact on the general size of the governor's legislative contingent. In the partial renovation systems where the executive who won in 1987 and 1991 was of the same partisan affiliation as the previous governor, the inheritance of one-half of the legislature from the previous administration's midterm is unlikely to have a negative impact on the size of the governor's legislative contingent. For governors who succeeded a governor of the same party, the ratio of the percentage of lower/single house seats won by their party in their concurrent election to the percentage of party seats inherited from the previous midterm was a mere 1.07 (i.e., the number of seats won in the concurrent election by the governor's party was only 7% greater than that won by the party in the midterm prior to his or her election).[12]

The one situation in which midterm elections do have a strong impact on the size of a governor's legislative contingent is when the candidate who wins the election for governor is of a different political party than the previous governor. Of the twenty-three elections in 1987 and 1991 which have occurred in the fourteen provinces which at the time were utilizing a system of partial renovation of the legislature, eighteen were won by a candidate of the same political party as the previous governor while five were won by candidates of a different party. The difference in the average size of the inheritance (i.e., the one-half of the lower/single house which these candidates receive from the previous midterm, and with which they must cope for the first half of the administration) received by these two groups is immense. The average size (i.e., the percentage of the seats) of the partisan inheritance of the governors who succeeded a coreligionist is 55.79% while that of the governors who replaced a governor of a different party is 26.43%. Significantly, whereas the ratio of the percentage of seats won by the governor's party in the concurrent election to that inherited from the previous midterm is a mere 1.07 for this former group, the ratio for the new party governors is over 100% greater at 2.24. The percentage of seats won by these governors' parties concurrent with their election is over twice the size of the number of seats which their parties won in the previous midterm (i.e., their inheritance).

Table 7.4 shows the electoral results for the five new party governors' political parties in the legislative elections. In every case, the governor's party fared better in the concurrent elections than it did in the previous midterm. In the cases of Chaco, Mendoza, and Salta the differences are impressive. For example in Mendoza, if instead of inheriting one-half of the legislature from the previous midterm, Governor José Octavio Bordón (PJ)

Table 7.4
The Legislative Contingent of New Party Governors in Partial Renovation Systems

Province	Term	Legislative Chamber	Seats Won by the Governor's Political Party		
			"Inheritance" Seats Won in Renovation prior to Election	Seats Won in Concurrent Renovation	Seats Won in Midterm Renovation
			(Seats Won of Total Seats Being Renewed)		
Buenos Aires					
	1987–91	Chamber	19 of 46	21 of 46	25 of 46
		Senate	7 of 23	12 of 23	14 of 23
Chaco					
	1991–95	Chamber	2 of 16	7 of 16	6 of 16
Mendoza					
	1987–91	Chamber	6 of 24	12 of 24	11 of 24
		Senate	4 of 19	10 of 19	10 of 19
Misiones					
	1987–91	Chamber	8 of 20	10 of 20	11 of 20
Salta					
	1991–95	Chamber	4 of 30	13 of 30	9 of 30
		Senate	1 of 12	2 of 11	1 of 12

Note: Elections are held every two years: 1983, 1985, 1987, 1989, 1991, 1993. In each election included here one-half of the legislature was renewed. The size of each governor's legislative contingent can be calculated by summing the totals of the two contiguous legislative renovations. Gubernatorial elections occurred in 1983, 1987, and 1991. The Buenos Aires data include a combination of two Peronist factions as one party.

The party which unseated the incumbent party in each province is as follows:

Buenos Aires: *Partido Justicialista*
Chaco: *Acción Chaqueña*
Mendoza: *Partido Justicialista*
Misiones: *Partido Justicialista*
Salta: *Partido Renovador de Salta*

Source: Data Files of the Argentine Ministerio del Interior, Dirección Nacional Electoral, Departamento de Estadísticas.

(1987–91) had received a legislature elected completely concurrent with his own election, then (based on an extrapolation from the 1987 data) he would have possessed 50% of the seats in the Chamber and 53% in the Senate. However, due to the small size of his partisan inheritance the respective composition of his contingent in these two bodies was only 38% and 37% of the seats. Clearly a noticeable difference. In Chapter Three the problems faced by Governor Roberto Ulloa in Salta, which in a large part were due to this meager inheritance, were detailed. Ulloa himself identified this system of partial renovation as one of the two most salient causes of his small legislative contingent (Ulloa 1993). Difficulties similar to those faced by Ulloa tend to confront all governors under this midterm system when they replace a governor of a different political party (Jiménez Peña 1993).

Three other ways in which timing affects the executive's relations with the legislature, while not directly related to the size of the executive's legislative contingent, nevertheless deserve mention. First, when legislative elections are held concurrently with those of the executive, legislators of the executive's party are more likely to be beholden to him or her than is the case when these deputies are elected at a separate time from the executive (especially if they are elected before he or she takes office). When legislators are beholden to the executive, it gives the executive greater control over the party's legislative bloc, making the implementation of the executive's policy program all the easier. Second, the problem of dual legitimacy (between the executive and legislative branches) has been mentioned by critics such as Linz (1994) as a severe problem for presidential systems. This problem of dual legitimacy is exacerbated when elections for the two constitutional branches are held at separate times, with the branch elected most recently being likely to claim a superior level of legitimacy (Shugart and Carey 1992). This situation can be particularly dangerous when the party (or parties) in control of the legislature do not correspond to the partisan affiliation of the president. As we have already noted, given the nonconcurrent systems' tendency to deprive the president of a legislative majority or near-majority, this scenario is highly plausible. Third, when elections are held during a president's tenure they often function as referenda on the president's performance in office (Kernell 1977). A president who must face these referenda elections often will be constrained in his or her ability to implement any type of unpopular reform (no matter how vital) out of fear of suffering severe losses in the midterm election (Hernández 1993). Thus midterms can in places lead to a certain degree of immobilism and the implementation of politically expedient policies in favor of sound constructive policies.

TIMING AND PRESIDENTIAL LEGISLATIVE SUPPORT: A REVIEW

Having examined the direct and indirect impact which timing has on the size of an executive's legislative contingent, we are now able to review the general impact of timing on presidential backing in the legislature. If a goal of a constitutional system is to provide the executive with a legislative majority or near-majority, then concurrent timing is the optimal choice. Not only will these concurrent elections constrain the level of multipartism in a system, but they will also allow the president's coattails to have their full effect (which can only occur when the executive and legislative elections are held at the same time).

Findings based on the mixed system of both concurrent and midterm elections used in many of Argentina's provinces suggest that the use of midterm elections does not have much of an effect on the size of presidential legislative contingents (except when a governor of a party different from that of the previous governor takes office). These findings tend to hold true to a lesser extent for Argentina II. In Ecuador II, however, midterm elections have a significant negative impact on the size of the president's legislative contingent.

These results are interesting since in general they tend to contradict the conventional wisdom derived from the experience of the United States where the presidential party's contingent in Congress tends to be reduced by the midterm election.[13] Campbell (1991) has suggested that this phenomenon in the United States is caused by a combination of the absence of presidential coattails (i.e., decline) and the use of the election by the public as a referenda on the president's tenure in office. Thus one is left to explain why (at least in the Argentine provinces) these effects in general do not occur. I would hypothesize that they do occur to a certain extent, but are at the same time counteracted by the activities of the governor.

Argentine governors have reasonably strong patronage powers. Thus during their first two years in office they spend a considerable amount of time awarding jobs and contracts and engaging in public works with the goal of succeeding in the upcoming election.[14] Thus governors can bolster their support in this manner and it is perhaps these efforts (as well as the fact that they are judged more on their work in the province than on macroeconomic policy over which they have little control) that account for the differential impact of midterm elections on the size of executive legislative contingents in the United States and in the Argentine provinces.

An additional factor which may account for the generally less potent impact of midterms on the legislative contingents of the Argentine governors is the use of multi-member PR electoral districts in these systems as opposed to the single-member plurality districts employed in the U.S. The use of multi-member PR districts should act to dampen the severity of the swing ratio associated with the drop in voter support for the governor's party (i.e., the decline) in the midterm election.

Based on the data examined, although a mixed arrangement is not as good as concurrent elections at providing the executive with strong legislative support, it does do a much better job than the nonconcurrent systems. Thus, if a system wished to combine concurrent elections with some type of midterm (perhaps to act as a referendum on the executive's performance, which is the reason most Argentines who endorse the system of partial renovation give for their support), this type of mixed concurrent/midterm system of elections would not have as negative an impact on the size of the presidential legislative contingent as would a nonconcurrent electoral cycle.

The timing of presidential and legislative elections is a prominent factor related to the size of the president's legislative contingent. Concurrent election systems are much more likely to provide the president with the strong legislative contingent which will enable him or her to govern effectively. Nonconcurrent elections are much more likely to endow the president with a weak legislative contingent which often leads to gridlock, inefficiency, and at times the deformation or termination of democratic government.

8
Legislative Effective Magnitude and Electoral Formula

The electoral laws which directly govern the conduct of legislative elections have an indirect impact on the size of a system's presidential legislative contingent. These electoral rules directly influence the level of multipartism in a system, which in turn influences the size of an executive's legislative contingent. There is a large assortment of electoral rules for legislative elections which have a hypothetical impact on multipartism. However, according to Arend Lijphart (1994a, 9) "there is broad agreement among electoral systems experts that the two most important dimensions of electoral systems are the electoral formula and the district magnitude."[1]

LEGISLATIVE EFFECTIVE MAGNITUDE

In proportional representation (PR) systems the average district magnitude (i.e., the number of representatives in the legislature divided by the number of electoral districts) is hypothesized to be positively related to legislative multipartism. As magnitude increases so does multipartism. Rein Taagepera and Matthew Shugart (1989) consider magnitude to be the decisive legislative electoral rule in regard to its impact on multipartism. Arend Lijphart has found the effective magnitude of a system to be the most important determinant of multipartism in parliamentary systems (Lijphart 1994a). In the opinion of Lijphart (1994a) and Taagepera and Shugart (1989), no other electoral dimension directly governing the legislative election has as much influence over the level of multipartism in an electoral system as does a system's effective magnitude.

The measurement of an electoral system's average district magnitude is quite simple in many cases (i.e., the number of legislative seats divided by the number of legislative districts). However, three additional dimensions of an electoral system often require the transformation of this average district magnitude into an "effective" district magnitude.

First, some of the systems in this study (i.e., Ecuador, El Salvador, Guatemala, and Venezuela, along with Rio Negro and San Juan II in Argentina) utilize two separate legislative tiers to elect the members of their respective lower or single house (i.e., complex districting). In Ecuador and Guatemala (along with Rio Negro and San Juan II in Argentina) separate elections are held at the district and national (provincial in Rio Negro and San Juan II) levels. In El Salvador a two-tiered district framework is employed (beginning in 1991) and in Venezuela compensatory seats are allocated to minor parties at the national level.[2] Aided by the work of Taagepera and Shugart (1989, 269), an effective magnitude was constructed for each system based on the geometric average of the magnitude of the systems' two levels or tiers.

Second, some systems (i.e., Argentina I and II along with many of the Argentine provinces) require a party to reach a specific electoral threshold in order to be eligible to receive legislative seats.[3] In reality this threshold is nothing more than another manner of expressing a cutoff level (which district magnitude signifies in terms of seats) below which no party may obtain seats. Once again following the lead of Taagepera and Shugart, the true "effective" magnitude of these systems was calculated based on these thresholds. This calculation merely involves dividing 50% (i.e., one-half of a quota, the lowest percentage of the vote with which a party could realistically be expected to win a seat in most cases) by the threshold at the level (i.e., district) where it is in force.[4] For example the Argentine I threshold of 8% (of the valid vote) results in an effective magnitude of 6.25 (i.e., 50% / 8%). If a district's average district magnitude is higher than this, then its effective magnitude becomes 6.25. If the district magnitude is lower than 6.25, the district's effective magnitude would be the same as its average district magnitude.

Third, a similar transformation was conducted for those systems which require that a party win a full electoral quota (the electoral quota equals the number of votes in an electoral district divided by the number of legislative seats being disputed) in order to receive any seats in a district (i.e., Bolivia [1989 only], Brazil Ia, Brazil Ib, Brazil II, and Buenos Aires province).[5] This third factor is really a threshold in disguise and can be expressed as the percentage of the vote needed to win a full quota in a district.

In the analysis which follows the effective magnitude of each system is employed. For many systems, the effective magnitude is the same as the average district magnitude. For others however, this effective magnitude is the product of the original average district magnitude transformed for one or more of the three reasons mentioned above.

The lower/single house effective magnitudes for the national systems range from a low of 2.00 for Chile II to a high of 99.00 for Uruguay. The mean effective magnitude for the national systems is 14.36 while the median is 7.04 and the standard deviation 22.56. For the Argentine (1983–95) provincial systems (which utilize PR) lower/single house effective magnitude ranges from a low of 1.30 in La Rioja to a high of 16.40 in Misiones. The mean effective magnitude for these provincial systems is 8.14 while the median is 8.24 and the standard deviation 4.42.

LEGISLATIVE ELECTORAL FORMULA

The electoral formula employed to allocate legislative seats has been linked to the number of parties in the assembly. The plurality formula tends to result in a two-party composition while majority runoff and, to a greater extent, proportional representation formulae are theorized to lead to multiple legislative parties. This distinction between plurality and proportional representation is the crucial one for multipartism. Furthermore, within the PR systems, certain seat allocation formulae are hypothesized to lead to higher levels of multipartism than others.

When discussing the impact of the legislative electoral formula on multipartism, there are two salient cleavages to examine. First is that between plurality and PR systems where the difference in regard to their impact on the level of multipartism in a system is likely to be quite large (Jones 1993; Lijphart 1990b). The plurality formula is hypothesized to lead to a two-party system (assuming the use of single-member districts) whereas PR is hypothesized to result in a multi-party system (Duverger 1986). However, the only use of the plurality formula among both the national and Argentine provincial systems (with one minor exception) occurs in a small number of the upper chambers of the bicameral systems. The second cleavage occurs within the proportional representation allocation formulae. There exists a large number of PR formulae which nations have used to allocate their legislative seats. In the systems included in this study (with four minor exceptions), the only PR allocation formulae employed are the highest average d'Hondt formula and the largest remainders Hare formula. Thirteen of the national systems (Argentina I, Argentina II, Brazil Ia, Brazil Ib, Brazil II, Chile I, Chile II, Dominican Republic, Guatemala, Paraguay, Peru, Uruguay, and Venezuela) use the highest average d'Hondt formula. The seven other national systems (Bolivia, Colombia, Costa Rica, Ecuador, El Salvador, Honduras, and Nicaragua) utilize the largest remainders Hare formula.[6] With one exception (the province of Buenos Aires 1985–) all of the Argentine provincial PR systems use the d'Hondt formula.

The LR-Hare formula uses a set of quotas (i.e., the number of votes in a district divided by the number of legislative seats apportioned to that district) to distribute seats, with political parties receiving one seat for every full quota won. A system of largest remainders is used to allocate the seats which remain after the population of full quotas has been exhausted. The Hagenbach-Bischoff formula operates in the same manner, except that the quota is calculated by dividing the votes cast in the district by the number of legislative seats apportioned to a district plus one.[7] The highest average d'Hondt formula utilizes a system of successive divisors $(1, 2, 3, \ldots)$ to allocate the legislative seats in sequential order to the political party with the highest average at each iteration until all seats are allocated. According to Lijphart (1994a) the d'Hondt formula benefits the larger parties (in terms of votes won) in an election while the LR-Hare formula favors smaller parties to a greater extent. The net result is that we would expect the use of the d'Hondt formula to lead to a lower level of multipartism and hence a larger executive legislative contingent than the use of the LR-Hare formula. Finally, while its primary influence is on the level of multipartism, the d'Hondt formula would be expected to be more likely to lead to larger presidential legislative contingents than the LR-Hare formula due to its stronger tendency to favor the larger parties in an electoral system.[8]

EFFECTIVE MAGNITUDE AND LEGISLATIVE MULTIPARTISM

The impact of effective magnitude on the size of an executive's legislative contingent occurs indirectly via its impact on the level of legislative multipartism in a system. In PR systems this impact is positive in nature, with increasing effective magnitudes leading to higher levels of legislative multipartism and hence smaller legislative contingents for the executive. This relationship is hypothesized to be of a log-log nature (i.e., the impact of an increase in the size of a system's magnitude on its level of legislative multipartism diminishes as one moves up the magnitude scale). Thus we examine the relationship between the logged values of the effective magnitude and multipartism variables in the statistical analysis.

The relationship between these two variables differs for the national and Argentine provincial systems' lower houses. For the national systems the bivariate correlation between a system's effective magnitude and its level of legislative multipartism for the national systems is quite low and insignificant (a correlation of .011). The same correlation for the Argentine provincial systems (.634) is much stronger as well as significant at the .01 level for a one-tailed t-test.[9] The cause of this divergence between the two sets is difficult to pinpoint, although a probable explanation is the absence of extreme outliers among the Argentine provincial systems such as exist in the national systems population (i.e., Uruguay, Nicaragua, and Venezuela). These three national systems have very high effective magnitudes (the log values of the effective magnitudes are in parentheses) 99 (1.996), 50 (1.699), and 25.65 (1.409) respectively, yet due at least in part to their use of the plurality formula for presidential elections along with concurrent election timing, they have reasonably low levels of multipartism. As none of the Argentine provincial systems has an effective magnitude approaching these extremely high levels (the highest is Misiones with 16.40 [1.215]), the Argentine set does not have this problem. The standard deviations, along with the differences between the mean and median effective magnitudes for the two populations, point to these outliers as the source of this divergence. The standard deviation for the national systems (22.56) is over five times the size of the standard deviation for the provincial systems (4.42). The difference between the mean and median effective magnitude for the national systems is quite high (7.32) while that for the Argentine provincial systems is very low (–0.10), primarily due to the lack of extreme cases in the Argentine provincial systems.

A better test of the general impact of effective magnitude on multipartism would control for those other factors such as election timing and executive electoral formula which also influence the level of legislative multipartism in a system. Two methods can be employed to accomplish this. One is to utilize some type of multivariate statistical analysis as is done in Chapter Ten. A second is the most similar cases approach, where one compares cases that are similar in all regards with the exception of the factor one wishes to examine. Among our electoral systems we are fortunate to have an ideal setting for such a comparison in many of the bicameral systems. In a select group of bicameral systems practically all salient exogenous variables, both electoral (e.g., election timing, executive electoral formula, legislative seat allocation formula) and non-electoral (e.g., historical, cultural, public opinion), are held constant except for the effective magnitude. Furthermore in each of these systems the senate is the constitutional equal of the lower house and thus the election for it "counts" as much as the chamber election.

Table 8.1 for the national systems and Table 8.2 for the Argentine provinces demonstrate the impact which a system's effective magnitude has on its level of legislative multipartism.[10] The differences in the level of multipartism in these systems are based almost solely on the difference in the two chambers' respective effective magnitudes. While some of the differences in magnitude are not enormous, one factor does stand out. In every case the chamber with the higher effective magnitude has a higher level of legislative multipartism. This finding demonstrates the salience of effective magnitude's impact on multipartism. The intra-system comparisons in Tables 8.1 and 8.2 demonstrate in a rough manner what impact a change in the effective magnitude of a system would have on a chamber's level of multipartism. For example, if the Venezuelan Chamber were to reduce its effective magnitude it could have a lower level of legislative multipartism similar to that of the Venezuelan Senate. Data from the Argentine provincial systems supply the same type of results. As was the case with all of the national systems, in each

Table 8.1

Bicameral Systems and Proportional Representation:
The Impact of Magnitude in the National Systems*

National System	Lower House Multipartism			Upper House Multipartism
Chile II	2.04			1.95
		2.00	*2.00*	
Colombia	2.09			2.03
		7.65	*5.01*	
Paraguay	2.44			2.69
		4.44	*45.00*	
Peru	2.92			3.39
		7.01	*60.00*	
Uruguay	2.75			2.56
		99.00	*30.00*	
Venezuela	3.19			2.54
		25.33	*6.46*	

* The effective magnitude of each chamber is below each legislative multipartism score in italics.

Note: For each pair of chambers, the two utilize the same proportional representation seat allocation formula. In Uruguay and Venezuela only one fused ballot is employed to elect the two branches (this is not the case for the 1993 Venezuelan election, and thus results from that election are not included in this table). In the other systems two separate ballots are used. In all cases the chamber possesses a larger number of members than does the senate. Chile I, while employing PR to elect both chambers, nevertheless also has partial renovation of the Senate every four years, which means that the electorates for the Lower and Upper Houses differ in any given election, with roughly one-half of the electorate voting for representatives in both houses and one-half voting in only the Lower House election. It is thus excluded from this portion of the analysis. For Chile II only data from the 1989 elections are used due to a similar problem of partial Senate renovation.

Sources: See Appendix A.

Table 8.2
Bicameral Systems and Proportional Representation: The Impact of Magnitude in the Argentine Provinces*

Argentine Provinces	Lower House Multipartism			Upper House Multipartism
Argentine Provinces 1983–95**				
Corrientes	2.52			1.89
		12.72	*1.77*	
Mendoza	2.38			2.24
		6.92	*5.54*	
Tucuman	2.16			1.99
		6.52	*4.15*	
Argentine Provinces 1973				
Buenos Aires	2.16			2.01
		6.25	*5.75*	
Catamarca	2.35			1.91
		6.25	*3.20*	
Cordoba	1.99			1.80
		6.25	*3.00*	
Corrientes	2.60			1.99
		6.25	*4.33*	
Entre Rios	2.51			1.85
		6.25	*4.67*	
Mendoza	2.34			2.24
		6.25	*6.25*	
Salta	2.02			1.59
		6.25	*5.75*	
Sante Fe	3.21			3.04
		6.25	*6.25*	
Tucuman	1.75			1.52
		6.25	*5.00*	

* The effective magnitude of each chamber is below each legislature multipartism score in italics.

** The Tucuman data are based only upon the 1983–89 elections since the new 1990 Tucuman constitution abolished the Senate.

Note: For each pair of chambers, the two utilize the same proportional representation seat allocation formula. The unit of analysis for the three post-1983 systems is the actual election, not the composition of the legislature, since each of these systems employs partial renovation of the legislature. In all cases the chamber possesses more members than the senate.

Source: Data Files of the Argentine Ministerio del Interior, Dirección Nacional Electoral, Departamento de Estadísticas.

of the twelve provincial cases where the lower and upper houses were elected using PR, the house with the higher effective magnitude had the higher level of legislative multipartism.

These results from the pairwise comparison of legislative chambers in bicameral systems, which differ solely in regard to their level of effective magnitude, provide complementary support for the hypothesis that a system's effective magnitude has a noticeable impact on its level of legislative multipartism. However, the overall strength of this relationship, outside of the Argentine provinces, is not extraordinary. The pairwise results tend to correspond with the evidence from the bivariate correlations. Both analyses detected a relationship between effective magnitude and legislative multipartism that was in the hypothesized direction, but strong only for the Argentine provincial systems. For example in Table 8.1 there is a large effective magnitude size difference between the two chambers in the Paraguayan, Peruvian, Uruguayan, and Venezuelan systems, yet on average the chamber with the much smaller magnitude has a level of multipartism which is within a half party of the other chamber except in Venezuela.[11]

In sum, the size of a system's effective magnitude does appear to be positively related to the system's level of legislative multipartism (i.e., an increase in the effective magnitude in a system increases its level of legislative multipartism which in turn reduces the size of the executive's legislative contingent). However, this relationship is not as strong as one might expect based on the prominence of magnitude in the theoretical literature on electoral systems (Lijphart 1994a, 1990b, 1985; Rae 1967; Taagepera and Shugart 1989).

One potential explanation for this weak impact of magnitude comes from work by Ordeshook and Shvetsova (1994). In an analysis of Western industrial democracies these authors found that district magnitude functioned as an intervening variable, mediating the impact of ethnic heterogeneity (as well as religious and linguistic heterogeneity) on the level of multipartism in a system. They concluded that in systems where ethnic heterogeneity is low, that district magnitude's impact on multipartism would be quite modest (except in extreme cases). Unlike in the Western industrial democracies examined by Ordeshook and Shvetsova however, in Latin America ethnic and religious-based parties are not very common. Those which do exist tend to receive very limited popular support at the polls, despite extremely high levels of ethnic, religious, and linguistic heterogeneity in many Latin American nations. Due to the historic (and current) discrimination against and oppression of the indigenous population and to a lesser extent evangelical Christians in many Latin American nations, the lack of strong ethnic and religious-based parties is not particularly surprising.[12] Thus the Ordeshook and Shvetsova thesis may be applicable to the Latin American nations, although at present this cannot be demonstrated empirically. The strong impact of magnitude in the Argentine provincial systems, however, suggests that their thesis does not work particularly well there since Argentina has an ethnic, linguistic, and religious population that is extremely homogenous.

An alternative explanation for this comparably tepid relationship between magnitude and multipartism is rooted in the influence which the rules governing the election of the executive in these systems have on the conduct of the legislative elections. The influence of the executive electoral formula and timing cycle seeps across institutional boundaries to affect the very nature of these legislative contests, to a greater extent than even their own electoral rules in many cases. This is of course not to say that the impact of the size of a system's effective magnitude is not very important in some instances. The very low level of legislative multipartism in Chile II (in spite of the use of the majority runoff formula for the presidential contest) is in all likelihood the product of the system's extremely low effective magnitude (2.00).

ELECTORAL FORMULA AND LEGISLATIVE MULTIPARTISM

Two dimensions of electoral formula are of cardinal importance when discussing multipartism. The first is the distinction between the plurality (with single-member districts) and proportional representation (with multi-member districts) formulas. Use of the plurality formula leads to lower levels of multipartism than does the use of PR formulae (Jones 1993; Lijphart 1990b). The second is the distinction within the PR family among the different electoral formulae used to allocate seats. The distinction which is of principal interest is between the use of the highest average d'Hondt formula and the largest remainders Hare formula, the latter of which is hypothesized to result in higher levels of multipartism (and hence indirectly smaller executive legislative contingents) than the former.

The lack of any system which uses a pure plurality formula for its lower/single house elections in all but one of our systems (the Argentine province of San Juan in 1983) limits our ability to compare the differential impact of plurality versus PR formulae on multipartism. The United States system does however offer an example of the impact of the plurality rule (with single-member districts) on legislative multipartism in a presidential system, with the level of U.S. multipartism continually hovering between 1.75 and 2.00 for both houses of the bicameral legislature. We can, however, in two cases compare the differential impact of the plurality formula versus the PR formula within a set of bicameral systems where lower house seats are allocated using PR and senate seats are allocated using the plurality rule (with elections for the two chambers occurring concurrently).[13] In the Dominican Republic Chamber legislative multipartism is 2.46 (PR formula and an effective magnitude of 3.95) while that of the Senate is 1.97 (plurality formula and an effective magnitude of 1.00). Very similar numbers exist for the Argentine province of Catamarca (1991) where the respective figures are 2.47 for the Chamber (PR formula and an effective magnitude of 13.02) and 1.97 for the Senate (plurality formula and an effective magnitude of 1.00).

The second dimension of comparison is between those PR systems which utilize the largest remainders Hare formula and those that employ the highest average d'Hondt formula. An examination of the bivariate relationship between the use of these two formulae (with the d'Hondt formula scored a zero and the LR-Hare formula scored a one) and the level of lower/single house multipartism in a system reveals a very weak relationship between the two variables for the national systems (a correlation of −.141) which is not even in the hypothesized direction.[14]

Electoral law variables influence legislative multipartism in two manners, mechanical and psychological (Blais and Carty 1991; Rae 1967). The mechanical effect involves the actual translation of votes into seats while the psychological effect is related to the impact of electoral rules on both party leaders (e.g., whether to form a new party, run in a coalition) and on voters (e.g., whether to vote for a party where they might waste their vote) as they make their strategic electoral calculations. The use of the LR-Hare formula in place of its most prominent alternative, the d'Hondt formula, has an obvious mechanical effect (Lijphart 1994a; Taagepera and Shugart 1989).[15] The differential use of the two formulae also influences the strategic calculations of party leaders. Theoretically use of the d'Hondt formula should cause party leaders/politicians to fragment less into multiple parties and coalesce more into a smaller number of parties than would be the case under the LR-Hare formula. Finally, since most political scientists have no real idea what the hypothesized effect of the use of these two formulae is, it is likely that the differential use of formula has very little effect on the vote choice of the general public. The difference in the use of the two formulae examined here is completely mechanical in nature, with the LR-Hare formula hypothesized to result in a higher level of multipartism than the d'Hondt formula.

To examine the mechanical impact of the differential use of formula I recalculated Costa Rican electoral results for its unicameral legislature in the same manner as done by the Costa Rican electoral authorities (the *Tribunal Supremo de Elecciones*: TSE) but instead of using the largest remainders Hare formula employed by the TSE to allocate the legislative seats among the political parties, I employed the highest average d'Hondt formula.[16]

Costa Rica possesses a wide range of electoral district sizes. The nation's seven electoral districts, during the eleven elections which have occurred under the 1949 constitution, have ranged in size from two to twenty-one deputies, with an average effective magnitude of 7.83. This variance in magnitude, along with the large number of elections, makes Costa Rica an ideal subject for an analysis of the differential impact of PR electoral formulae on legislative multipartism.

Under the use of the LR-Hare formula the Costa Rican system in the 1953–98 period has had an average level of legislative multipartism of 2.42. Use of the d'Hondt formula (mechanical effect only) would have resulted in a lower level of multipartism (2.19). The scope of this difference is shown in Figure 8.1, with the LR-Hare formula resulting in a higher level of legislative multipartism than the d'Hondt formula in every one of the eleven elections.

Figure 8.1

The Mechanical Effect of the Legislative Electoral Formula in Costa Rica: Actual and Hypothetical

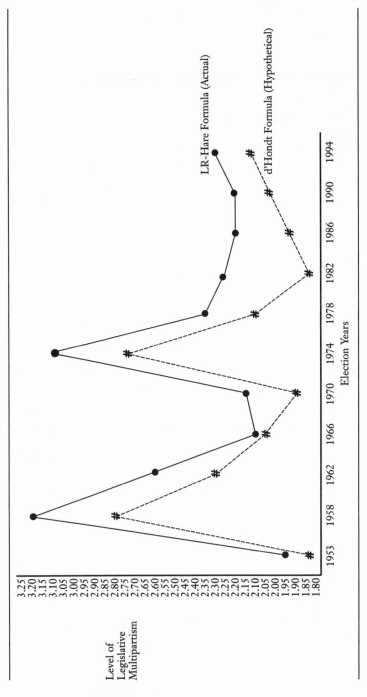

LR–Hare Formula (Actual)

d'Hondt Formula (Hypothetical)

Level of
Legislative
Multipartism

Election Years

• Represents the Actual Use of the LR-Hare Formula to allocate the seats.

Represents the Hypothetical Use of the d'Hondt Formula to allocate the seats.

Source: Elaboration by author based on the data contained in the official publications of the Costa Rican *Tribunal Supremo de Elecciónes*. For specific cite information, see Appendix A.

As hypothesized by Lijphart (1994a) the principal beneficiaries of this hypothetical change in formula were the largest two parties (the *Partido Liberación Nacional*) and various configurations of the center-right opposition (e.g., *Unificación Nacional, Unidad, Partido Unidad Social Cristiana*). The top two parties (i.e., the two which received the largest number of votes in the legislative contest) gained an average of 2.46 seats (out of an average of 54.57 seats) in each of the eleven elections as a consequence of the use of the d'Hondt formula in place of the LR-Hare formula. The impact of this change is also expressed by its hypothesized impact on the political Left in Costa Rica. Under the LR-Hare formula in the seven elections which have taken place since 1970 (when the Left first began to compete in elections), the leftist political parties combined have won an average of 2.43 legislative seats each election. If the d'Hondt formula had been used to allocate seats (mechanical effect only) the Left would have won an average of only 1.14 seats in each legislative election. Thus at least for the political parties of the Left, the change in formula would make a difference (although the overall significance of this for the electoral system is probably not great).[17] The hypothetical change (mechanical only) from the use of the LR-Hare to d'Hondt formula also affected the size of the president's legislative contingent, with the use of the d'Hondt formula raising it from its real level under the Hare formula of 49.55% of the seats to the higher level of 52.40%. While these data only represent the differential mechanical effect of formula use in one system, they do point to its potential impact in others.

While the bivariate findings for the impact of formula on multipartism were not particularly strong, evidence from the case of Costa Rica does demonstrate that at least in some instances the PR formula employed to allocate legislative seats can influence the level of multipartism in a system and indirectly influence the size of the president's legislative contingent.[18] The distinction between plurality and PR systems in regard to their impact on multipartism is strong although not particularly relevant here. Within the PR systems formula appears to possess partial importance in at least one case, although its general impact across systems (at least in a bivariate manner) is very weak.

Both the effective magnitude and electoral formula used in legislative elections have been hypothesized by many authors to have a strong impact on multipartism (Rae 1967; Taagepera and Shugart 1989). Within presidential systems the impact of these factors is likely to be partially diminished by the impact of the executive selection process. Factors such as the electoral formula employed to elect the executive as well as the timing of this executive election vis-à-vis the legislative contest would appear to travel across institutional boundaries to influence legislative elections, in many cases to a greater extent than the electoral laws which directly govern these legislative contests. Of course as the evidence from the Argentine provinces (effective magnitude), Chile II (low effective magnitude), and the United States (single-member plurality districts) demonstrates, these legislative rules are important in certain instances. Full confirmation of this comparison of effect must await the multiple regression analysis in Chapter Ten. However, based on the initial findings of this chapter, we would expect both effective magnitude and formula to have a mild independent impact on legislative multipartism.

9
Bicameral Versus Unicameral Legislatures

The number of legislative chambers in a constitutional system affects the likelihood of a president's possession of a legislative majority or near-majority in a fairly self-evident manner. It is more difficult to win a majority or near-majority in two legislative chambers than in one. This is particularly the case when the apportionment, term length, and formula/magnitude which govern the elections for the two chambers differ significantly, as is the case in many of the Latin American bicameral systems.

The impact of bicameralism on presidential legislative support has received virtually no scholarly attention. For instance, in their seminal work on executive-legislative relations in presidential systems Shugart and Carey (1992) do not examine bicameralism, and instead treat the legislature in bicameral systems as a single legislative actor. In general, bicameral systems due to their dual nature are hypothesized to be less likely to provide overall presidential legislative majorities or near-majorities than are their unicameral counterparts (Madison, *Federalist* 62). Of course, the tendency of bicameral systems to inhibit the achievement of overall presidential legislative majorities or near-majorities is highly conditioned by the electoral rules which a nation uses to govern the selection of its executive and legislature. The conclusions of this chapter are that the tendency of the presence of a bicameral system to influence the probability of a presidential legislative majority or near-majority is intertwined both with the electoral laws in a nation, but also with how some of these laws interact with the level and distribution of popular support for the president and his or her party. In short, while bicameralism in general appears to have a slightly negative impact on the achievement of a legislative majority (or close to it), this effect is intermixed with system-specific electoral law factors to such an extent as to make any generalizable comments on the impact of bicameralism difficult.

BICAMERALISM IN LATIN AMERICA AND THE ARGENTINE PROVINCES

Table 9.1 lists the distribution of bicameral and unicameral legislatures for the national systems. Bicameralism is employed in the majority of the systems with only the Central American republics and Ecuador (whose 1978 constitution abolished its Senate) lacking an upper chamber.[1] The popularity of bicameralism is probably due in large part to its historic use in the United States and France, the two constitutional systems (particularly the United States) which have served as models for Latin American constitution drafters. Added to this foreign influence is the issue of regionalism which was incorporated in the constitutions of many nations through the equal representation of the different constitutional administrative units in the upper chamber (e.g., Argentina, Bolivia, Brazil, and to a lesser extent Chile and Venezuela). The bicameral method is also popular among the Argentine provinces, with eight of twenty-three provinces currently possessing bicameral legislatures (see Table 9.2). Finally, unlike the case in most of the Anglo-European bicameral systems, all of the Latin American and Argentine provincial bicameral systems consist of two relatively equal (symmetrical in Lijphart's terms) chambers in regard to their constitutional power (Lijphart 1984).

BICAMERALISM AND PRESIDENTIAL LEGISLATIVE SUPPORT

Our comparison of legislatures with an unequal number of chambers prevents us from employing the preferred measure of a presi-

Table 9.1
Bicameral and Unicameral Legislatures in the National Systems

Bicameral Systems	Unicameral Systems
Argentina I	Costa Rica
Argentina II	Ecuador
Bolivia	El Salvador
Brazil Ia	Guatemala
Brazil Ib	Honduras
Brazil II	Nicaragua
Chile I	
Chile II	
Colombia	
Dominican Republic	
Paraguay	
Peru*	
Uruguay	
Venezuela	

* Peru's 1993 Constitution provides for a unicameral legislature.

dent's strength in the legislature (i.e., the average size of the presidential party's legislative contingent). In place of it I use a measure of the percentage of presidential years in which the president's party had an absolute majority in the legislature (in both chambers for bicameral systems).[2]

A very rough comparison of the impact of bicameralism on the tendency of a system to provide the president with a legislative majority compares the average percentage of presidential years in which the executive had an absolute majority for the two systems. During the period of study the unicameral system presidents had a legislative majority during 52.67% of their years in office while the comparable figure for the bicameral system presidents was 37.41%. While the difference is large, a strong possibility exists that it is the product not of the number of chambers in the systems, but rather of other aspects of the systems' electoral laws.[3]

A better method to analyze the impact of bicameralism on the tendency of a system to provide the executive with an overall legislative majority involves an intra-bicameral system examination. Theoretically, if bicameralism (i.e., the existence of a second chamber) is injurious to the prospects of a legislative majority, then we would

Table 9.2
Bicameral and Unicameral Argentine Provincial Systems: 1983–95*

Bicameral Systems	Unicameral Systems
Buenos Aires	Chaco
Catamarca II (1991–)	Formosa
Corrientes	Jujuy
Mendoza	La Pampa
San Luis II (1987–)	La Rioja
Tucuman I (1983–91)	Misiones
	Rio Negro
	San Juan
	San Luis I (1983–87)
	Santa Cruz
	Tierra del Fuego
	Tucuman II (1991–)

Systems which guarantee an absolute majority to the
plurality winner in the lower/single house

Cordoba	Chubut
Catamarca I (1983–91)	Neuquen**
Entre Rios	Santiago del Estero
Santa Fe	

* For provinces which changed either their number of legislative chambers or added/ annulled a rule providing an absolute majority of the legislative seats in the lower/single house to the plurality vote winner, separate entries (with the dates in which the system was in force in parentheses) are listed.

** Beginning in 1995 Neuquen will no longer provide a guaranteed majority to the plurality winner.

expect to find a large number of instances when the president's party possessed a majority in the lower house but lacked one in the senate, and thus failed to have an overall legislative majority due to the existence of this second chamber. In these cases, bicameralism would deprive the president of a legislative majority, thereby reducing his or her ability to govern.

Table 9.3 shows the average distribution of the legislative status (in percentage of presidential/gubernatorial years) for the national and Argentine provincial bicameral systems. Of principal importance are the two percentages in bold which represent instances where the existence of the second chamber cost the executive an overall legislative majority. The senate is guilty of executive majority deprivation in 9.18% of the presidential years and 3.70% of the gubernatorial years. In these cases, the executive was deprived of an overall majority due to the existence of a second chamber. However, also noteworthy is the fact that on average it is generally the chamber and not the senate which (where only one chamber deprives the executive of a majority) is more often the guilty party. In general, due primarily to their lower effective magnitudes and/or use of plurality and Sáenz Peña type formulas, as opposed to the higher magnitudes of the chambers along with their near universal use of proportional representation, senates tend to have a lower level of multipartism than their chamber counterparts and hence larger average presidential party legislative contingents.[4] For the bicameral systems the average size of the executive's chamber contingent is 41.20% of the seats for the national systems and 51.84% for the Argentine provincial systems while the average size of the executive's senate contingent is 44.09% and 62.73% respectively.[5]

The extent to which the presence of a second legislative chamber (i.e., bicameralism) makes the achievement of an overall absolute legislative majority or near-majority more or less likely covaries with the type of electoral laws employed by a system. The electoral formula used to select the executive, the timing of the executive

Table 9.3

Distribution of the Executive's Legislative Status in the National and Argentine Provincial (1983–95) Bicameral Systems

Legislative Status	The System Average of the Number of Years of Each Status in Percentages	
	National Systems	Argentine Provinces
Absolute Executive Majority	37.41	59.26
Majority in Chamber, but not in Senate	9.18	3.70
Majority in Senate, but not in Chamber	9.61	25.93
No Majority in Either Chamber	43.80	11.11
Total	100.00	100.00

Sources: See Appendix A.

and senate elections as well as their respective term lengths, and the effective magnitude/electoral formula employed to allocate the senate seats all influence the likelihood of a presidential legislative majority or near-majority to a greater extent than does the mere presence or absence of a second chamber. For example, in a hypothetical system where the lower house and upper house are elected in the exact same manner, the presence of a second chamber is likely to have very little impact on the tendency of the system to provide the president with sufficient legislative support.[6]

Of the four instances among the national systems where a president lacked an absolute majority in the senate but possessed one in the chamber, two can be attributed to the influence of the electoral laws discussed in the previous chapters. In the Peruvian election of 1980 President Fernando Belaúnde Terry won a majority in the Chamber which was elected from electoral districts with an effective magnitude of 7.20 using PR, but failed to do so in the Senate which was elected from a national district (with an effective magnitude of 60) using PR. As one might hypothesize, with all other electoral law factors (which have been previously discussed) held constant, the chamber (i.e., the Senate) with the higher district magnitude and hence the higher level of multipartism, was the body which deprived the executive of an overall legislative majority. In Chile (1965-69), as stated in Chapter Seven, President Eduardo Frei's lack of a majority in the Senate was due to the system's partial renovation of the Senate every four years. Thus the important issue in determining the relationship between bicameralism and the likelihood of a presidential legislative majority or near-majority is not the presence or absence of bicameralism per se, but rather where bicameralism exists what the electoral rules are that influence the composition of the second chamber.[7]

BICAMERALISM AND LEGISLATIVE SUPPORT: APPORTIONMENT

In addition to the electoral law dimensions which have been discussed in detail in the previous chapters, another factor takes on added significance when exploring the relationship between bicameralism and executive legislative majorities and near-majorities: the apportionment of senate seats. While most legislative chambers tend to possess some type of bias in regard to their representation of the populace, the senate tends to be the more malapportioned. The remaining two of our four cases where the lack of a senate majority denied the president of an overall legislative majority were the result of malapportionment: Argentina II (1983–87) and the Dominican Republic (1978–82).[8]

Any system which utilizes more than one electoral district to select members of a legislative body must have a method to apportion the seats to be contested. Holding all other factors constant, the more a legislative chamber deviates from the equal representation of the population (as exists in the presidential election), the greater the likelihood that the composition of the legislature will differ from national preferences and quite possibly lead to a lack of a legislative majority or near-majority for the president.[9] Theoretically then, the lower the degree of overrepresentation of certain regions in the legislature, the greater the likelihood of a presidential majority or near-majority in the legislature. As we will see, the levels of malapportionment of the systems tend to vary (in most bicameral systems the senate is the most malapportioned chamber), with the rationale for some of the more malapportioned cases (e.g., Argentina, Bolivia, and Brazil) rooted in a history of regional rivalries and conflict. This malapportionment, however, tends to have a salient impact on the partisan composition of the senate only when those units (i.e., provinces, states, or departments) which are overrepresented have a noticeably different set of political preferences than those units which are underrepresented. For example in the United States a plausible explanation for the lack of any serious public criticism of the highly unequal distribution of Senate seats is that on average the states which are overrepresented do not appear to be distinct in any politically significant manner from those which are underrepresented. If, however, such differences were to exist, the political salience of this unequal representation would take on new importance.

In Latin America roughly three methods have been employed to allocate senate seats. The first arrangement, used in Argentina, Bolivia, Brazil, and the Dominican Republic (as well as many of the Argentine provinces), allocates an equal number of seats to the principal administrative units of the system (i.e., provinces in Argentina and the Dominican Republic, states in Brazil, and departments in Bolivia and the Argentine provinces). The second method involves an equal allocation of seats to the administrative units of the country/province, but then an additional allocation based on the population of the administrative units (i.e., Colombia, one Argentine province, and to a lesser extent Venezuela through the use of compensatory seats).[10] Finally there are systems which use multiple districts to allocate senate seats in a manner similar to that used for the lower house (i.e., Chile and many of the Argentine provinces) as well as those which employ a single nation-wide district (i.e., Paraguay, Peru, and Uruguay).

It is useful to examine the degree of malapportionment in the first group of systems which allocate senate seats to all administrative units equally, regardless of population. It is in these systems (see Table 9.4) where the degree of malapportionment is the most extreme, and thus the potential for it to have an impact on the president's senate contingent highest.

Table 9.4 lists the smallest percentage of the population which can elect 50% of the seats in the senate of the nation/province. For each system, the population of the administrative units was progressively summed (moving from the least populated unit to the largest) until 50% of the senate seats had been accounted for. Also included are comparable percentages for the systems' chambers which in all cases are much less malapportioned than the senates. It is instructive that one of the most malapportioned senates (Argentina II) acted to deprive President Raúl Alfonsín of an overall legislative majority during the period 1983–87.

A review of Table 9.4 reveals a group of highly malapportioned senates, all of which allow for the election of at least 50% of the senators by less than 20% of the population. Among the national systems this level of malapportionment is particularly severe in present day Argentina II and Brazil II. In these nations the overrepresentation of the less populated provinces/states at the expense of the most populated provinces/states is an issue of current controversy. The fact that these less populated provinces/states tend to be more conservative politically than their more populous counterparts helps explain why the issue of senate malapportionment is a topic of greater political debate in these two nations than in the United States, despite relatively similar degrees of malapportionment.

Included in Table 9.4 are the apportionment data for the Argen-

Table 9.4
Senate Malapportionment in Nine Electoral Systems

		Smallest Percentage* of the Population which Can Elect 50% of the Legislative Body	
System**	Time Period***	Senate Percentage	Chamber Percentage
Argentina I	1973–76	13.53	35.61
Argentina II	1983–91	11.69	35.62
Bolivia	1985–94	17.56	33.45
Brazil Ib	1954–62	19.69	41.68
Brazil II	1990–94	13.53	39.60
Dominican Republic	1978–86	18.95	44.69
Province of Salta	1987–95	6.88	31.10
Province of San Luis	1987–95	13.02	24.20
United States	1992–94	16.24	49.98

* The percentage shown is the portion of the population from the least populated districts in a system which combined can elect 50% of the members of the legislative chamber.

** Only systems which provide equal senate representation to all constitutional administrative units are included in this table. However, Argentine provinces which meet this requisite but elect the chamber from a single province-wide electoral district are also excluded.

*** The time periods listed are those for which the calculation is valid. Many of the systems created new electoral districts and/or reapportioned seats as well as experienced demographic changes. Therefore only limited time periods could be used. However, the percentages for the other contemporary time periods are not noticeably different from those listed above.

Sources: Europa 1993; Europa 1963; Hoffman 1992; Marín and Rotay 1992; Paxton 1986. For electoral data sources see Appendix A.

tine province of Salta. Salta governor Roberto Ulloa (whose difficulties in governing effectively due to his lack of sufficient legislative support were detailed in Chapter Three) listed the malapportionment of the Salta legislative seats (particularly of the Senate) as one of the two principal causes of his deficient legislative contingent (Ulloa 1993). As stated earlier, malapportionment is only a problem for executive legislative majorities and near-majorities when the preferences of the overrepresented districts differ from those of the underrepresented districts. In Salta this difference in preferences exists, with Ulloa's *Partido Renovador de Salta* (PRS) highly popular in the provincial capital and in many of the other larger cities of the province where the majority of the population is concentrated, while the opposition *Partido Justicialista* (PJ) retains a great deal of support in the sparsely populated rural departments. In the 1991 gubernatorial election Ulloa received 45.05% of the vote in those departments which account for 50% of the Senate seats yet only 6.88% of the provincial population (i.e., the overrepresented departments), while his PJ opponent received 49.60% of the vote in these departments. Conversely, among the 93.12% of the provincial population which elect the other half of the Senate (i.e., the underrepresented departments), Ulloa was supported by 56.81% of the voters against only 34.77% who voted for his PJ opponent. This extreme level of malapportionment (6.88% of the population elects 50% of the senators) was deadly for Ulloa. Ulloa was supported by an absolute majority of the provincial population in the 1991 gubernatorial election, but his PRS was able to win only two of the eleven Senate seats contested in the same election (for the election results see Table 3.4).[11]

In sum, while malapportionment does not necessarily reduce the likelihood of a presidential legislative majority or near-majority in all cases, it does create the potential for a strong contradiction between the strength of the president in the national vote and his or her support in the senate. Where geographic differences in preferences exist (as was the case in both Salta and Argentina II) the consequence can be disastrous for an executive, whose ability to govern is severely restricted by the lack of sufficient partisan backing in the legislature.

The impact of bicameralism on the tendency of a system to provide the executive with an overall legislative majority or near-majority is negative. Since it is harder to win a majority or near-majority in two chambers rather than one, in general bicameralism has a negative impact on the executive's chances of achieving this level of legislative support. This negative impact, however, appears to depend to a considerable extent on system-specific factors, particularly the electoral laws used in a system (i.e., executive electoral formula, election timing, legislative magnitude/formula, apportionment). Also important, in regard to the impact of apportionment, is the geographic distribution of support for different political parties.

With the exceptions of Paraguay and Peru the electoral formula and magnitude of the senates examined in this study are more conducive to lower levels of multipartism than are those of their chamber counterparts. Therefore any negative impact which bicameralism has on the executive's likelihood of possessing a legislative majority or near-majority is primarily due either to (1) the use of partial renovation and/or senate term lengths which are longer than the term of the executive (such as in Argentina II, Brazil Ia, Brazil Ib, Brazil II, Chile I, and Chile II) and/or (2) malapportionment. The data indicate that in this latter case, as long as political preferences do not differentiate along the cleavage of over/under representation, malapportionment is not a problem. Thus the place of bicameralism in the debate over legislative majorities and near-majorities, while theoretically important, is not as prominent as was originally thought. However, the high level of malapportionment in many of these systems (particularly the systems listed in Table 9.4) should be a point of concern for those interested in the equality of the vote. While a certain level of overrepresentation to protect geographic entities is justifiable, the extreme levels listed in Table 9.4 are troubling.

10

Electoral Laws and Legislative Multipartism: A Multiple Regression Analysis

The impact of electoral laws on legislative multipartism was examined in the previous chapters in a bivariate manner. However, the overall impact of electoral laws on legislative multipartism is multivariate in nature. This chapter develops a multivariate model to examine the *independent* impact which the executive electoral formula, executive-legislative election timing, legislative effective magnitude, and legislative electoral formula have on the level of legislative multipartism in the lower/single house of an electoral system.

The units of analysis for this multiple regression analysis are nineteen Latin American national electoral systems (see Table 10.1) and nineteen Argentine provincial electoral systems (the same systems listed in Figure 5.2, with the addition of a second Tucuman system). The data are the averages for the systems since the goal of the study is to analyze the impact of institutional arrangements on representation and the party system, a task which is best accomplished by examining systems, not individual elections.[1] Ordinary least squares (OLS) regression analysis, with a log-log functional form assumed to exist between the independent and dependent (i.e., multipartism) variables, is employed.

OPERATIONALIZATION AND MEASURES[2]

For the national systems the impact of four electoral law variables (executive electoral formula, executive-legislative election timing,

145

Table 10.1
*Latin American Democratic Systems Included
in the Multiple Regression Analysis*

System	Time Period
Argentina I	1973–1976
Bolivia	1985–1997
Brazil Ia	1945–1954
Brazil Ib	1954–1964
Brazil II	1989–1994
Chile I	1945–1973
Chile II	1989–1997
Colombia	1974–1991
Costa Rica	1953–1998
Dominican Republic	1978–1994
Ecuador	1978–1986
El Salvador	1984–1997
Guatemala	1985–1995
Honduras	1981–1997
Nicaragua	1984–1996
Paraguay	1993–1998
Peru	1980–1992
Uruguay*	1942–1994
Venezuela	1959–1998

* The Uruguayan data exclude the elections of 1954, 1958, and 1962 when a collegial executive was employed, along with the years 1973–84, during which time the nation was governed by a military dictatorship.

legislative effective magnitude, legislative electoral formula) on the level of legislative multipartism in a system is examined.[3] Due to an almost complete lack of variance for two of these variables for the 1983–95 Argentine provincial systems (i.e., executive and legislative electoral formula), only the impact of a somewhat different version of the election timing variable and of the legislative effective magnitude variable is examined in the analysis of the Argentine provincial population.

The executive electoral formula is operationalized as a binary variable with the system scored zero if the executive is elected by a plurality vote (i.e., a relative majority in which the candidate/party receiving the most votes in the first and only round of voting wins the election) and one if the executive must receive an absolute majority (over 50% of the popular vote) in the first round to be elected.[4] In the majority systems, if no candidate receives an absolute majority in the first round, then in seven of the nine majority systems a runoff between the top two challengers is used to select the president. In two systems (Bolivia and Chile I), the president is then chosen by a majority vote in the legislature (with the upper and lower chambers meeting in joint session).

In the multiple regression analysis of the national systems timing is operationalized as a binary variable with concurrent presidential and legislative elections being scored as a zero and nonconcurrent presidential and legislative elections scored one. Concurrent elections are defined as elections where the first or only round of the presidential election and the election of the legislature are held on the same day.[5] Nonconcurrent elections are defined as elections where the popular selection of the legislature occurs in a separate year from the election of the president.[6] For the Argentine provincial systems concurrent elections are defined in the same manner as for the national systems (and scored zero). Distinct from the national systems, however, many Argentine provincial systems employ midterm elections to renew one-half of their legislatures. The systems which employ these partial midterm renovations are coded one.

The effective magnitude employed for the legislative election is calculated by dividing the number of legislative seats by the number of legislative districts with adjustments made for the use of multiple tiers of districts as well as electoral thresholds or quotas.[7] Legislative electoral formula is coded as a binary variable, with the highest average d'Hondt formula coded zero and the largest remainders Hare formula coded one.

Legislative multipartism is calculated utilizing a measure based on the percentage of legislative seats won by the various parties in the lower/single house elections (i.e., Laakso and Taagepera's measure of the "effective number of parties" in a party system [1979, 3–27]).[8] The values for the multipartism variable have a reasonably continuous distribution, with a mean for the national systems of 3.434 effective parties and a standard deviation of 1.618. Values for this dependent variable range from a low of 1.992 (which is the value for Chile II and corresponds to a little less than two effective parties) to a high of 7.464 (which is the value for Brazil II and corresponds to roughly seven and a half effective parties). This

Electoral Laws, Legislative Multipartism

Table 10.2
Legislative Multipartism in 19 Latin American Electoral Systems

	"Effective Number of Parties" in the Lower/Single House of the National Legislature*						
	1.99–2.50	2.51–3.00	3.01–3.50	3.51–4.00	4.01–4.50	4.51–5.00	5.01–
ELECTORAL SYSTEMS	Chile II Colombia Honduras Nicaragua Costa Rica Paraguay Dom Republic	El Salvador Uruguay Peru Argentina I	Venezuela Brazil Ia	Guatemala Bolivia		Brazil Ib	Ecuador Chile I Brazil II

* This is Laakso and Taagepera's (1979) "Effective Number of Parties" measure. For more information on its calculation, see note 8 of this chapter.

Sources: See Appendix A.

distribution is illustrated graphically in Table 10.2. For the Argentine provincial systems the mean level of multipartism is 2.266 effective parties with a standard deviation of 0.422. These provincial systems range in size from a low of 1.320 effective parties in La Rioja to a high of 3.116 effective parties in San Juan II.

DATA ANALYSIS

Plurality Versus Majority Presidential Electoral Systems

The formula used to elect the president is hypothesized to have a strong impact on the number of parties in a nation's legislature. The nineteen Latin American systems examined are almost evenly split between those which utilize a plurality selection process to elect their executive (ten) and those that employ a majority system to choose their executive (nine).

The basic multiple regression analysis combines the hypothesis of Duverger (1986) that plurality elections lead to two-party systems while majority systems favor multi-party systems with Shugart's (1988) assertion that presidential elections can have a strong impact on legislative elections in presidential systems. The result is a prediction that, holding other factors constant, systems which utilize the plurality presidential electoral formula will have lower levels of legislative multipartism than will systems which employ the majority formula. By extension, and using legislative multipartism as a proxy for the national party system, this choice of presidential election formula is hypothesized to influence the number of effective parties in the nation as well.

As is seen in the OLS regression results for the analysis of the Latin American national systems presented in Table 10.3, the presidential election formula (plurality or majority) does have a very strong impact on the number of effective parties in the legislature, with a t-ratio (1.822, 14-df) which is significant at less than .05 for a one-tailed test.[9] Here, the presence of a majority system results in a level of multipartism which is 1.331 times the level of multipartism of a plurality system (holding other factors constant).[10] For example, based on this model, in Honduras (multipartism: 2.087, with a plurality formula and concurrent timing) a 33.1% increase in multipartism from 2.087 to 2.778 would make Honduras's level of multipartism comparable to that of Peru (multipartism: 2.921, majority formula and concurrent timing). This change would amount to an increase of slightly less than three-fourths of an effective party and to a one column shift to the right in Table 10.2.

These data provide strong support for the hypothesis that the presidential electoral formula has a noticeable impact on the number of effective parties represented in the legislature and by extension in the nation. This implies that rules for elections for one constitutional office have an impact on the nature of elections and representation in other elective bodies.

Concurrent Versus Nonconcurrent Presidential and Legislative Elections

There is strong theoretical support for the hypothesis that in Presidential-PR systems the timing of presidential and legislative elections has a significant impact on the level of multipartism in the latter elections (Shugart 1988). Concurrent systems should be expected to have lower levels of multipartism than is the case when the two elections are held at different times when the restraining impact of the executive selection process is much weaker.

Multiple regression analysis of the Latin American national systems provides solid support for the hypothesis that election timing has a strong impact on legislative multipartism, with a *t*-ratio (2.612, 14-*df*) which is significant at less than .05 for a one-tailed test. Table 10.3 indicates that the use of nonconcurrent elections results in a level of multipartism that is 1.611 times the level of multipartism that occurs when concurrent elections are used (holding other factors constant).[11] Here the model indicates that a shift to a nonconcurrent electoral cycle in Uruguay (multipartism: 2.749, plurality formula and concurrent timing) would lead to an increase in multipartism from 2.749 to 4.429. This change would result in a transformation of Uruguay's party system (with slightly less than three effective parties) to a situation similar to that of Brazil Ib (multipartism: 4.539, plurality formula and nonconcurrent timing), with the difference being the presence of roughly one and two-thirds more effective parties in the legislature. On Table 10.2 this change would shift Uruguay three columns to the right.

For the Argentine provincial analysis, the use of completely con-current election timing is coded zero and the utilization of partial renovation (where one-half of the legislature is elected concurrently with the governor and the other half is selected in a midterm elec-tion) is scored one. The findings of this analysis are neither in the hypothesized direction nor significant. The use of the partially nonconcurrent system (holding other factors constant) results in a 3.5% reduction in the level of multipartism in the legislature (exponential 0.965, *t*-ratio -0.189 with 16-*df*). The use of a mixed timing cycle (at least in this case) appears to be quite distinct in regard to its effect on legislative multipartism from the use of the nonconcurrent electoral cycle.

Effective Magnitude

In an examination of thirty-one Anglo-European systems, Arend Lijphart detected a small positive relationship between district mag-

Table 10.3
Ordinary Least Squares Estimates of Institutional Determinants
of Legislative Multipartism

Independent Variables	Estimated Coefficient	Exponential of Estimated Coefficient[1]	T-Ratio (14 DF)
Election Timing	0.207	1.611	2.612*
Presidential Formula	0.124	1.331	1.822*
Effective Magnitude	0.079		0.899
Legislative Formula	−0.044	0.893	−0.659
Constant	0.340		3.222**

R-Square = .507
**p < .01 one-tailed test
*p < .05 one-tailed test

Note: a Log-Log functional form is employed.

1. Note that the exponential of the estimated coefficient indicates the ratio of the expected value of Y (i.e., the dependent variable multipartism) when the binary variable (i.e., presidential formula, election timing, or legislative formula) equals one to the expected value of Y when the binary variable equals zero. The effective magnitude variable coefficient (as is the case with all continuous variables) is interpreted via its elasticity. In a log-log model however, one cannot interpret the binary variable coefficients using their elasticities, and thus for purposes of interpretation, the exponentials of the estimated coefficients of the binary variables are employed. For more information on the interpretation of these coefficients, see notes 10 and 11 of this chapter.

Sources: See Appendix A.

nitude and electoral multipartism (Lijphart 1990b). A replication of Lijphart's study using data from twenty-two Latin American and Caribbean nations revealed the same positive relationship, albeit in an even more limited status (Jones 1993).

Table 10.3 shows the impact of effective magnitude on legislative multipartism to be in the hypothesized direction, but not significantly strong. The estimated coefficient (0.079, t-ratio: 0.899, 14-df) does however reveal that effective magnitude influences legislative multipartism to a certain extent.

Data from the analysis of the Argentine provincial systems provide a divergent finding. The impact of effective magnitude on the level of legislative multipartism in the lower/single house is in the hypothesized direction and significant at the .01 level for a one-tailed t-test (estimated coefficient: 0.177, t-ratio: 3.312, 16-df).

Legislative Electoral Formula: D'Hondt Versus LR-Hare

The electoral formula utilized to allocate legislative seats is hypothesized to influence the level of legislative multipartism via its impact on the degree of proportionality of the translation of votes into seats (Lijphart 1990b). Due to its more proportional nature the LR-Hare formula is hypothesized to result in a higher level of legislative multipartism than the less proportional d'Hondt formula.

Multiple regression analysis indicates that the PR legislative electoral formula employed to allocate legislative seats has an impact on multipartism which is very weak (i.e., an exponential of 0.893, with a t-ratio of −0.659). This finding is furthermore not even in the hypothesized direction. This suggests that within the parameters of the most commonly used PR formulae, the use of one versus the other is not of tremendous importance for the level of legislative multipartism in presidential systems.

DISCUSSION

Four important conclusions can be drawn from this analysis. First, the choice between a plurality and majority presidential election formula has a strong impact on the level of legislative multipartism and, by inference, on the number of relevant parties in a nation's party system. Plurality systems clearly possess lower levels of legislative multipartism than do majority systems. Second, Shugart's hypothesis regarding the salience of presidential and legislative election timing was supported by these data. Systems in which these elections were held concurrently have lower levels of multipartism than do those systems where these two elections were held at separate times. This finding does not however hold true for the use of partial midterm elections which have only a marginal impact on the level of legislative multipartism. Third, effective magnitude was found to have an impact on multipartism in the hypothesized direction (positive) in the national and Argentine systems, but only of significant strength in the latter population. Finally, the PR electoral formula employed to allocate the seats in the legislative elections was found to have a very weak effect on the number of relevant legislative parties in a system.

An important test of multiple regression results is their predictive value. In 1991 Colombia engaged in a substantial modification of its constitutional system. As part of this modification, two of the important dimensions examined here were changed. First, to elect the president the majority runoff method was selected to replace the plurality formula. Second, the effective magnitude of the electoral districts for the Chamber election was lowered from 7.654 to 4.878. The other two electoral dimensions examined here, election timing and legislative formula, remained unchanged.[12] Based on the results in Table 10.3 we would expect the change in presidential formula to lead to an increase in legislative multipartism in the lower house, an increase that would be slightly counteracted by the small decrease in effective magnitude.

In the 1990 Chamber election the level of legislative multipartism was 1.976.[13] In a previous work (Jones 1994, 214–15) utilizing the multivariate results from a table which is the predecessor of Table 10.3, I predicted that the level of Colombian multipartism in the 1994 Chamber elections would be 2.506.[14] Of course many other factors beyond the four electoral law dimensions discussed here work to influence the level of legislative multipartism in a nation. However, based solely on the changes in the rules governing the elections, an increase of roughly one-half of an effective political party was the predicted consequence of the recent change of the electoral formula employed to select the executive and the effective magnitude for the Chamber election. In the 1994 Chamber election the actual level of legislative multipartism was 2.451, very close to the predicted value of 2.506. This finding increases our confidence in the validity of the model used in this study.

While many of the results reported in this chapter were quite strong, given the strength of the theoretical argument, why were they not stronger? A partial explanation would be based around four points: (1) Many of the systems have only experienced a few elections under the current rules; and it may take time for both voters and party elites to conform to the electoral rules through a learning process; (2) there are electoral rules which were not examined here but may influence the level of multipartism in specific systems; (3) the small size of the population examined increases the probability of partial outliers exerting a strong influence on the results; (4) many other factors in a nation (e.g., socioeconomic, religious, cultural, regional, ethnic) can also affect the level of multipartism in a nation.

11

Electoral Laws and Electoral Engineering

The first portion of this work discussed the difficulties posed by divided government for the functioning of presidential systems. It was noted that contrary to the case in parliamentary systems, the institutional features of presidentialism actively discourage the formation of coalitions aimed at reducing the friction and gridlock associated with divided government. Parliamentary systems are able to function quite adequately when the executive's political party lacks a majority or near-majority in the legislature. This is not the case in presidential systems.

The theoretical literature on divided government, with some minor exceptions, highlights the potent negative impact which deficient partisan legislative support has on the functioning of presidential government. Literature based on the U.S. experience as well as on cross-national and country-specific analyses tends to concur that when the president lacks a legislative majority or near-majority, democratic government is less effective, less efficient, more conflictive, and outside of the United States more likely to break down than is the case when the president possesses a legislative majority or near-majority. Contrary to the U.S. experience, it was demonstrated that electoral laws are the principal source of divided government in the Latin American presidential systems.

In this study data were utilized from two populations: Latin American national electoral systems and Argentine provincial electoral systems. Using these data the study discussed in considerable

155

detail the impact of a set of key electoral law dimensions on the tendency of a system to provide the executive with a healthy level of support in the legislature. These electoral dimensions have both an indirect effect (via the intervening variable of multipartism) and in places a direct effect on the size of the executive's legislative contingent.

The analysis section began with an examination of the strong relationship between the key intervening variable of legislative multipartism and the average size of the executive's legislative contingent. The remaining analysis chapters examined the indirect and in certain instances direct impact which electoral laws have on the size of the executive's legislative contingent. Four chapters devoted to the in-depth analysis of the specific dimensions, combined with Chapter Ten which utilized multiple regression analysis, provided a thorough examination of the differential impact of these prominent electoral law dimensions on the tendency of a system to provide the executive with a legislative majority or near-majority.

REVIEW OF ELECTORAL DIMENSIONS

The electoral formula used by a system to select its executive has a direct (in concurrent timing systems only) and indirect (via the intervening variable of multipartism) effect on the size of the executive's legislative contingent. From the perspective of providing the president with a legislative majority or near-majority, of the formulae for which there exist empirical referents, the plurality formula is the only method suitable for the selection of the executive. Its principal alternative, the majority runoff formula, results in a higher level of multipartism as well as a decreased linkage between the executive and legislative elections (in concurrent systems) which has the end result of supplying legislative contingents which are inferior to those provided under the plurality arrangement.[1]

The electoral timing cycle employed by a system for presidential and legislative elections influences the size of the presidential legislative contingent both indirectly and directly. Presidential and legislative elections which are held concurrently are optimal from a standpoint of assuring a strong executive legislative contingent. The mixed timing cycle, with both concurrent and midterm elections, provides the next strongest legislative contingent. Finally, the non-concurrent electoral cycle encourages high levels of multipartism and reduces the degree of linkage between the executive and legislative elections. This cycle is extremely detrimental to the provision of a strong legislative contingent for the executive.

The indirect impact of the electoral formula and effective magnitude used for the legislative elections is most salient along the divide of single-member plurality districts versus multi-member PR districts. Among the latter systems, however, the differential use of the prominent PR formulas and effective magnitudes is of reduced import for the size of the executive's legislative contingent. In the national and Argentine provincial systems the size of a system's effective magnitude has a modest and strong impact respectively on the level of legislative multipartism (and hence on the size of the executive's contingent). The employment of different PR formulas (d'Hondt versus LR-Hare) was found not to have a salient impact on the level of legislative multipartism in these systems.

While theoretically an important factor, the impact of the number of legislative chambers on the tendency of a system to endow the executive with sufficient legislative support is deeply intertwined with other electoral dimensions to a great extent which makes this factor much less problematic for executive majorities or near-majorities than might be expected. As a general rule in the bicameral systems, senators are elected under rules which make an executive majority in them more likely than in the lower houses (in this population Paraguay and Peru are two exceptions). However, bicameralism can have a very prominent impact where the malapportionment of senate seats coincides with a cleavage in the distribution of partisan support in a system as was the case in Argentina II and the province of Salta.

The Electoral Engineering Option

Often in the discussion of electoral laws there is an overweighted emphasis on the political consequences of legislature specific electoral dimensions such as effective magnitude and intra-PR legislative electoral formula. The study of electoral systems was initiated by scholars studying parliamentary systems for whom an exclusive focus on legislative electoral rules made perfect sense. Unfortunately many scholars studying electoral rules in presidential systems have maintained this overweighted focus on legislative electoral rules. In the study of the impact of electoral laws in presidential-PR systems, while these legislature specific rules are undoubtedly important, this study has shown that, in most cases, the electoral dimensions which have the strongest impact on legislative multipartism in presidential systems (and hence indirectly, and in places directly, on the tendency of a system to provide the executive with a strong legislative contingent) are the electoral rules governing the election of the president.

The timing of the executive and legislative elections along with the formula employed to select the executive were demonstrated to be the two most important factors in terms of their impact on the tendency to provide the executive with a legislative majority or near-majority. Both dimensions influence this tendency directly through the degree of linkage between the executive and legislative elections and indirectly via the intervening variable of multipartism.

Table 11.1 provides a brief review of the most common combinations of executive electoral formulas and election timing cycles. Assuming a PR system with an effective magnitude within normal parameters (roughly greater than four and less than twelve) only one of the combinations listed in Table 11.1 is able to consistently provide the executive with a legislative majority or near-majority: the plurality-concurrent arrangement. All of the other arrangements are sufficiently problematic as to recommend against their use. Of these inferior methods, some are however more detrimental to the provision of a legislative majority or near-majority than others. The plurality–mixed timing arrangement should provide the next largest contingent, while the majority runoff–nonconcurrent timing arrangement is the nadir from the standpoint of providing a president with strong partisan legislative support. Of course as the case of Chile II demonstrates, the potentially negative consequences of at least the use of the majority runoff formula can be partially ameliorated through the use of a very small effective magnitude. Likewise, the use of an extremely high effective magnitude can act to undermine the plurality–concurrent arrangement's general tendency to provide a strong executive contingent (e.g., Uruguay,

Table 11.1
Electoral Rules and Legislative Support: The Two Key Dimensions

Assuming a PR legislative electoral formula and an effective magnitude within normal parameters (i.e., above four but below twelve), the following diagram assesses the impact of the two key electoral dimensions on the level of legislative multipartism and degree of executive-legislative election linkage.

Executive
Electoral
Formula   The Timing of the Executive and Legislative Elections

	Concurrent	Mixed	Nonconcurrent
Plurality	Low levels of multipartism. Highest degree of linkage between the presidential and legislative elections.	Low levels of multipartism although not as low as those of the Plurality-Concurrent arrangement. Only partial linkage between the presidential and legislative elections.	High levels of multipartism. No linkage between the presidential and legislative elections.
Majority Runoff	Moderate to high levels of multipartism. High degree of linkage between the presidential and legislative elections, although not as high as that of the Plurality-Concurrent arrangement.	High levels of multipartism. Only marginal linkage between the presidential and legislative elections.	Highest levels of multipartism. No linkage between the presidential and legislative elections.

Venezuela). Finally, the utilization of single-member plurality districts for the election of members of the legislature could partially counteract the negative impact of the nonconcurrent electoral cycle and/or of the use of the majority runoff formula for the election of the executive. However, as the single-member plurality method has many highly negative consequences (e.g., partisan gerrymandering, severe disproportionality, a negative impact on the executive's relationship with members of his or her party's legislative bloc), its use is not recommended.

I agree with Linz (1994) and Stepan and Skach (1993) that multi-party democracy and presidential government in most cases are incompatible. Their solution to this incompatibility is parliamentary government. I suggest an alternative. For many of these multi-party systems the solution is not to jettison presidential government, but rather to change the electoral laws of the nation to encourage a reduced number of parties.

In presidential systems, electoral laws can be employed to promote a less fractionalized party system in three principal ways. Where electoral laws currently encourage a two-party dominant system, they should not be changed unless it is to strengthen this two-party dominant arrangement. In emerging democratic presidential systems, electoral laws which foster a two-party dominant system should be adopted to help mold the structure of the party system in order to enhance the probability of a two-party dominant system in the short and long term. Finally, the electoral laws of the current multi-party presidential systems should be redesigned in an attempt to reduce the number of political parties to a level compatible with successful presidential government.

AN IDEAL ELECTORAL ARRANGEMENT
FOR PRESIDENTIAL SYSTEMS

If the goal of a presidential system is to provide for an effective, stable, and democratic form of government that will survive for more than a few elections, then the system must typically provide the president with a legislative majority or near-majority. Is this type of system majoritarian? Of course, since presidential systems that emphasize their majoritarian nature have been shown, with the partial exception of the United States, to be the only strain of presidentialism that has proven to be even partially immune to democratic decay.

The sage use of electoral laws can neither save a democracy nor guarantee its survival. Electoral laws are, however, an important component for the overall functioning of a democratic system. It is argued here that the choices regarding five electoral rules can have a profound impact on the stability, effectiveness, and life span of democratic presidential systems.

Within the framework of the five electoral dimensions examined here, the ideal electoral arrangement for presidential systems would employ: (1) the plurality electoral formula to select the president, (2) presidential and legislative elections held concurrently, (3) proportional representation with (4) multi-member districts with a moderate effective magnitude to elect legislators, and (5) a unicameral legislature. Employing the plurality formula to elect the president and concurrent timing is of cardinal importance if a system is to have a hope of consistently providing the president with a legislative majority or near-majority.[2] This is particularly the case when any relatively proportional type of PR-effective magnitude arrangement is used. The plurality formula constrains the level of legislative multipartism in a system to a much greater extent than the majority runoff formula. It furthermore provides a stronger degree of linkage between the presidential and legislative contests than does the majority runoff method. Concurrent timing is much preferable to nonconcurrent timing due to its tendency to limit the degree of legislative multipartism as well as provide a tighter linkage between the presidential and legislative contests.

Use of a moderate effective magnitude (roughly between five and eight) aids the maintenance of a low level of multipartism while at the same time guaranteeing at least partial representation of minor political parties. The more disproportional PR formulae, such as the highest average d'Hondt formula, are theoretically likely to lead to the lowest level of multipartism. However, given the very mild salience of the intra-PR choice the largest remainders Hare formula is perhaps preferable due solely to its more easily understood (for the general public) method (i.e., its use of simple quotas in place of either divisors or complex quotas). Finally, unicameral legislatures are more likely to lead to an overall legislative majority or near-majority than are bicameral ones. However, the negative theoretical impact of bicameralism can be moderated by electing the upper house by methods which are similar to or less proportional than those used for the lower house election. This negative impact can also be countered by holding the upper house election concurrent with the executive contest. In this way federal systems can maintain their federal senates while at the same time reducing the potentially negative impact of bicameralism on the provision of a legislative majority or near-majority.[3] Examples of systems which approach this type of ideal arrangement include unicameral Costa Rica and Honduras and, with one minor exception, both bicameral Colombia (pre-1991) and Paraguay.

Many democratizing nations are currently exploring the potential use of different constitutional arrangements (e.g., Bolivia, Philippines, Russia, South Africa, Taiwan). On the surface it would appear that when a presidential format is selected there exist a broad array of possible options for methods to select the executive and legislature. However, as the findings of this study indicate, if a desideratum of those implementing this constitutional framework is effective and successful government, then these choices are in fact quite limited. The ideal arrangement presented in the previous paragraph is the only framework which can be consistently relied upon to provide the executive with a legislative majority or near-majority. It has the added advantage of allowing at least partial representation of minor parties as was discussed in Chapter Five. In terms of the executive electoral formula and timing cycle for executive and legislative elections, the plurality formula and concurrent cycle respectively stand out as the preferred options. While perhaps the mixed electoral cycle could be utilized with only marginal damage to the size of the presidential contingent, this method is not highly recommended. The scope of options is wider in regard to the rules governing the selection of the legislature, although a unicameral legislature which elects its members from moderately sized electoral districts (i.e., with a moderate effective magnitude) using PR is the ideal arrangement.

Use of either the majority runoff formula or nonconcurrent timing cycle, except possibly when combined with the election of the legislature via single-member plurality (or majority runoff) districts or a PR formula with a very low effective magnitude, is likely to lead to a presidential system which normally fails to provide the president with a legislative majority or near-majority. While the use of either the majority runoff formula or nonconcurrent electoral cycle separately is likely to be problematic, the joint use of these two methods invites disaster. Unfortunately, it is this exact framework, combined with a legislature elected using PR with a relatively high effective magnitude, which has been chosen by many recently democratizing nations such as Brazil (chosen in 1988; partially reformed in 1994) and the premier-presidential systems of Poland and Russia. The extreme crises of government which have recently afflicted these three systems should serve as a warning to present and future constitutional architects.

With an overwhelming majority of democratizing presidential and premier-presidential systems choosing the majority runoff formula to select their executive and some also employing nonconcurrent presidential and legislative elections (while at the same time using a PR or majority runoff formula to elect members of the legislature), the situation is urgent. In the short run the use of the majority runoff formula to elect the president and/or nonconcurrent election timing may appear to be a good strategy for initiating elections. Both the often inchoate state of the party system in a nation as well as a desire to avoid the concentration of power (i.e., the presidency and legislature controlled by the same party), appear to argue for such electoral arrangements. Nonetheless, the selection of either or both of these methods represents a marginal short-term gain with pernicious medium and long-term consequences which are often apparent almost immediately following the first post-election legislative session.

Attenuating Majoritarianism When the President has a Legislative Majority or Near-Majority

According to the findings of this book, the ideal presidential system will regularly provide the president with a legislative majority or near-majority. The most prominent critique of this arrangement is that it reinforces the "winner-take-all" nature of presidential elections, and in general leads to an extremely majoritarian form of government. To a certain extent this is correct. However, as stated earlier, all evidence indicates the functioning of presidential systems is greatly enhanced when the president is provided with a majority or near-majority in the legislature. There are however two factors which weaken the critique that presidential systems where the president possesses a legislative majority or near-majority are extremely majoritarian.

First, when the president has a legislative majority or near-majority, this does not imply that the president has a pliant legislature. In all systems, regardless of the rules governing elections and intra-party control, there exist differences among party members with presidential party deputies likely to act as a filter and check on presidential power. The advantage is that being of the same party, both the president and particularly the deputies, have an incentive to cooperate (to safeguard the party image, etc.) which does not exist in relations between a president and opposition deputies. It must be remembered that a president has a weaker level of control over members of his or her legislative party than does a prime minister. Unlike prime ministers, in practically all systems presidents lack the tool of the confidence vote to keep party members in line.

Second, in the past decade there has been a growing decentralization of political power in Latin American presidential systems (as well as in presidential and premier-presidential systems elsewhere) from the national government to sub-national governments. For example, since 1985 Colombia, Guatemala, Nicaragua, Paraguay, and Venezuela have all held their first popular election of mayors, while Colombia, Paraguay, and Venezuela also conducted their first election of governors. While true sub-national autonomy depends on both electoral and fiscal independence, this electoral trend, along with some increased fiscal decentralization (e.g., Argentina, Bolivia) has increased the ability of provincial and municipal governments to provide opposition parties with opportunities to govern and exert a greater degree of political influence, thus reducing the majoritarian and zero-sum nature of the system. The presence of popularly elected governors (Argentina, Brazil, Colombia, Paraguay, Uruguay, Venezuela) and mayors (virtually all nations, although some are elected indirectly by the municipal council) who are not from the president's party represents a strong check on the president's power, even when he or she has a partisan majority or near-majority in the legislature. This decentralization reduces the threat of a "winner-take-all" or "extreme majoritarian system."[4]

Thus even a president who possesses a legislative majority is still checked by: (1) members of the president's party in the legislature, and (2) the sub-national branches of government. As one might expect, these two factors vary extensively across different nations. The checks on the president are greatest where the president has the least amount of control over members of his or her party (e.g., Brazil, Colombia) and in systems which most closely approach true federalism (e.g., Argentina, Brazil). While the latter type of check is desirable, the former is perhaps too extreme, defeating the original purpose of having a presidential majority or near-majority in the first place. The probable ideal level of control is where the president exercises sufficient control over the party's legislators so as to govern effectively, but not so much so as to stifle all dissent by and freedom of action of the party's congressional bloc.

Concluding Remarks

Despite academic criticism of the presidential form of democratic government, presidentialism continues to enjoy a considerable degree of popularity throughout the world. Given this reality of presidential government, it is important to focus on the ways in which democratic governance can be both safeguarded and enhanced in these systems. The employment of electoral laws represents one prominent method which can be utilized to foster democracy in these nations. While the use of electoral rules to achieve the relatively consistent provision of a presidential legislative majority or near-majority will not work in all countries, it represents a gradual yet viable method to aid the entrenchment of democracy in presidential systems.

Evidence from nations as diverse as Argentina, Brazil, Mexico, Nigeria, Poland, Russia, South Africa, and Taiwan demonstrates that the concept of utilizing electoral rules to influence the number of political parties in a system and its tendency to provide the president with a legislative majority or near-majority is not a topic of interest to academics only. Debate over the electoral dimensions discussed in this work is occurring in the legislatures, think tanks, and mass media in these nations as well as others. It is thus imperative that a more comprehensive understanding of the political conse-quences of electoral laws for the functioning of presidential govern-ment be provided. The goal of this work has been to identify the impact of electoral laws in presidential systems on the systems' tendency to provide the executive with a legislative majority or near-majority. It was demonstrated that the electoral laws employed have a profound impact on this tendency. Given the salience of strong partisan legislative support to the functioning of presidential democracies, these electoral rules have a strong effect on the effectiveness and survival of democratic presidential systems.

Electoral rules such as the majority runoff formula of executive election and the nonconcurrent timing cycle are inimical to the successful functioning of democratic presidential government. Conversely the employment of a plurality electoral formula to select the president and concurrent election timing is much more likely to ensure a stable and effective presidential democracy.

Certain electoral arrangements are hazardous for the health of presidential democracy. This fact must be realized by those responsible for the creation of electoral laws in the different nations of the world. All too often electoral laws are selected based on mistaken assumptions regarding their political consequences. These choices are also often made for partisan political reasons which have little to do with the goal of a successful presidential democracy. Academics must work to correct any mistaken assumptions as well as attempt to impress upon politicians that what may appear to be to their political advantage in the short run (e.g., a system which aids and abets the survival of a large number of political parties), in the long run is likely to lead to the collapse of the democratic political system, after which the demand for party politicians will be much lower than under a democratic framework.

The goal of enhancing democracy by replacing the presidential form of government with a parliamentary system should not be forgotten in all cases. However, given the unlikely prospects for this type of shift in many countries, it is also useful to focus on electoral law reform as a method for facilitating the proper functioning and survival of democratic systems. That has been the purpose of this work.

APPENDIX A
Sources of Electoral Data
by Country

Argentina

Dirección Nacional Electoral, Departamento de Estadísticas. Ministerio del Interior, República Argentina. Department data files.

Bolivia

Embajada de Bolivia. 1993. Washington, D.C.
Honorable Corte Nacional Electoral. 1990. *Elecciones Generales 1985–1989*. La Paz: Honorable Corte Nacional Electoral.
Mesa Gisbert, Carlos D. 1990. *Presidentes de Bolivia: Entre Urnas y Fusiles*, 2nd ed. La Paz: Editorial Gisbert.

Brazil

Costa Porto, Wálter. 1989. *O Voto No Brasil: Da Colonia a 5a República*. Brasilia: Grafica do Senado Nacional.
Guimares, Cesár, et al. 1991. *O Novo Congreso e os Rumos da Política*. Rio de Janeiro: Instituto Universitario de Pesquisas de Rio de Janeiro.
Jornal do Brasil. 1989. 22 November.
Lamounier, Bolívar, and Judith Muszynski. 1993. "Brasil." In Dieter Nohlen, ed., *Enciclopedia Electoral Latinoamericana y Del Caribe*. San José: Instituto Interamericano de Derechos Humanos.
Laverada, Antonio. 1991. A Democracia nas Urnas. *O Proceso Partidario Eleitoral Brasileiro*. Rio de Janeiro: Rio Fundo Editora.

Mainwaring, Scott. 1994. "Brazil: Weak Parties, Feckless Democracy." In Scott Mainwaring and Timothy Scully, eds., *Building Democratic Institutions: Parties and Party Systems in Latin America*. Stanford: Stanford University Press.

Oliveira, Luia M. Lippi. 1973. "Partidos Politicos Brasileiros: O Partido Social Democrático." Tese de Mestrado, Instituto Universitario de Pesquisas de Rio de Janeiro.

Smith, William C. 1990. "Brazil." In James M. Malloy and Eduardo A. Gamarra, eds., *Latin America and Caribbean Contemporary Record*, volume VII, 1987–1988. New York: Holmes & Meier.

Tribunal Superior Eleitoral. 1964. *Dados Estatísticos: Eleições Federal, Estadual e Municipal Realizadas no Brasil a partir de 1945*. Volumes 1–4. Rio de Janeiro: Departamento de Imprensa Nacional.

Chile

Caviedes, Cesar. 1979. *The Politics of Chile: A Sociogeographical Assessment*. Boulder: Westview.

Cope, III, Orville G. 1967. "Politics in Chile: A Study of Political Factions and Parties and Election Procedures." Ph.D. Dissertation, Claremont Graduate School and University Center.

Cruz-Coke, Ricardo. 1984. *Historia Electoral de Chile: 1925–1973*. Santiago de Chile: Editorial Jurídica de Chile.

Embajada de Chile. 1994. Washington, D.C.

El Mercurio, Edición Internacional (Santiago de Chile). 1993. Week of December 9–15.

Nohlen, Dieter. 1993. "Chile." In Dieter Nohlen, ed., *Enciclopedia Electoral Latinoamericana y Del Caribe*. San José: Instituto Interamericano de Derechos Humanos.

Urzúa Valenzuela, Germán. 1986. *Historia Política Electoral de Chile 1931–1973*. Santiago de Chile: Tarmacos.

Urzúa Valenzuela, Germán. 1968. *Los Partidos Políticos Chilenos*. Santiago de Chile: Editorial Jurídica de Chile.

Colombia

Archer, Ronald P. 1991. Unpublished Manuscript. Durham: Duke University.

Delgado, Oscar. 1987. *Colombia Elige: Mitaca/84–Perspectivas/86*. Bogota: Pontificia Universitaria Javeriana.

Embajada de Colombia. 1994. Washington, D.C.

Osterling, Jorge P. 1989. *Democracy in Colombia: Clientalist Politics and Guerrilla Warfare.* New Brunswick: Transaction Publishers.

Registraduría Nacional del Estado Civil. 1991. *Estadísticas Electorales 1990: Asamblea Constitucional.* Bogota.

Registraduría Nacional del Estado Civil. 1990. *Estadísticas Electorales 1990.* Bogota.

Registraduría Nacional del Estado Civil. 1988. *Historia Electoral Colombiano.* Bogota.

Costa Rica

Tribunal Supremo de Elecciones. 1994. *Cómputo de Votos y Declatorias de Elección para Presidente, Vicepresidentes, Diputados a la Asamblea Legislativa, Regidores y Síndicos Municipales (1994).* San José: TSE.

Tribunal Supremo de Elecciones. 1990. *Cómputo de Votos y Declatorias de Elección para Presidente, Vicepresidentes, Diputados a la Asamblea Legislativa, Regidores y Síndicos Municipales (1990).* San José: TSE.

Tribunal Supremo de Elecciones. 1986. *Cómputo de Votos y Declatorias de Elección para Presidente, Vicepresidentes, Diputados a la Asamblea Legislativa, Regidores y Síndicos Municipales (1986).* San José: TSE.

Tribunal Supremo de Elecciones. 1982. *Cómputo de Votos y Declatorias de Elección para Presidente, Vicepresidentes, Diputados a la Asamblea Legislativa, Regidores y Síndicos Municipales (1982).* San José: TSE.

Tribunal Supremo de Elecciones. 1978. *Elecciones en Cifras: 1953, 1958, 1962, 1966, 1970, 1974, 1978.* San José: TSE.

Tribunal Supremo de Elecciones. 1978. *Cómputo de Votos y Declatorias de Elección para Presidente, Vicepresidentes, Diputados a la Asamblea Legislativa, Regidores y Síndicos Municipales (1978).* San José: TSE.

Tribunal Supremo de Elecciones. 1974. *Cómputo de Votos y Declatorias de Elección para Presidente, Vicepresidentes, Diputados a la Asamblea Legislativa, Regidores y Síndicos Municipales (1974).* San José: TSE.

Tribunal Supremo de Elecciones. 1970. *Cómputo de Votos y Declato-*

rias de Elección para Presidente, Vicepresidentes, Diputados a la Asamblea Legislativa, Regidores y Síndicos Municipales (1970). San José: TSE.

Tribunal Supremo de Elecciones. 1969. *Cómputo de Votos y Declatorias de Elección para Presidente, Vicepresidentes, Diputados a la Asamblea Legislativa, Regidores y Síndicos Municipales (1953–1966)*. San José: TSE.

Dominican Republic

Brea Franco, Julio. 1987. *Administración y Elecciones: La Experiencia Dominicana de 1986*. San José: CAPEL.

Campillo Pérez, Julio G. 1986. *Historia Electoral Dominicana: 1848–1986*. Santo Domingo: Junta Central Electoral.

Contreras, Dario. 1986. *Comportamiento Electoral Dominicano: Elecciones Dominicanas 1962–1982*. Santo Domingo: Editora Corripio.

Junta Central Electoral. 1990. *Elecciones Generales del 16 de Mayo*. Santo Domingo.

Listin Diario (Santo Domingo). 1990. 12 June, 12.

Ecuador

Darlić Mardesić, Vjekoslav. 1989. *Estadísticas Electorales del Ecuador 1978–1989*. 2d ed. Quito: SENAC/ILDIS.

Economist Intelligence Unit. 1992. *Ecuador Country Report, No. 3*. London: EIU.

Embajada de Ecuador. 1994. Washington, D.C.

Inter-Parliamentary Union. 1991. *Chronicle of Parliamentary Elections and Developments*. Volume 24. Geneva: International Centre for Parliamentary Documentation.

Latin American Weekly Report, number 28, July 23, 1992.

Weekly Analysis of Ecuadoran Issues, volume 22, #20, May 25, 1992.

El Salvador

Arriaza Meléndez, Jorge. 1989. *Historia de los Procesos Electorales en El Salvador (1811–1989)*. San Salvador: ISEP.

Estudios Centroamericanos. 1994. "Las Elecciones Generales del 20 de Marzo 1994." #545–546.

Estudios Centroamericanos. 1991. "Las Elecciones del 10 de Marzo 1991: Sus Resultados y Su Significado." #509.

Estudios Centroamericanos. 1989. "Las Elecciones Presidenciales del 19 de Marzo 1989." #485.

Estudios Centroamericanos. 1988. "Elecciones del Diputados del 20 de Marzo 1988." #473.

Estudios Centroamericanos. 1984. Cómputos Oficiales, 6 de Mayo de 1984: Elecciones para Presidente y Vice-Presidente." #426.

Jiménez, Edgar C., et al. 1988. *El Salvador: Guerra, Política y Paz (1979–1988)*. San Salvador: CINAS.

National Republican Institute for International Affairs. 1992. *The 1991 Elections in El Salvador: Report on the Observer Delegation*. Washington, D.C.

Guatemala

Bendel, Petra, and Michael Krennerich. 1993. "Guatemala." In Dieter Nohlen, ed., *Enciclopedia Electoral Latinoamericana y Del Caribe*. San José: Instituto Interamericano de Derechos Humanos.

Guatemala Watch, volume 5, no. 12, 1991. "Special Elections Issue, 1991."

Inforpress Centroamericana (Guatemala City). 1991. *Central America Report*, 11 January.

National Democratic Institute for International Affairs. 1991. *The 1990 Elections in Guatemala*. Washington, D.C.

Tribunal Supremo Electoral. 1985. *Memoria de las Elecciones Celebradas en los Meses de Noviembre y Diciembre de 1985*. Antigua: Libreria Mafcuense.

Honduras

Bendel, Petra. 1993. "Honduras." In Dieter Nohlen, ed., *Enciclopedia Electoral Latinoamericana y Del Caribe*. San José: Instituto Interamericano de Derechos Humanos.

Delgado Fiallos, Anibal. 1986. *Honduras Elecciones (Más allá de la fiesta cívica) 85*. Tegucigalpa: Editorial Guaymuras.

Embajada de Honduras. 1994. Washington, D.C.

Fernández, Oscar. 1990. "Elecciones Generales en Honduras, 26 de Noviembre 1989." Boletín Electoral Latinoamericano, no. 2.

Inter-Parliamentary Union. 1990. *Chronicle of Parliamentary Elections and Developments*. Volume 23. Geneva: International Centre for Parliamentary Documentation.

United States House of Representatives, Committee on Foreign Affairs. 1982. *Report on Congressional Study Mission, November 28–30, 1981.* Washington, D.C.: U.S. Government Printing Office.

Nicaragua

Consejo Supremo Electoral. 1989. *Elecciones 1984.* Managua: CSE.
Council of Freely Elected Heads of Government. 1990. *Observing Nicaragua's Elections 1989–90,* Special Report #1, Atlanta: The Carter Center of Emory University.
Krennerich, Michael. 1993. "Nicaragua." In Dieter Nohlen, ed., *Enciclopedia Electoral Latinoamericana y Del Caribe.* San José: Instituto Interamericano de Derechos Humanos.
Latin American Studies Association. 1990. *Electoral Democracy under International Pressure: The Report of the Latin American Studies Association Commission to Observe the 1990 Nicaraguan Election.* Pittsburgh: LASA.

Paraguay

Riquelme, Marcial A. 1994. *Negotiating Democratic Corridors in Paraguay: The Report of the Latin American Studies Association Delegation to Observe the 1993 Paraguayan National Elections.* Pittsburgh: LASA.

Peru

El Comercio (Lima). 1990. May 13, p. A6.
International Foundation for Electoral Systems. 1992. Unpublished foundation data file for Peru.
Tuesta Soldevilla, Fernando. 1993. "Perú." In Dieter Nohlen, ed., *Enciclopedia Electoral Latinoamericana y Del Caribe.* San José: Instituto Interamericano de Derechos Humanos.
Tuesta Soldevilla, Fernando. 1987. *Perú Político en Cifras: Elite Política y Elecciones.* Lima: Fundación Friedrich Ebert.

Philippines

Council on Foreign Relations. 1946–1968. *Political Handbook and Atlas of the World* (annual). New York: Simon and Schuster.
Inter-Parliamentary Union. 1968–1973. *Chronicle of Parliamentary*

Elections and Developments (annual). Geneva: International Centre for Parliamentary Documentation.

United States

Congressional Quarterly. 1991. *Guide To Congress*, 4th ed. Washington, D.C.: Congressional Quarterly.
Mackie, Thomas T., and Richard Rose. 1991. *The International Almanac of Electoral History*, 3rd ed. Washington, D.C.: Congressional Quarterly.

Uruguay

Albornoz, Alfredo. 1989. *Elecciones Generales: 25 de Noviembre 1984*. Montevideo: Tradinco.
Fabregat, Julio T. 1968. *Elecciones Uruguayas: Plebiscito y Elecciones de 27 de Noviembre 1966*. Montevideo: República Oriental de Uruguay, Cámara de Senadores.
Fabregat, Julio T. 1964. *Elecciones Uruguayas de 25 de Noviembre 1962*. Montevideo: República Oriental de Uruguay, Cámara de Senadores.
Fabregat, Julio T. 1957. *Elecciones Uruguayas de Noviembre de 1950 a Noviembre de 1954*. Montevideo: República Oriental de Uruguay, Cámara de Representantes.
Fabregat, Julio T. 1950. *Elecciones Uruguayas: Febrero de 1925 a Noviembre de 1946*. Montevideo: República Oriental de Uruguay, Poder Legislativo.
Libreria Linardi y Risso. 1989. *Uruguay: Elecciones Nacionales, 26 de Noviembre de 1989*. Montevideo.
Rial, Juan. 1986. *Elecciones de 1984: Sistema Electoral y Resultados*. San José: CAPEL.
Venturini, Angel R. 1989. *Estadísticas Electorales, 1917–1982*. Montevideo: EBO.

Venezuela

Chang Mota, Roberto. 1985. *El Sistema Electoral Venozolano: Su Diseño, Implantación y Resultados*. Caracas: Consejo Supremo Electoral.
Consejo Supremo Electoral. 1990. *Elecciones 1988*. Caracas: CSE.

Consejo Supremo Electoral. 1987. *Los Partidos Políticos y Sus Estadísticas Electorales 1946–1984.* 2 vols. Caracas: CSE.

Consejo Supremo Electoral. 1983. *La Estadística Evolutiva de los Partidos Políticos en Venezuela 1958–1979.* Caracas: CSE.

Embajada de Venezuela. 1994. Washington, D.C.

APPENDIX B
Choosing Electoral Laws: A "Rational" Process?

In this appendix I briefly examine one particular case of electoral law reform: the selection of a new gubernatorial electoral law in the Argentine province of Corrientes. Evidence from Corrientes provides support for the general rational choice position that electoral laws selected in any reform process are the product of the rational self-interests of politicians.

Following the return to democracy in 1983 Corrientes employed an electoral college to select its governor every four years. Twenty-six electors were chosen from three multi-member districts in the province and allocated among the parties using PR, with a de facto absolute majority of the electors required to elect the governor. In the first two gubernatorial elections (1983 and 1987) the *Pacto Autonomista Liberal* (PAL) won an absolute majority of the electors, and its candidate became governor. In 1991 however the PAL failed to garner an absolute majority of the electors, winning thirteen, with the *Partido Justicialista* (PJ) and *Unión Cívica Radical* (UCR) winning nine and four electors respectively. Thus there was a tie, with the parties unable to agree on a candidate (to open the electoral college a quorum of one-half of the electors plus one [i.e., fourteen] was required). Unfortunately, the drafters of the 1960 provincial constitution had not envisioned this scenario and thus a stalemate ensued. Given the severity of this constitutional crisis, the federal government intervened in the province and called new gubernatorial elections along with elections for a constituent assembly to reform selected portions of the provincial constitution. The results of this 1992 gubernatorial election gave twelve electors to the PJ, eleven to the PAL, and three to the UCR. After a potential deal between the PAL and UCR was wrecked by the mysterious flight of one of the UCR electors to Paraguay (rumors have him both leaving after he received a substantial bribe from the PJ, as well as fleeing to prevent the UCR from being hoodwinked by the PAL), deadlock once again set in. The federal intervener then decided that new gubernatorial elections would be held in October 1993 concurrent with the renewal of one-half of the national Chamber of Deputies under rules to be established by the Constituent Assembly.

In the Constituent Assembly the PAL held eighteen seats, the PJ sixteen seats, and the UCR five seats. Given that the old electoral college system was no longer an attractive option, the principal alternatives articulated by the Constituent Assembly delegates were the plurality and majority runoff formulas. The PAL supported the use of the plurality formula, modified as in Costa Rica so that if the plurality winner fails to win more than 40% of the vote, a runoff is held between the top two candidates (Romero Feris 1993). The PJ and UCR on the other hand supported the implementation of the majority runoff formula (Durañona y Vedia 1993). The electoral data in Table AB.1 reveal the strategic logic behind the different formulas supported by the two sides. Since 1983 (under the electoral

Table AB.1
*Electoral Results for Gubernatorial Elections
in the Province of Corrientes, 1983–92*

Political Party	Percentage of the Vote Won in Each Gubernatorial Election				
	1983	1987	1991	1992	Average
Pacto Autonomista Liberal	46.61	44.35	43.86	42.93	44.44
Partido Justicialista	22.94	18.44	33.97	39.20	28.64
Unión Cívica Radical	20.70	24.85	17.84	13.86	19.31
Others	9.75	12.36	4.33	4.01	7.61
Total	100.00	100.00	100.00	100.00	100.00

Source: Data Files of the Argentine Ministerio del Interior, Dirección Nacional Electoral, Departamento de Estadísticas.

college framework) the PAL consistently received the support of over 40% of the electorate in the gubernatorial elections, averaging 44.44% of the vote. In no case, however, was either of the two principal opposition parties able to crack the 40% ceiling.

Given the absolute majority of the combined PJ and UCR forces in the Constituent Assembly (they held twenty-one of the thirty-nine seats), the majority runoff formula was chosen. It is easy to see why the PAL argued for the plurality formula and the PJ and UCR championed the majority runoff formula, even though nationally the PJ is against the use of the majority runoff formula. Use of the plurality formula probably would have assured continued PAL possession of the governor's office. The employment of the majority runoff method gives the PJ a real chance of winning the governor's office. Furthermore, its use allows the UCR to continue to be an important actor in Corrientes, whereas the utilization of the plurality formula, following Duverger's law, would in all likelihood have resulted in the marginalization of the UCR as a political force in the province.

The gubernatorial election of October 3, 1993 partially vindicated the decision of the PJ and UCR to implement the majority runoff formula. In this election the PAL won 47.73% of the vote with the PJ coming in second with 37.62% and the UCR in third with 11.61%. While the PJ declined to participate in the runoff after failing to obtain the support of the UCR, its prospects for the future are brighter than would be the case if the plurality formula had been implemented. In a different vein, the UCR was able to sustain itself as a viable political force in the province, winning 11.61% of the vote in the gubernatorial race and one of the thirteen Lower House seats being contested. Its continued vitality is evidenced by the attempts of the PJ to gain its endorsement for the second round along with the PJ's subsequent withdrawal from the runoff when this endorsement failed to materialize.

For the case of Corrientes, a rational choice–based explanation of the selection of the gubernatorial electoral formula works quite well. Whether rational choice–style analysis is equally powerful in its ability to explain reforms in other systems awaits further testing.

APPENDIX C
Significant Electoral Law Changes in Latin America 1990–94

This table lists the significant electoral law changes which occurred in the sixteen current Latin American democracies included in this study during the period 1990–94. They correspond to those changes identified by a check mark in the first three columns of Table 1.1.

COUNTRY	ELECTED INSTITUTION	PRE-REFORM ARRANGEMENT	POST-REFORM ARRANGEMENT
Argentina	President	Indirect election via an Electoral College.	Direct election using a hybrid form of the double complement rule.
	Senate	48 senators elected indirectly from 24 districts using the plurality rule.	72 senators elected directly by an incomplete list system from 24 three member districts (2 seats for the plurality winner, 1 seat for the first minority).*
	Chamber	One concurrent and two nonconcurrent elections each presidential term.	One concurrent and one nonconcurrent election each presidential term.
Bolivia	President	If no candidate receives an absolute majority in the first round a runoff is held in Congress between the top three finishers.	If no candidate receives an absolute majority in the first round a runoff is held in Congress between the top two finishers.

COUNTRY	ELECTED INSTITUTION	PRE-REFORM ARRANGEMENT	POST-REFORM ARRANGEMENT
Bolivia	Chamber	PR from multi-member districts.	German-style mixed system.
Brazil	Senate	Nonconcurrent election timing.	One-half of elections concurrent and one-half nonconcurrent.**
	Chamber	Nonconcurrent election timing.	Concurrent election timing.
Chile	Chamber (1/2) Senate	One-half of elections concurrent and one-half nonconcurrent.	Nonconcurrent election timing.
Colombia	President	Plurality formula.	Majority Runoff formula.
	Senate	114 senators elected from 23 districts using PR.	100 senators elected from one national district using PR plus two senators elected from a special district for the indigenous population.
Nicaragua	President	Plurality formula.	If no candidate receives at least 45% of the vote in the first round a runoff is held between the top two candidates.***
Paraguay	President (1990)	Plurality formula.	Majority runoff formula.
	President (1992)	Majority runoff formula.	Plurality formula.
	Senate/Chamber	Senators and deputies elected from a national district. The plurality winner receives two-thirds of the seats with the remainder allocated among the remaining parties using PR.	Senators elected from a national district using PR. Chamber deputies elected from 18 multi-member districts using PR. (This is the 1990 reform as modified in 1992)
Peru	Senate	Existed.	Abolished.
	Chamber	180 deputies elected from 26 districts using PR.	120 deputies elected from a national district using PR.

COUNTRY	ELECTED INSTITUTION	PRE-REFORM ARRANGEMENT	POST-REFORM ARRANGEMENT
Venezuela	Chamber	PR from multi-member districts.	German-style mixed system.

* Following a transition period.

** Senators are elected for an eight-year term, with two-thirds then one-third of the Senate renewed concurrent with the presidential contest.

*** Not officially approved until 1995.

APPENDIX D
Conflict Articles

This appendix contains ten randomly selected summaries of the executive-legislative conflict articles which formed the basis for the measure employed in Chapter Three in the cross-national analysis of executive-legislative conflict. It is included to provide a better understanding of the measures employed in the analysis as well as of the type of executive-legislative conflict which has occurred in Latin America over the past decade. For each article summary the country, month, year, and president are provided. For reasons of convenience the summaries are placed in chronological order.

1. Argentina. March 1984. President Raúl Alfonsín.
   Alfonsín has his union reform law defeated in the Senate where he lacks a majority, after the law had already passed the Lower House where he has a majority. This is Alfonsín's first defeat. It helps to restore some prestige to the principal opposition party, the *Partido Justicialista*.

2. Uruguay. February 1986. President Julio Sanguinetti.
   The opposition in Congress pushed through the budget bill which was subsequently vetoed by Sanguinetti. As the opposition does not have sufficient legislative strength to override the veto, negotiations between the two sides have begun.

3. Ecuador. July 1987. President León Febres Cordero.
   The President and Congress are involved in a dispute over the legality of the presence of U.S. troops carrying out a road construction project in Ecuador.

4. Ecuador. October 1987. President León Febres Cordero.

Few are surprised by the opposition-controlled Congress's ordering of the dismissal of the interior minister. Having failed to impeach the President, Congress has used the impeachment of his ministers as a weapon. Febres has countered by refusing to recognize the legality of the dismissal proceedings.

5. Argentina. December 1989. President Carlos Menem.
The government's tax legislation has been slowed down in Congress, as legislators (mainly UCR) want more details on its contents, particularly related to changes in the value added tax.

6. Venezuela. April 1990. President Carlos Andrés Pérez.
Pérez is very frustrated with Congress's refusal/reluctance to approve the government's investment program designed to pull the country out of debt. The opposition keeps delaying and blocking the bill. The government criticizes Congress as jeopardizing the nation's economic recovery.

7. Brazil. May 1990. President Fernando Collor de Mello.
The Congress modifies in a considerable manner two economic reform bills submitted by Collor.

8. Ecuador. April 1991. President Rodrigo Borja.
Once again conflict between Borja and Congress takes place as the opposition-controlled Congress has renewed its war of attrition against the government, this time targeting the Vice President with impeachment.

9. Brazil. September 1991. President Fernando Collor de Mello.
The Congress rebuffs Collor and passes legislation doubling the minimum wage and reintroducing the indexation of salaries. Collor views these bills as harmful to his economic program and vetoes them.

10. Chile. January 1993. President Patricio Aylwin.
The Senate (the opposition has a majority there) votes down the government's electoral reform bill which had earlier been approved in the Chamber where the government has a majority.

APPENDIX E
Coding Rules for "Difficult" Cases

Chile I

1. Chilean President Carlos Ibáñez (1952–58) ran as an independent. His candidacy was supported by a number of political parties and groups. His legislative contingent was calculated based on the number of seats won/held by those parties which directly supported his candidacy: *Acción Renovadora, Movimiento Nacional Ibañista, Movimiento Nacional del Pueblo, Movimiento Republicano, Partido Agrario, Partido Agrario Laborista, Partido Laborista, Partido Nacional, Partido Nacional Cristiano, Partido del Trabajo.*

2. Chilean President Arturo Alessandri (1958–64) also ran as an independent. His candidacy was supported by two political parties: *Partido Liberal* and *Partido Conservador Unido.* Alessandri's legislative contingent was calculated by summing the seats held by these two parties.

Chile II

For legislative elections, the party/coalition lists are treated as parties (e.g., *Concertación por la Democracia, Democracia y Progreso, Unidad para la Democracia*).

The Chilean electoral coalitions (i.e., those parties that share the same party list) are treated as parties due to the many characteristics which they share with political parties (i.e., internal primaries, participation on the same party list, distribution of cabinet seats in a proportional manner among coalition members, relatively cohesive voting in the legislature). Faced with the choice of calculating

183

multipartism and related statistics using the coalition as the unit of analysis or the parties of the individual coalition members as the unit of analysis, the former is the most logical choice. In fact, the large number of individual parties which hold legislative seats is a product of the presence of these two large coalitions. Without coalition rules governing the placement of candidates, it is doubtful that such a large number of parties would have achieved legislative representation due to the use of binomial districts (this is particularly the case for the smaller members of the two coalitions).

Nicaragua

The *Unión Nacional Opositora* of President Violeta Barrios de Chamorro is treated as one party.

Venezuela

In 1994 Venezuelan President Rafael Caldera ran as an independent candidate supported by two political parties: *Convergencia* and *Movimiento al Socialismo*. Additionally, these two parties shared a legislative ticket for the Chamber and Senate elections in many districts. In the analysis, the combined legislative contingent of these two parties is considered to be Caldera's legislative contingent.

Brazil Ib, Brazil II, Chile I, Colombia, Guatemala, Peru, Uruguay, Venezuela

In instances where a president's and/or legislature's term ended prematurely, the legislative contingent is nevertheless calculated as if that president and/or legislature served a full term.

APPENDIX F
The Robust Presidential Electoral Mandate: Analysis

The most frequently argued advantage of the majority runoff formula is its ability to assure a strong popular mandate for the executive (Light 1982; Linz 1992; Suárez 1982). The mirror image of this position is that it avoids those highly negative situations where a president is elected with a very low percentage of the popular vote such as the often cited 36.61% of the vote which Chilean President Salvador Allende received in 1970. Such extremely low mandates are particularly troublesome since as Linz (1994) notes, directly elected executives are likely to think of themselves as possessing a type of plebiscitarian majority.[1]

This justification for the adoption of the majority runoff formula can be divided into two sub-components. The first hypothesized advantage of the majority runoff formula over its plurality counterpart is its ability to consistently provide executives with a large mandate which endows them with broad-based public support. Second, the runoff provision virtually assures that no executive will be elected with a dangerously low percentage of the vote. Placing its other flaws aside for a moment, it is instructive to see how well the majority runoff formula succeeds in these two related tasks in relation to the other prominent electoral formulae which have been used in Latin America to select the executive.

Majority runoff systems require a runoff if no presidential candidate receives an absolute majority of the popular vote in the first round of elections. Thus it is logical to expect them to provide the executive with an electoral mandate that is larger (and hence more broad based as well) than that provided by plurality systems. However, the difference in the size of the mandate is not as large as one might suppose because of the impact of Duverger's law which states that the plurality formula will encourage a two-party system, and hence two relevant presidential candidates, leading to a reasonably strong mandate for the winning candidate in the plurality systems (Duverger 1986).

Furthermore, as Linz (1992) has pointed out, the mandate won in a runoff is not the same thing as a mandate won in the first and only round in a plurality formula system. The electoral majority won by the executive in the runoff represents no unified coalition, party, group, or even a homogeneous electorate (Linz 1992). Runoff majorities are in a sense manufactured majorities. The relative strength of an electoral mandate received in the second round of the runoff systems cannot easily be compared to that won in the only round in the plurality systems. It is clear, however, that the two are not equivalent (i.e., a mandate of 53% of the vote in a plurality system is stronger than a mandate of 53% won in a runoff), but the degree of difference cannot be accurately calculated.[2]

As Table AF.1 demonstrates, the majority runoff systems on average provide the president with a mandate of 57.47% of the vote while the plurality systems provide an average mandate of 48.77% of the vote.[3] Since we have already noted that the valence of the plurality formula mandates is superior to that of the mandates received by presidents in the runoff systems who are elected in a second round runoff (ten of the fifteen presidents who have been elected in the majority runoff systems in this study were elected in this second round), this difference is relatively marginal.[4] These data challenge the claim made by scholars such as Hauriou (1971) and McClintock (1989) that the majority runoff formula provides superior electoral mandates and endows presidents with more broad-based support than their plurality counterparts. Due to Duverger's law, plurality systems tend to provide mandates that are reasonably similar in size to those of the runoff systems. In turn, they have the added advantage of being much truer mandates than the hastily manufactured ones received by executives in the runoff elections. Also noteworthy is the marked inferiority of the majority congressional systems (currently used only in Bolivia) in terms of the size of their presidential mandates.

Table AF.1
Presidential Electoral Formula and Presidential Electoral Mandates *

Majority Runoff Systems		Plurality Systems		Majority Congressional Systems	
Electoral System	Mean Mandate (percentages)	Electoral System	Mean Mandate (percentages)	Electoral System	Mean Mandate (percentages)
Guatemala (2)	68.23	Nicaragua (2)	60.86	Chile I (5)	42.26
Ecuador (4)	58.59	Honduras (4)	52.66	Bolivia (3)	29.16
El Salvador (3)	58.54	Costa Rica (11)	52.08		
Peru (2)	57.81	Brazil Ia (2)	52.05		
Chile II (2)	56.59	Colombia (5)	52.03		
Brazil II (1)	53.03	Uruguay (7)	46.82		
Argentina I (1)	49.53	Dom. Republic (4)	43.97		
		Venezuela (8)	43.59		
		Brazil Ib (2)	41.97		
		Paraguay (1)	41.63		
Average	57.47	Average	48.77	Average	35.71

* For the time period for the elections from which these means were derived see Table 4.1. The number of elections upon which each country's mean is based is in parentheses.

Note: The Argentine II Electoral College system has provided the president with a mean mandate of 49.62% of the vote. In 1994 Argentina adopted a modified version of the double complement rule. For more information on the rule see note 5 in Chapter Six. In 1991 Colombia switched to the majority runoff formula. In 1994/95 Nicaragua adopted a new presidential electoral formula. For information on the formula adopted see Appendix C.

Sources: See Appendix A.

Table AF.1 illustrates the ability of many of the plurality systems to provide their executives with majoritarian electoral mandates. Nicaragua, Honduras, Costa Rica, Brazil Ia, and Colombia all have provided an average mandate above the 50% threshold. Even those plurality systems which fail to provide an average mandate greater than 50% of the vote still manage to supply average mandates that are more than 40% in all cases.

The second hypothesized advantage of the majority runoff formula is that it avoids the election of candidates with small mandates, who are often supported by a narrow segment of the population, through the use of the runoff provision. In 13.04% (6 of 46) of the elections which have occurred in the ten plurality national systems during the period of study the president failed to receive over 40% of the vote.[5] In 6.78% (4 of 59) of the plurality formula gubernatorial elections in twenty-one Argentine provinces (1983–95), the governor failed to receive a mandate of over 40% of the vote. While these low mandates are not necessarily incompatible with effective executive rule, they do make it more difficult. Nevertheless, such an event appears to only occur in roughly one of every ten plurality formula elections.

In sum, the only explanation for the use of the majority runoff formula which is justifiable in terms of having a beneficial impact on the functioning of the democratic system is its ability to prevent a candidate from winning with a precariously low percentage of the vote. A weak electoral mandate can lead to presidents whose rule is at least initially considered illegitimate, who are elected into office with the support of only a narrow spectrum of the population, and/ or who will in all likelihood believe that they have a mandate which outstrips their actual level of popular support. However, precariously low mandates occur only rarely in plurality formula systems, and so far have not been associated with the disintegration of democratic government in any. Two potential solutions to this dilemma of low mandates for the plurality systems are: (1) the use of a 40% threshold such as is employed in Costa Rica, although the efficacy of this arrangement in other systems remains untested, and (2) the use of the untried double complement rule (Shugart and Taagepera 1994).

APPENDIX G

An Alternative Statistical Test: OLS Results from Analysis Using the Individual Elections as the Units of Analysis

The results below, with the individual elections as the units of analysis, are relatively similar in regard to their significance to those presented in Chapter Ten based on systems as the units of analysis. The two key variables (Election Timing and Executive Formula) are very similar in terms of impact and significance and Legislative Formula is even futher in conflict with its hypothesized impact, although still insignificant. Additional statistical analysis identified the principal cause of the increased strength and significance of the Effective Magnitude coefficient in this test compared to that in Table 10.3. This cause was the holding constant of the country variable for each election, most importantly that of Ecuador, Nicaragua, and Uruguay. For more on this point see Chapter Eight. Also noteworthy is that none of the individual country dummy variables had a significant impact on legislative multipartism, which suggests that the potential problem of "country-specific" factors skewing the results is not a serious threat to the validity of the findings in Chapter Ten. The two country dummy variables which have the most notable impact are those of Ecuador and Uruguay.

| | Ordinary Least Squares Estimates of Institutional Determinants of Legislative Multipartism | |
Independent Variables	Estimated Coefficient	T-Ratio (53 DF)
Election Timing	0.216	3.100**
Presidential Formula	0.152	1.939*
Effective Magnitude	0.334	2.115*
Legislative Formula	−0.272	−1.348
Country Dummy Variables		
Argentina	−0.092	−0.590
Bolivia	0.194	0.928
Brazil	0.035	0.318
Chile	−0.072	−0.529
Colombia	0.125	0.613
Costa Rica	0.182	0.906
Dominican Republic	0.016	0.146
Ecuador	0.382	1.622
El Salvador	−0.098	−0.382
Guatemala	−0.094	−0.628
Honduras	0.156	0.732
Nicaragua	−0.193	−1.327
Paraguay	0.170	1.220
Peru	−0.102	−0.812
Uruguay	−0.301	−1.550
Venezuela	−0.128	−0.818

R-Square = .749
**$p < .01$ one-tailed test
*$p < .05$ one-tailed test

Note: a Log-Log functional form is employed.

Sources: See Appendix A.

Notes

1. LEGISLATIVE SUPPORT AND PRESIDENTIAL SYSTEMS

1. There are two prominent types of government where presidents play a significant role in governance: presidentialism (i.e., pure presidentialism) and premier-presidentialism (i.e., semi-presidentialism). Presidential systems are where the president is the supreme executive, popularly elected for a fixed term, and appoints and then administers a cabinet. Premier-presidentialism also provides for a popularly elected president for a fixed term, but the president must co-govern with a prime minister and cabinet who perform many governmental functions and at the same time are subject to parliamentary confidence (Duverger 1980; Shugart and Carey 1992). This study focuses almost exclusively on presidential systems, although many of its findings are applicable to premier-presidential systems. All of the Latin American systems are presidential (although with constitutions which grant varying degrees of power to the president). Premier-presidentialism is used in France, several African, Asian, and Eastern European democratizing nations, and enjoys considerable popularity in the European portion of the former Soviet Union.

2. When modifications of the constitutional system are proposed in most presidential systems, they predominantly involve a movement to make the system more premier-presidential and less presidential (Council for the Consolidation of Democracy 1992; González 1991; Kline 1992; Lamounier 1994; Molinelli 1994; Nino 1989). In most instances this modification does not affect the issues that are basic to our argument.

3. The discussion of the utilization of constitutional reform to alter the power relations between constitutional units normally focuses on the distribution of constitutional power between the executive and the legislature and between the national government and sub-national administrative

191

units (i.e., states/provinces and municipalities). The goal of power decentralization can be achieved via this method either by strengthening the constitutional power of the legislature and/or delegating increasing amounts of power to sub-national administrative units. Prospects for the enhancement of the functioning of democratic presidential systems via the route of decentralization are in all likelihood greatest using the latter method of decentralization rather than the former. When the president lacks a legislative majority (or close to it), any prior efforts to strengthen the legislative branch will inevitably exacerbate the problems associated with divided government.

4. Presidential and premier-presidential systems are those where the constitutionally powerful executive is (1) elected by a popular vote, and (2) not dependent on legislative confidence (i.e., in office for a fixed term). Parliamentary regimes are those where the constitutionally powerful executive is (1) selected by the legislature, and (2) dependent on the confidence of the legislature. For a more refined distinction between presidential and parliamentary systems see Linz et al. (1990) and Shugart and Carey (1992). For a critical analysis of the principal parliamentarist critiques of presidentialism, see Niou and Ordeshook (1993).

5. Presidential systems enhance accountability by making the responsibility for governmental policy much easier to assess than is the case in multi-party parliamentary systems. In presidential systems it is easier for voters to know who the rascals are (thereby making it easier for voters to "throw them out" if they so desire), although divided government does often undercut this advantage of presidentialism. Presidential systems enhance identifiability by making the link between the government alternatives presented at the ballot box and the government alternatives possible after the election much stronger. Multi-party parliamentary systems suffer from low identifiability, that is the voter often has a difficult time determining how his or her vote will be translated into the formation of a government (Strom 1990). In presidential systems identifiability is enhanced since it is much easier for voters to identify the various governmental alternatives (i.e., potential presidents).

6. The issue of dual legitimacies can be more serious in the premier-presidential systems, since the legislature in these systems possesses more constitutional power vis-à-vis the president than is the case in presidential systems.

7. For now the term 'legislature' is used to refer to the legislative branch of government, with no distinction made between bicameral and unicameral systems. Later analysis takes this factor into account, but in this section all references to the legislature are directed toward it as a body, or where specifics are involved to the lower or single house.

8. While this has not been particularly the case in the United States beginning with President Richard Nixon's first administration in 1968 (although it was quite common prior to this period), the United States has been able to avoid many, although not all, of the severe problems associated with divided government for a variety of reasons which are discussed in Chapter Two.

9. When a president has a near-majority in the legislature it is generally much less problematic to gain support sufficient to form a cohesive and stable working majority. Two prominent methods utilized by presidents with near-majorities are: (1) secure the support of minor party legislators (who are present in virtually all of the Latin American systems), (2) obtain the support of dissidents from the main opposition party or parties. Both methods are quite feasible and do not require the president to expend many resources or sacrifice much autonomy.

10. The parliamentary alternative was actually much more a premier-presidential than parliamentary model of government. The campaign in Brazil however tended to portray the choice as one between presidential and parliamentary government.

11. Through the combination of a moderate degree of proportional representation and other electoral rules, a system can theoretically both endow the president with a strong legislative contingent as well as provide minor parties with at least some legislative representation. An ideal electoral arrangement for presidential systems is presented in Chapter Eleven.

12. See Linz (1994) for a critique of premier-presidentialism. The recent difficult experiences of premier-presidential systems in Eastern Europe and the former Soviet Union buttress Linz's position regarding the regime type (Rodkey 1995).

13. For example, El Salvador increased the number of deputies elected at the district level from 60 to 64 and added a separate national district with 20 seats for a total of 84 seats.

14. These and other advantages of the plurality formula for the selection of the president are discussed in Chapters Six and Eleven. In Chapter Eleven the potential of an untested, yet promising, formula (the double complement rule) is explored.

15. While the extreme end of concurrency would utilize a single fused ballot for the election of the two branches, this method reduces voter choice as well as requires the voter to participate in both a plurality (or majority runoff) and PR election in the same vote, which is problematic.

16. In a slightly related manner, nonconcurrent elections are likely to exacerbate the problem of dual legitimacies, with the branch elected most recently having the ability to claim the possession of a superior popular mandate (Shugart and Carey 1992).

17. The effective magnitude is first calculated by dividing the number of legislative seats by the number of legislative electoral districts. Where necessary this sum is transformed to take into account the existence of multiple tiers of electoral districts and the use of electoral thresholds/quotas.

18. The degree of correspondence between the electoral laws used to select the executive and members of the legislature is also an important issue (Sabsay 1991). However, since PR with multi-member districts is increasingly the predominant form of legislative selection throughout the world and is used exclusively to select the lower/single house in all of the Latin American systems included in this study, while a single president cannot be directly elected using PR, this discontinuity is in most cases irreparable. It should be noted that the German-style mixed system is still at its core a PR arrangement.

19. The functional form for the relationship between effective magnitude and legislative multipartism is log-log.

20. A moderate effective magnitude would be roughly between five and eight. This issue is discussed in much greater detail in Chapter Eight.

2. Perspectives on Divided Government

1. This includes the United States. The U.S. has been able to avoid some, although most certainly not all, of the more negative consequences of divided government due to a variety of unique traits (e.g., weak political parties, a strong federal system). For further discussion of U.S. exceptionalism see Lijphart (1994b), Riggs (1988), and Shafer (1989).

2. All of the literature reviewed in this chapter was written prior to the Republican landslide in the 1994 midterm election which gave the GOP a majority of the seats in the U.S. House and Senate. This event is likely to cause a reevaluation of the literature on the causes of divided government in the United States.

3. As a result of the 1994 Congressional election the position of those advocating a structural explanation of divided government has been strengthened, while that of those positing a political explanation has been weakened.

4. The Philippines also conforms to this arrangement, although with weaker political parties.

5. For the senates in the bicameral systems, only in Brazil do the electoral laws and level of party control converge to provide a context which approaches that of the United States.

6. The Chile I and Chile II apportionment schemes are also based on administrative boundaries, but allow in theory a greater opportunity for apportionment schemes. However, in Chile I for political reasons only one very modest reapportionment occurred during the entire period under study.

7. The use of a German-style mixed system, if the German case is instructive (Kaase 1984), is not likely to dramatically increase the focus on candidate specific traits.

8. These generalizations tend to hold true for the Latin American senates as well.

9. Where split-ticket voting occurs in Latin America, it tends to be much more the product of the electoral system (presidential elections combined with PR for the legislature) where a subset of citizens vote in the presidential contest (single-member district) for a candidate with a chance at victory and in the legislative contest (multi-member districts) for a smaller party which more closely matches their policy preferences. Even this split-ticket voting however tends to occur less frequently than might be expected (Shugart and Carey 1992).

10. Both Brazil and Colombia come closest to the United States in terms of the incentives to and ability of members of congress to represent district interests over those of the party (see Table 2.1). Nevertheless, important differences remain between these two systems and the U.S. For more information on the behavior of Brazilian deputies, see Ames (1994, 1987).

11. Mainwaring (1993) also makes a point similar to that of this work: when divided government occurs, the size of the president's partisan contingent in the legislature is very important. He suggests that the relatively large size of this contingent in the United States is perhaps an explanation for why divided government has not had more serious consequences in this country. Between 1950 and 1994 in the United States the average partisan contingent in the House of Representatives of presidents who lacked an absolute majority of the seats in this body was 41% of the seats. The comparable figure for the Senate was an average of 44% of the seats. This contrasts with the situation in many Latin American nations (e.g., Chile I, Brazil, Ecuador, Guatemala, Peru) where the president's legislative contingent has at times been below 20% of the seats in a legislative chamber.

12. Illustrative of this major thesis, the consequences of divided government for policymaking in Argentina in general and in the Argentine province of Salta in particular are examined in the next chapter.

3. PRESIDENTIAL LEGISLATIVE SUPPORT AND THE FUNCTIONING OF PRESIDENTIAL SYSTEMS

1. Additional differences such as the normally larger legislative contingent held by minority U.S. presidents as well as the generally weaker level of party discipline in the U.S. (which makes "wooing" easier) have already been noted.

2. The population at risk (i.e., the number of systems which potentially could have been included in each category) for each of the four categories in Table 3.1 is as follows: Parliamentary–Majoritarian 18; Parliamentary–Consensual 19; Presidential–Majoritarian 16; Presidential–Conflictual 16. These populations at risk are rough estimates based on Mainwaring (1993). The important point to gather from them is that the populations at risk for all four of the cells in Table 3.1 are relatively equal.

3. The cutoff point of 45% was chosen to underscore the importance of both majorities and near-majorities. In any event this is only a rough measurement, which does nevertheless correspond quite closely to Lijphart's (1984) categorization of majoritarian and consensual systems. Use of either a 50% or 40% cutoff point would not dramatically change the placement of the systems in Table 3.1. For the six bicameral presidential systems (Costa Rica is unicameral) the average percentage of seats held by the president's party in the legislature was calculated by adding the percentage of seats held by the party in the lower house to the percentage held in the senate and dividing by two. This was done only in the presidential systems since the second chamber's constitutional power in these systems is roughly equal (i.e., symmetrical) to that of the lower chamber. This is not the case in any of the bicameral parliamentary systems where the lower chamber is the dominant chamber (although to varying degrees).

4. As of January 1995 Ecuador, which over the past decade has experienced serious divisive executive-legislative conflict (Martz 1990; Schodt 1989), had the longest streak (fifteen years) of continuous democratic government within a system which has consistently provided the president with a weak legislative contingent (i.e., on average less than 45% of the legislative seats).

5. For related information on the issue of measuring executive-legislative relations see McKay (1994).

6. Only complete presidential years are examined except when the presidential year was terminated prematurely due to either a coup (Peru 1992), the impeachment of the president (Brazil 1992, Guatemala 1993), or the early exit of the president from power (Argentina 1989). In all of these cases a weighted measure was employed for purposes of comparabil-

ity. No presidential year which would have extended into 1994 is examined. Also, presidents who were not popularly elected (directly or indirectly) were excluded from the analysis. For Argentina, the presidential year 1983–84 began after the final 1983 regular LAWR issue had gone to press and thus is included in the analysis.

7. The 21 presidential years excluded were distributed as follows: Dominican Republic (9), Costa Rica (6), Honduras (4), Guatemala (2).

8. An article was considered to be any reporting which had a separate title in bold. The LAWR has two types of articles: (1) relatively long articles, and (2) relatively short articles which are one or two paragraphs in length, the overwhelming majority of which are located on the back page of the report. The difference between the two types of articles is very straightforward in most cases, although in a very few instances on the interior pages some judgment had to be employed in terms of length. In this analysis only the longer type of articles is included. Whether or not an article involved politics as one of its principal themes was defined as follows. For most longer articles the LAWR utilizes headings which include: Politics, Politics and Labor, Politics and War, Politics and Finance, etc. With the minor exceptions listed below, any heading with the term 'politics' in it was included in the analysis. Furthermore, regardless of the heading employed, articles were included if they discussed as their principal or secondary topic the political role of the executive, legislature, courts, political parties, interest groups, military, church, insurgent groups, subnational governments, civic groups, business groups, or labor groups. Articles on purely military conflict were not included if they did not deal with the political aspects of the conflict. As the focus of this study is on domestic politics, no articles on international politics were included unless they involved some type of domestic political issue. In the excluded articles the focus is on the nation as a single actor rather than on intra-national politics. Finally, only articles reporting on a single country are included. Broad comparative articles containing one or two paragraphs on different countries were excluded since the focus is on the coverage of events in the individual countries.

9. An article was considered to have executive-legislative conflict as a principal or secondary subject if it met one of the following criteria (that is in the article one or more of the following themes was present). (1) The legislature defeated/was going to defeat, delayed/was delaying to a serious extent, blocked/was blocking, or modified/was modifying in a significant manner a bill either proposed or strongly supported by the president. (2) The president either was going to veto/vetoed a bill passed by the legislature or made a credible threat of such a veto. (3) The legislature credibly threatened or actually engaged in the censure or impeachment of a govern-

ment minister or the president. (4) The president threatened to dissolve the legislature either constitutionally or unconstitutionally. (5) There was general conflict between the president and the legislature or there were generic problems which the president was having with the legislature (and vice versa). For a summary of ten randomly selected conflict articles see Appendix D.

10. The conflict scores for the 99 presidential years range from a high of 63 to a low of 0 with a mean of 9.75 and a standard deviation of 13.19.

11. In bicameral systems, the chamber where the president has the weakest level of support generally is the principal source of conflict, particularly when the partisan seat distributions in the chambers differ substantially (e.g., Argentina 1983–93, Chile 1989–93).

12. Brazilian President Fernando Collor's political party did not exist when the legislature which sat between 1987 and 1991 was elected.

13. The presidential years included in this study of Alberto Fujimori and Carlos Menem were prior to their respective initiations of constitutional reforms to obtain the right to seek immediate reelection which was previously prohibited by both the Peruvian and Argentine constitutions. Similarly, the presidential years of President Violeta Barrios de Chamorro examined took place prior to the 1995 Nicaraguan constitutional reform which barred immediate reelection. The Dominican Republic president can seek unlimited reelection, although no Dominican presidential years are included in the analysis.

14. In those instances where the president possesses a strong veto power in all areas with the exception of budgetary matters, the system is coded as a strong veto system.

15. Following a 1994 constitutional reform the runoff will henceforth be between the top two candidates.

16. The results of analysis excluding the Bolivia dummy variable are very similar to those presented in Table 3.3. In each of the two regressions, however, the variables measuring presidential legislative support along with legislative censure power were less robust, although still significant at the same levels as in Table 3.3.

17. No multicollinearity problems were detected. Additional analysis was conducted separating the conflict articles by whether or not conflict was the primary theme of the article or a secondary theme. The findings for the two sub-analyses proved to be very similar to each other as well as to the results reported in this chapter.

18. These interviews consisted of semi-structured discussions which focused on the salience of presidential support in the legislature, the political consequences of electoral laws, and the relations between the federal government and the provincial governments. Those interviewed were chosen based on their reputations as having a high degree of knowledge

regarding one or more of the three principal themes. In addition, a concerted effort was made to interview politicians from a broad range of Argentine political parties. Where the ideas or opinions of those interviewed are used in the text, they are duly cited, giving the last name of the interviewee and the year of the interview. Direct quotes come from notes transcribed immediately following the interview.

19. The Peronist party is officially called the *Partido Justicialista*.

20. Salta is located in the northwest of Argentina, bordering five other provinces as well as Bolivia and Paraguay on the north and Chile on the west. It is Argentina's seventh most populous province with 866,153 (1991) inhabitants. Its capital, Salta, is considered to be the economic center of the entire northwest region.

21. I thank Enrique Zuleta Puceiro for his help in identifying Salta as an ideal case for analysis.

22. I am very grateful for the assistance and hospitality provided by Governor Roberto Ulloa and members of the *Partido Renovador de Salta* in facilitating the interviews with key party officials as well as other types of access and information during my stay in Salta.

23. The 75% estimate is from FIEL (1991, 251) while the 90% estimate is from Donat Hirsch (Director of the *Cámara de Comercio de Exterior de Salta*) representing his best estimate and is Senator Pontussi's best estimate based on Senate files (Hirsch 1993; Pontussi 1993).

24. Since the legislature quite literally would not pass most of this type of legislation, Ulloa often had to resort to the issuing of decrees of a state of urgency and necessity, provided for in Article 142 of the Salta Constitution (Ulloa 1993). In general Ulloa would issue a decree which would remain in force until the legislature either approved or rejected it (or after 90 days of legislative inaction it would become law) (Constitución de la Provincia de Salta 1986). Nevertheless, the PJ legislature tended to reject (thereby nullifying) practically all of Ulloa's decrees (Ulloa 1993).

25. Following the 1993 provincial elections Ulloa's legislative position remained mostly unchanged for the second half of his term. Of the 23 Senate seats the PJ held 20 and the PRS 3. Of the 60 Chamber seats the PJ held 37, the PRS 22, and the UCR 1.

4. The Latin American and Argentine Provincial Systems

1. No changes were however made for the Argentine provinces of Corrientes, Mendoza, and Tucuman when they switched from the use of an electoral college to the plurality formula (Mendoza, Tucuman) or majority

runoff formula (Corrientes) to elect their governor. Due to limited variance, the electoral formula used to select the executive is not incorporated as an explanatory variable for most of the analysis involving the Argentine provincial systems. For purposes of comparability all legislature-related aggregate data analysis only includes the 1978–79 and 1984 elections for Ecuador.

2. Results from elections which took place after May 1, 1994 are not included in order to ensure the accuracy of the data used. Furthermore, only elections for governments which held office in the post–World War II era are included.

3. All of the provincial systems which provide the plurality party with a guaranteed majority in the lower/single house elect the members of this chamber from a single province-wide district.

4. All of the 1973 Argentine provincial systems utilize PR to allocate their lower/single house legislative seats.

5. The three nations and five provinces which provide more than one system (with the electoral dimensions which underwent a significant change in parentheses) are: Argentina, two systems (presidential electoral formula, election timing); Brazil, three systems (election timing is the dimension which changed during the life span of Brazil I, while Brazil II differs from Brazil I in terms of the presidential electoral formula); Chile, two systems (election timing, effective magnitude, and to a lesser extent presidential electoral formula); Catamarca, two systems (guaranteed absolute majority in the legislature provided until 1991); San Juan, two systems (electoral formula and effective magnitude for the legislative contest); San Luis, two systems (number of legislative chambers); Santiago del Estero, two systems (election timing); Tucuman, two systems (number of legislative chambers, election timing).

6. Unless otherwise stated all references to presidential systems are equally applicable to the Argentine provincial systems and vice versa.

7. These minor critiques should not detract from the path-breaking work of Shugart and Carey. Their book represents a major contribution and a significant advance in the comparative study of constitutional institutions. The logic behind these classifications is very important and should be kept in mind when examining the salience of presidential majorities and near-majorities in any presidential system.

8. An attempt by the author to measure the president's power and effectiveness based on the type, topic, and quantity of legislative output (e.g., laws, decrees) issued in the systems included in the study was unsuccessful. The method, meaning, and procedure of the legislative process of the systems in this study differs to such an extent that a comparison of factors such as executive decree output, the number of laws passed by congress, and the issue area of these legislative acts supplies results whose only real contribution is to highlight the differences in the legislative

processes in the different nations, and reveals very little about the actual level of constitutional power distribution in the different systems. Even intra-system analysis of different presidencies ran into difficulty.

9. I nonetheless think that the constitution-based methodology used by Shugart and Carey is superior to all other alternatives.

10. Indicators of presidential control currently used in the scholarly literature all have serious flaws. For example, problems with the closed list/open list binary variable employed in Chapter Two include: (1) within closed and open ballot systems there is considerable variation in terms of the control exercised by the president/presidential candidate over list formation, (2) the measure does not work well in bicameral systems where the senate is not elected using a party list, and (3) even within systems the effect of the list format can differ dramatically depending on the party in question.

5. LEGISLATIVE MULTIPARTISM AND PRESIDENTIAL LEGISLATIVE SUPPORT

1. The distinction between two-party dominant and multi-party systems in Latin America and elsewhere is between those systems which have two dominant parties and a varying number of minor parties, and systems whose level of multipartism is anything larger than this. In terms of the legislative multipartism scale, a two-party dominant system is considered to be any system with an average level of multipartism of 2.50 or less, and a multi-party system anything above this. This definition corresponds with those of authors such as Linz (1992), Mainwaring (1991), and Remmer (1991). Also, as Sartori (1976) has pointed out, a distinction should be made among the multi-party systems between those with moderate levels of multipartism and those with extreme levels. Sartori places the dividing line between these two categories at five parties. Of the systems included in this study only three (using the Laakso and Taagepera measure of multipartism) have on average possessed an extreme level of legislative multipartism. They are Brazil II, Chile I, and Ecuador.

2. Linz (1992) has many other critiques of presidentialism which make it in his mind inferior to parliamentarism in practically all instances. This, however, is a separate topic beyond the scope of this work.

3. An additional, non–electoral law oriented explanation for this large number of conservative parties is possibly the *de facto* inability of any party located on the left half of the political spectrum to effectively compete electorally in Guatemala.

4. There is some disagreement over whether or not the Chilean law encourages a system with two dominant coalitions/parties. However, if one assumes consistent preferences among the members of the two current coalitions (see Appendix E) then the maintenance of each coalition is clearly the dominant strategy for the different members of the two coalitions. Hence the rule encourages the maintenance of two dominant coalitions/parties. Put differently, if one coalition broke apart while the other remained cohesive, the members of the former coalition would receive a payoff which is less than that which they would have received had they maintained the coalition. If both coalitions broke apart, the members of the two former coalitions would receive payoffs equal to those which they had received under the coalition. Given this payoff matrix the dominant strategy for the members of the two coalitions is to maintain their respective coalition.

5. In Costa Rica the next largest party, the *Partido Demócrata*, won 35.3% of the presidential vote and 24.4% of the seats in the unicameral legislature. In Venezuela the next largest party, the *Unión Republicana Democrática*, won 34.6% of the presidential vote, 25.6% of the seats in the Chamber, and 21.5% of the seats in the Senate.

6. The legislative contingent inherited by the new DLP president Kim Young Sam consisted of 49.83% of the legislative seats (Banks 1992).

7. Both Nohlen (1984) and Irvine (1984) note that over the past century the international trend in electoral systems has been toward PR with virtually no system switching from the use of PR to the use of single-member plurality districts. Italy's 1993 electoral law reform represents a partial exception, although given the Italian system's negative experience with an extremely proportional version of PR, this partial move away from PR is not surprising. It must finally be stressed that the German-style mixed system is still very much a PR system.

8. With the exception of Chile (particularly Chile II), the issue of district creation in the Latin American systems included in this study is relatively non-controversial since the multi-member districts are based on the nations' sub-national geographic units (i.e., provinces/states/departments). Where disputes exist, they tend to focus more on the number of seats apportioned to these units, with particular emphasis on the minimum number of seats per unit (and hence the degree of overrepresentation of the least populated sub-national units). The employment of single-member plurality districts as part of the German-style mixed system used in Venezuela in 1993 and scheduled to be employed in Bolivia in 1997 makes the issue of gerrymandering of some importance in these nations. However, as the second, party list ballot (like in Germany) is the crucial one for seat allocation purposes, the political consequences of these districts are much less noteworthy than in a SMPD system like the United States.

9. Furthermore, most Latin American nations lack the tradition of judicial neutrality and independence characteristic of the courts in the United States, which often are called upon to resolve disputes and deadlocks over redistricting plans.

10. In the five largest electoral districts the two candidates who received the largest number of votes yet did not win a seat in a single-member plurality contest were each awarded a legislative seat. Of these ten seats, the UCR won 8 and the Peronists 2. In the 1951 election the Peronist Party also won every one of the 30 seats in the Senate.

11. Following the 1954 partial renovation of the Chamber, the PJ possessed 143 of the 155 seats (92.3%) while the UCR held only 12 seats (7.7%).

12. For more on this point see Chapter Two.

13. The equation used for the measure of legislative multipartism (N) is: $N = 1/(1-F)$, where N represents the "effective number of parties," F represents the index of fractionalization, and $F = 1-$ the sum of the squared seat shares of each party. Since a log-log functional form is employed (using logarithms to the base 10), the log values of the legislative multipartism and effective district magnitude measures are used in the quantitative analysis.

14. Electoral multipartism measures the effective number of parties in a system based on the votes won by each party in an election, as opposed to legislative multipartism which is derived from the number of seats won by each party in an election.

15. Brazil Ia, Ib, and II as well as Colombia (only the 1986 and 1990 elections) would have to be excluded if electoral multipartism were used. The widespread use of alliances in Brazil (as well as in Colombia beginning with the 1986 election) where the vote is often recorded for the alliances, not the parties, prevents the use of vote-based data. Finally, the Peruvian 1990 and Venezuelan 1993 elections also would have to be excluded due to a lack of adequate vote data for these contests.

16. Legislative multipartism is also considered to be a good proxy for the number of relevant political parties operating in a nation.

17. This value for San Juan II is the result of the province's switch from the use of single-member plurality districts to a mixed system with two separate electoral district tiers. Slightly less than half of the deputies are chosen from single-member plurality districts with the remainder elected at the province-wide level utilizing the d'Hondt PR formula with a 3% threshold.

18. The correlation between lower house legislative multipartism and the size of the executive's lower house contingent for the 1973 Argentine provincial systems is a similar $-.909$.

6. THE EXECUTIVE ELECTORAL FORMULA

1. In Bolivia and Chile I only the first round represents a true popular vote. Nevertheless the election remains very close to a popular election, even when the president is elected by the congress. First, it is the voters who decide the two (Chile I) or three (Bolivia) candidates who will compete in the runoff. Second, the first round vote provides legislators/congressional parties with very important cues regarding the level and distribution of support for the different candidates which influences their second round vote (this was particularly the case in Chile I). Finally, in Bolivia the fact that the president and members of congress are elected concurrently on a single fused ballot makes the actual vote by Congress similar to an electoral college vote in many respects. Given these factors, the Bolivian and Chilean I majority-congressional electoral formula is considered much more similar to a popular election than to any type of non-popular electoral method.

2. The electoral college method of executive selection used until recently by Argentina II (1983–94) and by three of its provinces (Mendoza 1983–85, Tucuman 1983–90, and Corrientes 1983–93) is distinct from either a plurality or majority system (since a candidate could win with less than 50% of the popular vote, but needed a majority of the seats in the college to be elected). This is particularly the case since in these systems delegates to the electoral college were elected by a system of PR at the electoral district level. This electoral college method is considered to be in its functioning intermediate between the majority and plurality systems. In its tendency to encourage multiple presidential candidates it is, however, most similar to the majority systems.

3. Unlike the case in the pure plurality systems, the Costa Rican constitution specifies that to be elected a candidate must receive more than 40% of the vote. Costa Rica is, however, classified as a plurality system due to the low level of this threshold which makes the system much more similar to plurality than majority systems. It should be noted that in the eleven presidential elections which have occurred under the Costa Rican 1949 constitution, at no time has this 40% threshold not been surpassed.

4. The Peruvian 1979 constitution specified that to be elected in the first round of voting a presidential candidate must receive over 50% of the vote. For the 1980 election a one-time exception lowered this threshold to 36%. For the 1985 and 1990 elections the rule was interpreted to require that to win in the first round, a candidate needed to obtain over 50% of all votes emitted (including null and blank votes). This fact, combined with Peru's mandatory voting requirement which for the most part is

obeyed due to the stiff sanctions for non-voting (which logically will result in a high level of null and blank votes), resulted in an effective threshold for 1985 and 1990 of 58% and 59% respectively (i.e., to win 50% of the total vote, a candidate needed to win 58%/59% of the valid vote in the first round of the two elections). Nevertheless Peru is classified as a majority runoff system. The rules governing the Argentina I majority runoff system included a provision for more than two candidates in the runoff if certain conditions arose (i.e., if the top two finishers in the first round combined did not receive two-thirds or more of the vote, and at the same time there was a third candidate who had received at least 15% of the vote). In the first 1973 presidential election, however, the planned runoff only included two candidates. Furthermore, only the first presidential election which took place in Argentina in 1973 is included, since the second one was much more similar to a runoff than a first round election due to its close temporal proximity to the first election. The second presidential contest took place slightly more than six months after the first election.

5. As part of its 1994 partial constitutional reform Argentina switched from the indirect to direct election of the president. Under this new arrangement if in the first round no candidate receives (1) over 45% of the valid vote, or (2) a minimum of 40% of the valid vote and at the same time is more than 10% ahead of the second place candidate, then a runoff is held between the top two candidates. In 1994 Bolivia maintained its majority congressional formula in modified form, with the runoff henceforth to be between the top two candidates in the first round. In 1994–95 Nicaragua reformed its constitution replacing the plurality formula with a system where if no candidate receives at least 45% of the vote in the first round, a runoff is held between the top two candidates. Colombia switched from the plurality formula to the majority runoff formula to elect the president with the promulgation of the nation's new constitution in 1991. The first use of this new formula occurred in May and June 1994.

6. This is the most important of the direct effects. Other effects, which are partially contingent on this factor, are discussed later in the chapter.

7. This corollary, in a manner slightly different than that proposed by Riker, is partially applicable to the Argentine provincial systems. For an enhanced discussion of this point, see Chapter Four.

8. A Condorcet winner is a candidate/party that can defeat any other candidate/party in a pairwise contest (Riker 1986).

9. The twentieth system is Argentina II which up until 1994 employed an electoral college for the selection of the president. Argentina II is excluded from much of the following analysis.

10. For Ecuador results from the 1988 and 1992 presidential elections

(in addition to those from 1978 and 1984) were used in this portion of the analysis.

11. For the Argentine provincial systems, 1983 (plurality) versus 1973 (majority runoff), the percentages were 80.23% and 73.84% respectively.

12. This analysis of the 22 Argentine provinces includes the 1973 elections and the 1983 elections. Only the 1983 elections (and not the others which occurred in 1987 and 1991) were utilized in this portion of the analysis for two reasons. First, by using only the 1983 elections the important variable of election timing (a majority of the post-1983 provinces utilize partial renovation for their legislature) is held constant. Second, the 1973 and 1983 elections are the first elections following a period of military rule, a factor which is also held constant if only the 1983 elections are employed. One problem associated with the use of the 1973 data is that these elections involved (for all intensive purposes) one dominant party (the *Partido Justicialista*) without any effective opposition (the *Unión Cívica Radical* was quite weak in 1973) and thus the results tended to be quite lopsided. The extent of the Peronist victory at the provincial level is exemplified by the fact that the PJ won 21 of the 22 governorships, coming in a close second to a provincial party in the race for the one it lost. Lopsided results make it difficult to examine the impact of electoral laws in many instances and thus this election is excluded from much of the later analysis. However, in this section the use in 1973 of the majority runoff formula contrasted with the prevalence of the plurality formula in the 1983 elections (in 19 of the 22 systems) justifies the inclusion of the 1973 elections in this portion of the analysis. In fact we should be encouraged by any manner in which the results correspond to the theoretical propositions given the unique circumstances surrounding the 1973 elections.

13. The three electoral college systems are excluded from the statistical portion of this analysis.

14. For purposes of comparability this percentage is based on lower/ single house elections only. The comparable figure for the 23 Argentine provinces for the period 1983–95 is 90%. These percentages like all others used, unless otherwise noted, are based on the system averages, not on the average of the individual elections.

15. The focus of this portion of the analysis is on the majority runoff systems due to the fact that several of the secondary effects of electoral formula occur only in the runoff systems. Thus the majority congressional case of Bolivia, where in both 1985 and 1989 the person elected president was not the one who won the plurality of the vote in the first round, is excluded from this part of the analysis. Also, a one time exception led to the holding of the 1979 Ecuadoran legislative election (for district level legislators) concurrent with the presidential runoff (not the first round as

established in the constitution, where however in 1978 the national level legislators were elected). This 1978/79 election is not included in this portion of the analysis, although Ecuadoran presidential elections from 1984, 1988, and 1992 are. Finally, while not a concurrent system, the 1994 presidential and legislative elections were held concurrently in El Salvador, and thus this election is included in this part of the analysis.

16. The negative impact which the weak nature of their parties (particularly in regard to organizational and candidate matters) had on Fujimori and Serrano's legislative success is demonstrated by a comparison of two separate legislative votes held in each system. In both Guatemala and Peru one legislative race was held at the national level (i.e., with the nation serving as a single district), the national list of deputies in Guatemala and the Senate in Peru. Likewise, in each nation an election was also held at the district level, for the departmental deputies in Guatemala and the Chamber in Peru. Party organization as well as candidate quality/recognition is obviously more important in the latter elections, and it is exactly in these elections where Serrano and Fujimori fared the worst. Serrano's MAS won 24.2% and Fujimori's CAMBIO 90 21.7% of the vote in the national level elections while winning only 14.0% and 16.9% respectively in the district level elections.

17. Of course the degree of party discipline in these "outsider" parties is also likely to be low (to mention one of many possible consequences) given the uncertainty involved in candidate selection, a factor which can worsen the situation of the executive vis-à-vis the legislature. This topic is however beyond the scope of this work.

18. In two of the cases where the first round plurality winner won in the second round, he did so by default due to the withdrawal of the other candidate prior to the runoff election.

19. In the one bicameral system, Peru, Fujimori's Cambio 90 won 22.56% of the seats in the Senate.

20. The Ecuadoran Congress renewed 59 of its members in the 1986 midterm election. Febres Cordero's PSC won 12 of the 59 seats (20.34%) raising the size of his legislative contingent to 19.72% of the seats.

21. Of course, for reasons which are discussed in the next chapter, the use of nonconcurrent elections has even more deleterious results. This critique is an indictment of the problematic nature of the majority formula, not of the concurrent election timing cycle.

22. While Guatemalan president Serrano quickly resigned in the face of international, popular, and military pressure, his attempted *autogolpe* nevertheless represented a severe reversal for the development of the Guatemalan democratic system.

7. The Timing of Executive
and Legislative Elections

1. In all of the nonconcurrent systems in this study, the nonconcurrent elections take place in a separate year from the presidential contest.

2. For the 1989 and 1993 elections the Chilean II system held its presidential and Chamber elections concurrently. In early 1994 Chile established a six-year presidential term. Until further reforms are made (such reforms are likely), Chilean presidential and legislative elections will be nonconcurrent. In 1994 Brazil reduced the president's term length from five to four years. Henceforth, presidential and Chamber, and alternating two-thirds/one-third Senate elections will be concurrent. The near-concurrent case of Colombia is coded as concurrent due to the close temporal proximity of the presidential and legislative contests.

3. This focus is on the timing cycle for the election of the lower/single house only. Among the national bicameral systems, concurrent timing is also the cycle for the election of the majority of the senates. Of the fourteen national bicameral systems in this study, senate elections are held concurrently with those of the president in seven of the systems (Argentina I, Bolivia, Dominican Republic, Paraguay, Peru, Uruguay, Venezuela), nonconcurrently in four (Argentina II, Brazil Ib, Brazil II, Chile I), on a mixed basis in two (Brazil Ia, Chile II), and near-concurrently in Colombia. Following the Brazilian (1994) and Chilean (1993) constitutional reforms, their senates will be elected on a mixed and nonconcurrent basis respectively. Peru abolished its Senate in 1993.

4. In the statistical analysis Ecuador I (1978–84) and Colombia are included with the concurrent systems.

5. This point was discussed in detail in Chapter Two.

6. This statistic excludes the 1994 Salvadoran election where the president and legislature were elected concurrently.

7. This honeymoon election can, however, very well be a counter-midterm for the next president. As stated earlier, a single nonconcurrent election can often affect more than one president. Here the analysis treats the impact of a single nonconcurrent election on two presidents as two separate events. An example of this duality is the 1988 Salvadoran legislative election which was a midterm election for President Duarte and cost him his legislative majority, and at the same time was a counter-honeymoon election for President Cristiani who inherited a legislative majority when he took office in 1989.

8. This refers only to the lower/single house. The most extreme cases of counter-midterm elections lie with the Argentine, Brazilian, and Chilean

Senates. In Brazil Ia, Brazil Ib, Brazil II, Chile I, and Chile II the senators are elected to eight-year terms with a portion renewed every four years. In some of the worst cases (e.g., Chile I) a president for part of his tenure had to contend with a Senate in which close to one-half of its members were elected seven years prior to his election. In fact, the one Chilean Chamber majority did not result in an overall legislative majority due to President Frei's lack of a majority in the Senate. In 1965 Frei's *Partido Demócrata Cristiano* (PDC) won 12 of the 21 (57%) Senate seats being contested. However in 1961 when the other portion of the Senate was elected, the PDC won only 2 of the 25 seats (one of the two PDC Senators resigned to become Frei's ambassador to the U.S.). Thus despite its success in the honeymoon election of 1965, Frei's PDC still only possessed 29% of the seats in the Senate. In this regard the Argentine II system is probably the worst, since senators are elected by the provincial legislatures for nine-year terms (with one-third renewed every three years). A president thus could face during his or her term a situation where two-thirds of the Senate was selected either three or six years prior to his or her assumption of office. The 1994 Argentine constitutional reform reduced the term length of senators to six years.

9. A small number of representatives did however affiliate/had already affiliated with Collor's *Partido Reconstruçao Nacional* (PRN), with this contingent prior to the 1990 legislative elections comprising 6.26% of the seats in the Lower House (Power 1991). However, calculations using the election-based measure employed in this study place Collor as having a contingent of zero at the time of his assumption of office.

10. The 1994 constitutional reform reduced the president's term length to four years.

11. The Ecuadoran legislature renews completely concurrently with each executive election, and thus there exists no inheritance from a previous midterm. The Argentine national system has had only one inheritance. President Carlos Menem inherited a legislative contingent with 48% of the seats in the Lower House when he took office in 1989. Menem's PJ won 53% of the seats in the legislative elections concurrent with his 1989 victory in the presidential contest.

12. During the period 1983–91 all but a few provincial constitutions prevented the governor from seeking immediate reelection. In recent years many governors have engaged in the reform of their province's constitution to permit them to seek immediate reelection.

13. We must be cautious of these findings since they are extrapolated primarily from one set of cases, the Argentine provinces.

14. It should be remembered that in 1991 the national average percentage of the economically able population employed by provincial govern-

ment was 10%. It will be interesting to see if the economic restructuring currently taking place at the provincial level in Argentina (which involves the privatization of many provincial government enterprises as well as layoffs for those concerns which remain under provincial control) reduces the ability of governors to continue avoiding midterm losses.

8. LEGISLATIVE EFFECTIVE MAGNITUDE AND ELECTORAL FORMULA

1. Lijphart is referring to the rules directly governing legislative elections. Much of his research as well as the majority of electoral systems research is based on the study of parliamentary systems. In presidential systems the rules governing the executive selection process have a profound influence on legislative elections and in part diminish the salience of legislature specific rules such as the PR electoral formula and effective magnitude for a system's level of legislative multipartism.

2. In the 1993 Chamber election Venezuela employed its new German style mixed system, maintaining the use of national level compensatory seats. Unlike Germany, however, the vote calculation for the distribution of party list seats was done at the state (i.e., electoral district) level (not the national level as is Germany). Hence, the 1993 effective magnitude was calculated in the same manner as for the previous elections.

3. For Argentina II as well as most of the 1983–95 provinces which employ thresholds, the threshold percentage is not based on the number of valid votes in the electoral district, but rather on the number of registered voters (*padrón electoral*) in the district. Thus the effective threshold is higher than the listed threshold in terms of the percentage of the actual vote needed to qualify to receive a legislative seat. This effective threshold is calculated for each electoral district as the percentage of the actual valid vote needed by a party in order to achieve the threshold percentage of all registered voters. Thus the Argentina II threshold of 3% at the district level has been effectively as high as 5% of the valid vote in districts where voter turnout lagged.

4. From Taagepera and Shugart, a base threshold of one-half of a quota is assumed to be the normal threshold for representation in a system.

5. In the calculation of its district level quota Brazil Ia, Ib, and II include both valid and blank votes.

6. For its 1945 election Brazil Ia used a modified version of the Hare formula which favored the largest party in an electoral district

to a greater extent than the normal LR-Hare method since it allocated all remainder seats to the plurality party in the district. For its 1990 election Nicaragua employed a somewhat similar method, allocating remainder seats in descending order to the parties (one per party) which received the largest number of votes in the district. In 1990 for two of its smaller electoral districts (out of a total of nine districts), with three and two seats respectively, Nicaragua employed the Droop formula. In the statistical analysis Nicaragua is coded with the d'Hondt systems. For its 1993 election Bolivia employed the pure Sainte Lagüe formula (a divisor formula using odd integers). Given this formula's high degree of functional similarity to the LR-Hare formula in terms of its impact on seat allocation, Bolivia is coded as a LR-Hare formula. In two-member districts Colombia employs the Hagenbach-Bischoff formula (which favors minor parties slightly less than the Hare formula). Given the scope of the difference along with the small number of districts in which it applies, this minor deviation from the Hare formula is not particularly relevant. Since 1991 Colombia has used the Hare formula in all districts.

7. With the number of votes cast in a district (v) and the number of seats to be allocated (s), the Hare formula is calculated by (v / s) and the Hagenbach-Bischoff formula ($v / (s + 1)$). The Hagenbach-Bischoff formula is also known as the Droop formula. The two formulas are functionally identical.

8. One method of semi-proportional representation used in Bolivia for Senate elections is a variant of the Sáenz Peña formula. Two-thirds of the seats in a district are allocated to the plurality winner and one-third to the second place finisher.

9. This correlation could not be examined for the Argentine 1973 provincial systems due to a complete lack of variance for the effective magnitude category.

10. For the three Argentine 1983–95 systems which utilize partial renovation where all districts in the province have legislators from both branches being elected (Corrientes, Mendoza, and Tucuman), the levels of multipartism are based on the average of each of the elections, not of the composition following each election. The levels of multipartism for Peru and Venezuela are calculated excluding the members of the senate who as ex-presidents have the status of senators for life (*senadores vitalicios*). The Uruguayan Senate data exclude the Vice-President who is a full voting member of the Senate.

11. Effective magnitude's impact is in all likelihood diminished by the two chambers exerting a strong pull on multipartism toward an equilibrium between the two chambers' effective magnitudes. This link is particularly

strong for the Uruguayan and Venezuelan (prior to 1993) systems where the two chambers are elected from a single shared ballot (in Uruguay the President is also elected on this ballot). This conditioning factor does not take away from the salience of these findings. It does help explain the somewhat weaker than hypothesized impact of effective magnitude on multipartism for these pairwise cases.

12. Evangelical Christians are the most prominent non-Catholic religious group in every nation included in this study.

13. Of course the differences in effective magnitude between the senate and lower house influence the level of multipartism also. As it is impossible to separate the impact of formula from that of magnitude in these two cases, it is easiest to consider the comparison as one of PR with multi-member districts versus plurality with single-member districts.

14. This variable could not be examined for the Argentine provincial systems due to their almost universal use of the d'Hondt formula.

15. The d'Hondt formula favors the largest parties in a district in the seat allocation process to a greater extent than the LR-Hare formula.

16. Costa Rican electoral data were taken from official TSE publications of electoral results. For more details see Appendix A.

17. If in fact the d'Hondt formula actually had been used it is likely that (due to the psychological effect) the political leaders of the Left would have at least in part limited some of the splintering which occurred in this sector out of a desire to succeed electorally. Thus both the drop in Left legislative seats from 2.43 to 1.14 as well as the increase in the size of the presidential legislative contingent from 49.55% to 52.40% probably overstate what the impact of the d'Hondt formula would have been had it been employed. Since party leaders react to the electoral formula employed, their response would have had a "psychological dampening" influence on the mechanical effect which has been identified here.

18. In a quasi-direct manner, although also linked to multipartism, use of the d'Hondt formula in place of the LR-Hare formula aids the executive's legislative party due to the d'Hondt formula's tendency to favor the largest political parties in an election, one of which is almost always the party of the executive.

9. BICAMERAL VERSUS UNICAMERAL LEGISLATURES

1. Prior to the 1979 Sandinista revolution, Nicaragua possessed a bicameral legislature. Of course, at no time during this period did Nicaragua function as a democracy. Peru abolished its Senate in 1993.

2. The absolute majority threshold was employed in place of the near-majority threshold because in this one instance its use was considered to enhance the clarity of the analysis.

3. For the Argentine provincial systems the comparable percentage (excluding those provinces which provide an absolute majority of the legislative seats to the plurality winner in the lower/single house) for the unicameral systems is 54.17% and for the bicameral systems is 59.26%. These figures provide support for the premise that the bivariate comparison of unicameral versus bicameral systems is not a particularly useful way to determine the impact of bicameralism on the president's legislative presence.

4. Two exceptions to this generalization are Paraguay and Peru where the chamber and senate use the same electoral methods except the senate has a higher effective magnitude and hence a higher level of legislative multipartism (this is also the case for Colombia under its 1991 Constitution). Two cases included in this portion of the analysis where a lower house in a bicameral system did not employ PR to allocate the legislative seats are in the Argentine provinces of Salta (1985–87) and San Luis (1987–89). For these elections they used a modified version of the Sáenz Peña formula to allocate seats in their multi-member districts.

5. The Argentine data are only for those systems which do not provide the plurality winner in the lower/single house with an absolute majority of the seats.

6. The Latin American system which most closely approximates this hypothetical case is Uruguay.

7. When discussing the impact of bicameralism on a system's tendency to provide the president with a healthy legislative contingent, the influence which the electoral laws of a system have on the lower/single house of a system is held constant. Since all of the systems have such a chamber, comparison of the lower/single chambers is not germane to this portion of the analysis.

8. The failure of Dominican President Silvestre Antonio Guzmán's *Partido Revolucionario Dominicano* to win a majority in the Senate was also due in part to the quasi-legal manipulation of the electoral results by the *Junta Central Electoral* under pressure from the Dominican Armed Forces which did not want Guzmán to have an overall legislative majority (Barrios 1993).

9. The Argentine II system and the three electoral college provincial systems deviate from the equal representation of the population to a certain extent, although the impact of the popular vote is still quite strong due to the use of PR to distribute the electoral college seats. The malapportionment of the electoral college seats in Argentina II was, however, itself a

source of concern. This electoral college malapportionment was a product of the malapportionment of the Chamber and Senate seats since a district received a number of electoral college seats equal to double its number of Chamber and Senate seats.

10. Since 1991 the Colombian Senate, with the exception of a two-member district for the nation's indigenous population, has been elected from a single nation-wide district.

11. The partial renovation of the Senate also played a contributing role to the small number of Senate seats won. However, even if all twenty-three Senate seats had been renewed, Ulloa's PRS would have at best won between six and eight seats.

10. ELECTORAL LAWS AND LEGISLATIVE MULTIPARTISM

1. An alternative statistical test utilizing all of the individual elections in the different nations as independent cases, while controlling for country, was also conducted. This test yielded results (see Appendix G) which with one partial exception are remarkably similar to those of the test using system averages as the units of analysis.

2. For more detailed information on these operationalizations and the classification of specific systems based on them, please see the respective chapter on the variable in question.

3. A variable measuring the presence or absence of a fused ballot, where a single vote registers support for both the presidential and legislative candidates, was excluded from the analysis after preliminary findings yielded null results.

4. Unlike the case in the pure plurality systems, the Costa Rican constitution specifies that to be elected a candidate must receive more than 40% of the vote. Costa Rica is however classified as a plurality system due to the low level of this threshold which makes the system much more similar to plurality than majority systems.

5. An exception to this rule was made in the case of Colombia where the legislative elections are on average held three months prior to those for the president. The short time period between these two contests leaves the legislative contests deeply influenced by the presidential election. Thus these elections are coded as concurrent.

6. For Ecuador, only the 1978–79 and 1984 elections are included in the analysis. During the period 1978–84 the Ecuadoran system had only

concurrent presidential and legislative elections (in 1979, 57 of the deputies were elected concurrent with the presidential runoff and 12 concurrent with the first round of the presidential contest in 1978 while in 1984 all deputies were elected contemporaneously with the first round of the presidential elections). Beginning in 1986 Ecuador also employed midterm elections for the district level congressional deputies which renders the post-1984 Ecuadoran system un-amenable to the analysis used in this portion of the study.

7. For more information on the calculation of the effective magnitude measure, see Chapter Eight.

8. The equation used for the measure of legislative multipartism (N) is: $N = 1/(1-F)$, where N represents the "effective number of parties," F represents the index of fractionalization, and $F = 1-$ the sum of the squared seat shares of each party. Since a log-log functional form is employed (using logarithms to the base 10), the log values of the legislative multipartism and effective magnitude measures are used in the quantitative analysis.

9. The possibility of the existence of multicollinearity was examined. These tests revealed low R-Squares when each independent variable was regressed on all of the other independent variables, with the highest R-Square being .172 (Lewis-Beck 1980, 58–62).

10. 1.331 is merely the exponential of the estimated coefficient (i.e., Exponential .124 = 1.331). The value 1.331 indicates that the expected value of the multipartism variable, when the presidential formula variable equals one (i.e., a majority system), is 1.331 times the expected value of the multipartism variable when the presidential formula variable equals zero (i.e., a plurality system). Since logarithms to the base 10 are employed, this exponential is given by 10 raised to the power of the estimated coefficient for the formula variable (.124). I am indebted to John E. Jackson for his advice regarding the general use and interpretation of dummy variables in a log-log model.

11. Similar to the case of the presidential formula variable, the value 1.611 indicates that the expected value of the multipartism variable, when the election timing variable equals one (i.e., a nonconcurrent system), is 1.611 times the expected value of the multipartism variable when the election timing variable equals zero (i.e., a concurrent system). This ratio is given by 10 raised to the power of the estimated coefficient for the timing variable (.207).

12. Colombia employs a near-concurrent electoral cycle (with the legislative election held approximately three months prior to the presidential contest) and the LR-Hare formula to allocate seats in the lower house elections. Between the 1990 and 1994 elections there was a slight change in the legislative electoral formula used. In the 1990 and previous elections

districts with two seats utilized the Droop formula in place of the LR-Hare formula. In 1994 the LR-Hare formula was employed in all districts. This change is, however, very minor.

13. The special 1991 legislative elections are not used since they took place separately from the presidential contest and under the new magnitude rules.

14. Prior to the 1994 election, Colombia made a minor change in its effective magnitude (it went from the 4.878 used in the Jones [1994] calculation to 4.794). Taking this change into consideration does not alter the prediction of 2.506.

11. ELECTORAL LAWS AND ELECTORAL ENGINEERING

1. A promising alternative method of presidential election, the double complement rule (DCR), has been proposed by Shugart and Carey (1992) and Shugart and Taagepera (1994). Offered as a compromise between the plurality and majority runoff formulas, the double complement rule has not been utilized in any nation. However, a modified version of the DCR has been adopted by Argentina and was used in its May 1995 presidential election. The DCR has a number of desirable qualities and should be considered in any discussion of electoral law reform. However, due to the lack of any empirical referents, the DCR is not focused on in this study. For example, these empirical referents are needed to determine the impact of the DCR on the level of legislative multipartism in a system and hence its indirect impact on the provision of a presidential legislative majority or near-majority.

2. While it is not discussed more fully here due to the lack of empirical referents, the reader is reminded of the DCR's potential as a method of presidential election.

3. Nevertheless, inherent in the use of a federal arrangement where each geographic administrative unit receives an equal number of senators, regardless of population, exists the potential risk that the malapportionment of senate seats will coincide with a salient partisan cleavage.

4. For example, since 1991 in Argentina President Carlos Menem (PJ) has had an absolute majority of the seats in the Senate and near-majority in the Chamber. Despite this control of the national government, members of his party during the 1991–95 period have held the governorship in only fourteen of the nation's twenty-three provinces. Of the remaining nine provinces, four have governors from the principal opposition party, the UCR, and five others are run by governors from provincial parties which

contest elections only in that specific province. These opposition governors have shown themselves in many instances to be an effective check on presidential power. Furthermore, due to their distinct electoral constituencies, Menem also has been checked at times by PJ governors (e.g., Eduardo Duhalde, PJ Governor of Buenos Aires province) in situations where they were in disagreement with his administration's policies.

APPENDIX F. THE ROBUST PRESIDENTIAL ELECTORAL MANDATE

1. These low mandates can be particularly dangerous when the supporters of the winning candidate represent a distinct, narrow sector of the population.

2. Although it is true that the plurality formula systems most often are dominated by two parties which themselves are composed of diverse societal groups, they nevertheless represent two cohesive and identifiable forces to a much greater extent than the two groupings supporting the candidates in the second round elections of the majority runoff systems. Thus while one could perhaps criticize the artificial nature of the dominant parties in a two-party dominant system due to their tendency towards catchall status, these parties are in no way similar to the ephemeral groupings which line up behind the two opposing candidates in the runoffs of the majority systems.

3. The average size of the mandate provided by the Argentine provincial plurality systems (1983–95) is 48.98% of the vote.

4. Two of the five remaining presidents elected in majority runoff systems avoided a second round runoff due to the withdrawal of the second place finisher (Argentina I 1973, Peru 1985). The remaining three presidents received an absolute majority of the vote in the first round of elections (Chile II 1989, Chile II 1993, El Salvador 1989).

5. The choice of 40% as the threshold for below which a mandate is deemed to be precariously low and above which it is considered acceptable is somewhat arbitrary. However, the use of a 40% threshold in Costa Rica as well as its popularity among academics (e.g., Peirce and Longley 1981) and politicians (e.g., Romero Feris 1993) suggests that it does represent a rough dividing line.

References

Abramowitz, Alan I. 1983. "Partisan Redistricting and the 1982 Congressional Elections." *Journal of Politics* 45:767–70.

Adrogué, Gerardo. 1993. "Los Ex-Militares en Política. Bases Sociales y Cambios de Representación Política." *Desarrollo Económico* 33:425–42.

Albornoz, Alfredo. 1989. *Elecciones Generales: 25 de Noviembre 1984.* Montevideo: Tradinco.

Ames, Barry. 1994. "The Reverse Coattails Effect: Local Party Organization in the 1989 Brazilian Presidential Election." *American Political Science Review* 88:95–117.

Ames, Barry. 1987. *Political Survival in Latin America.* Berkeley: University of California Press.

Archer, Ronald P. 1991. Unpublished Manuscript. Durham: Duke University.

Arriaza Meléndez, Jorge. 1989. *Historia de los Procesos Electorales en El Salvador (1811–1989).* San Salvador: ISEP.

Axelrod, Robert. 1970. *Conflict of Interest: A Theory of Divergent Goals with Applications to Politics.* Chicago: Markham.

Baglini, Raúl. 1993. Interview (02/25, Buenos Aires, Argentina) with Baglini, former President of the *Unión Cívica Radical* bloc in the Chamber and a deputy between 1983 and 1993.

Banco Mundial. 1991. *Argentina: Finanzas de los Gobiernos Provinciales.* Washington, D.C.: Banco Mundial.

Banks, Arthur S., ed. 1992. *Political Handbook of the World: 1992.* Binghamton: CSA Publications.

Barrios, Harald. 1993. "República Dominicana." In Dieter Nohlen, ed., *Enciclopedia Electoral Latinoamericana y Del Caribe.* San José: Instituto Interamericano de Derechos Humanos.

Bendel, Petra. 1993. "Honduras." In Dieter Nohlen, ed., *Enciclopedia Electoral Latinoamericana y Del Caribe.* San José: Instituto Interamericano de Derechos Humanos.

219

Bendel, Petra, and Michael Krennerich. 1993. "Guatemala." In Dieter Nohlen, ed., *Enciclopedia Electoral Latinoamericana y Del Caribe*. San José: Instituto Interamericano de Derechos Humanos.

Blais, André, and R. K. Carty. 1991. "The Psychological Impact of Electoral Laws: Measuring Duverger's Elusive Factor." *British Journal of Political Science* 21:79–93.

Bond, Jon R., and Richard Fleisher. 1990. *The President in the Legislative Arena*. Chicago: University of Chicago Press.

Brady, David W. 1993. "The Causes and Consequences of Divided Government: Toward a New Theory of American Politics?" *American Political Science Review* 87:189–94.

Brady, David W. 1988. *Critical Elections and Congressional Policy Making*. Stanford: Stanford University Press.

Brea Franco, Julio. 1987. *Administración y Elecciones: La Experiencia Dominicana de 1986*. San José, Costa Rica: CAPEL.

Bryce, James. 1921. *Modern Democracies*, volume 2. New York: Macmillan.

Burns, James MacGregor. 1993. "Political Party Reform." In James L. Sundquist, ed., *Beyond Gridlock? Prospects for Governance in the Clinton Years—and After*. Washington, D.C.: Brookings Institution.

Burns, James MacGregor. 1963. *The Deadlock of Democracy: Four-Party Politics in America*. Englewood Cliffs, N.J.: Prentice-Hall.

Campbell, James E. 1991. "The Presidential Surge and Its Midterm Decline in Congressional Elections, 1868–1988." *Journal of Politics* 53:477–87.

Campbell, James E. 1985. "Explaining Presidential Losses in Midterm Congressional Elections." *Journal of Politics* 47:1140–57.

Campillo Pérez, Julio G. 1986. *Historia Electoral Dominicana: 1848–1986*. Santo Domingo: Junta Central Electoral.

Carey, John, and Matthew Soberg Shugart. 1993. "A General Scoring System for Leadership-Rank-and-File Relations in Competitive Political Parties." Paper presented at the annual convention of the American Political Science Association, Washington, D.C.

Caviedes, Cesar. 1979. *The Politics of Chile: A Sociogeographical Assessment*. Boulder: Westview.

Chang Mota, Roberto. 1985. *El Sistema Electoral Venezolano: Su Diseño, Implantación y Resultados*. Caracas: Consejo Supremo Electoral.

Clarín. Buenos Aires, Argentina. Various issues during 1992.

El Comercio. (Lima, Peru). 1990. May 13, p. A6.

Conaghan, Catherine M. 1994. "Loose Parties, Floating Politicians, and Institutional Stress: Presidentialism in Ecuador, 1979–88." In Juan J. Linz and Arturo Valenzuela, eds., *The Failure of Presidential Democracy*. Baltimore: Johns Hopkins University Press.

Congressional Quarterly. 1991. *Guide To Congress*, 4th ed. Washington, D.C.: Congressional Quarterly.

Consejo Supremo Electoral. 1989. *Elecciones 1984*. Managua: CSE.

Consejo Supremo Electoral. 1990. *Elecciones 1988*. Caracas: CSE.

Consejo Supremo Electoral. 1987. *Los Partidos Políticos y Sus Estadísticas Electorales 1946-1984*. 2 vols. Caracas: CSE.

Consejo Supremo Electoral. 1983. *La Estadística Evolutiva de los Partidos Políticos en Venezuela 1958-1979*. Caracas: CSE.

Contreras, Dario. 1986. *Comportamiento Electoral Dominicano: Elecciones Dominicanas 1962-1982*. Santo Domingo: Editora Corripio.

Cope, Orville G., III. 1967. "Politics in Chile: A Study of Political Factions and Parties and Election Procedures." Ph.D. Dissertation, Claremont Graduate School and University Center.

Coppedge, Michael. 1994. "Venezuela: Democratic Despite Presidentialism." In Juan J. Linz and Arturo Valenzuela, eds., *The Failure of Presidential Democracy*. Baltimore: Johns Hopkins University Press.

Coppedge, Michael. 1988. "Strong Parties and Lame Ducks: A Study of the Quality and Stability of Venezuelan Democracy." Ph.D. dissertation, Yale University.

Costa Porto, Wálter. 1989. *O Voto No Brasil: Da Colonia a 5a República*. Brasilia: Gráfica do Senado Nacional.

Council for the Consolidation of Democracy. 1992. "Constitutional Reform in Argentina." In Arend Lijphart, ed., *Parliamentary Versus Presidential Government*. Oxford: Oxford University Press.

Council of Freely Elected Heads of Government. 1990. "Observing Nicaragua's Elections 1989-90" Special Report #1. Atlanta: The Carter Center of Emory University.

Council on Foreign Relations. 1946-1968. *Political Handbook and Atlas of the World* (annual). New York: Simon and Schuster.

Cox, Gary W., and Samuel Kernell. 1991. "Conclusion." In Gary W. Cox and Samuel Kernell, eds., *The Politics of Divided Government*. Boulder: Westview Press.

Cox, Gary W., and Mathew D. McCubbins. 1991. "Divided Control of Fiscal Policy." In Gary W. Cox and Samuel Kernell, eds., *The Politics of Divided Government*. Boulder: Westview Press.

Cruz-Coke, Ricardo. 1984. *Historia Electoral de Chile: 1925-1973*. Santiago de Chile: Editorial Jurídica de Chile.

Cutler, Lloyd N. 1988. "Some Reflections about Divided Government." *Presidential Studies Quarterly* 18:489-90.

D'Agostino, Thomas J. 1992. "The Evolution of an Emerging Political Party System: A Study of Party Politics in the Dominican Republic

1961–90." Paper presented at the International Congress of the Latin American Studies Association, Los Angeles.

Darlić Mardesić, Vjekoslav. 1989. *Estadísticas Electorales de Ecuador 1978–1989*. 2nd, ed. Quito: SENAC/ILDIS.

Davidson, Roger H. 1991. "The Presidency and Three Eras of the Modern Congress." In James A. Thurber, ed., *Divided Democracy: Cooperation and Conflict between the President and Congress*. Washington, D.C.: Congressional Quarterly.

Delgado Fiallos, Anibal. 1986. *Honduras Elecciones (Más allá de la fiesta cívica) 85*. Tegucigalpa: Editorial Guaymuras.

Delgado, Oscar. 1987. *Colombia Elige: Mitaca/84-Perspectivas/86*. Bogota: Pontificia Universitaria Javeriana.

Diamond, Larry, Juan J. Linz, and Seymour Martin Lipset, eds. 1990. *Politics in Developing Nations: Comparing Experiences with Democracy*. Boulder: Lynne Rienner.

Dirección Nacional Electoral, Departamento de Estadísticas. Ministerio del Interior, República Argentina. Department data files.

Durañona y Vedia, Francisco de. 1993. Interview (03/01, Buenos Aires, Argentina) with Duranona, president of the bloc of the *Unión del Centro Democrático* in the Argentine Chamber, president of the Chamber Justice Commission and a deputy since 1987, former federal intervener in the province of Corrientes (1991–92).

Duverger, Maurice. 1986. "Duverger's Law: Forty Years Later." In Bernard Grofman and Arend Lijphart, eds., *Electoral Laws and Their Political Consequences*. New York: Agathon Press.

Duverger, Maurice. 1980. "A New Political System Model: Semi-presidential Government." *European Journal of Political Research* 8:165–87.

Duverger, Maurice. 1954. *Political Parties: Their Organization and Activity in the Modern State*. New York: Wiley.

Economist Intelligence Unit. 1992. *Ecuador Country Report, No. 3*. London.

Economist Intelligence Unit. 1991. *Brazil: Country Profile, 1991–92*. London.

Embajada de Bolivia. 1993. Washington, D.C.

Embajada de Chile. 1994. Washington, D.C.

Embajada de Colombia. 1994. Washington, D.C.

Embajada de Ecuador. 1994. Washington, D.C.

Embajada de Honduras. 1994. Washington, D.C.

Embajada de Venezuela. 1993. Washington, D.C.

Estudios Centroamericanos. 1994. "Las Elecciones Generales del 20 de Marzo 1994." #545–546.

Estudios Centroamericanos. 1991. "Las Elecciones del 10 de Marzo 1991: Sus Resultados y Su Significado." #509.

Estudios Centroamericanos. 1989. "Las Elecciones Presidenciales del 19 de Marzo 1989." #485.

Estudios Centroamericanos. 1988. "Elecciones del Diputados del 20 de Marzo 1988." #473.

Estudios Centroamericanos. 1984. Cómputos Oficiales, 6 de Mayo de 1984: Elecciones para Presidente y Vice-Presidente." #426.

Europa Publications Limited. 1993. *The Europa World Year Book*. London.

Europa Publications Limited. 1963. *The Europa Year Book*. London.

Fabregat, Julio T. 1968. *Elecciones Uruguayas: Plebiscito y Elecciones de 27 de Noviembre 1966*. Montevideo: República Oriental de Uruguay, Cámara de Senadores.

Fabregat, Julio T. 1964. *Elecciones Uruguayas de 25 de Noviembre 1962*. Montevideo: República Oriental de Uruguay, Cámara de Senadores.

Fabregat, Julio T. 1957. *Elecciones Uruguayas de Noviembre de 1950 a Noviembre de 1954*. Montevideo: República Oriental de Uruguay, Cámara de Representantes.

Fabregat, Julio T. 1950. *Elecciones Uruguayas: Febrero de 1925 a Noviembre de 1946*. Montevideo: República Oriental de Uruguay, Poder Legislativo.

Federalist Papers, The. 1961. (Alexander Hamilton, James Madison, and John Jay), Clinton Rossiter, ed. New York: New American Library.

Fernández, Oscar. 1990. "Elecciones Generales en Honduras, 26 de Noviembre 1989." Boletín Electoral Latinoamericano, no. 2.

Ferreira Rubio, Delia, and Matteo Goretti. 1994. "Government by Decree in Argentina (1989–1993)." Paper presented at the International Congress of the Latin American Studies Association, Atlanta.

Fiorina, Morris P. 1992. *Divided Government*. New York: Macmillan.

Fiorina, Morris P. 1977. *Congress: Keystone of the Washington Establishment*. New Haven: Yale University Press.

Foreign Broadcast Information Service—Latin America (FBIS-LAT), 05/03/93, 085.

Fundación de Investigaciones Económicas Latinoamericanas (FIEL). 1991. *El Gasto Público en la Argentina 1960–1988*. Buenos Aires: FIEL.

Gammara, Eduardo. 1995. "Hybrid-Presidentialism and Democratization: The Case of Bolivia." In Scott Mainwaring and Matthew Soberg Shugart, eds., *Presidentialism and Democracy in Latin America*. Forthcoming.

Geddes, Barbara. 1994. *Politician's Dilemma: Building State Capacity in Latin America*. Berkeley: University of California Press.

González, Luis E. 1991. *Political Structures and Democracy in Uruguay*. Notre Dame: University of Notre Dame Press.

González, Luis Eduardo, and Charles Guy Gillespie. 1994. "Presidentialism and Democratic Stability in Uruguay." In Juan J. Linz and

Arturo Valenzuela, eds., *The Failure of Presidential Democracy*. Baltimore: Johns Hopkins University Press.

Guatemala Watch, volume 5 no. 12, 1991. "Special Elections Issue, 1991."

Guimares, Cesár, et al. 1991. *O Novo Congreso e os Rumos da Política*. Rio de Janeiro: Instituto Universitario de Pesquisas de Rio de Janeiro.

Haggard, Stephan, and Robert R. Kaufman. 1994. "The Challenges of Consolidation." *Journal of Democracy* 5 (October):5–16.

Hauriou, André. 1971. "Derecho Constitucional e Instituciones Políticas." In *Biblioteca de la Ciencia Política*. Barcelona: Ariel.

Hernández, Antonio María. 1993. Interview (04/15, Buenos Aires, Argentina) with Hernández, a *Unión Cívica Radical* deputy (1991–) and UCR Vice Presidential candidate for the 1995 presidential election.

Hirsch, Donat. 1993. Interview (04/01, Salta, Argentina) with Hirsch, director of the *Cámara de Comercio Exterior de Salta*.

Hoffman, Mark S., ed. 1992. *The World Almanac and Book of Facts 1993*. New York: Pharos Books.

Honorable Corte Nacional Electoral. 1990. *Elecciones Generales 1985–1989*. La Paz: Honorable Corte Nacional Electoral.

Hughes, Steven W., and Kenneth J. Mijeski. 1973. *Legislative-Executive Policy-Making: The Cases of Chile and Costa Rica*. Beverly Hills: Sage Publications.

Hurtado, Osvaldo. 1989. "Changing Latin American Attitudes: Prerequisite to Institutionalizing Democracy." In Robert A. Pastor, ed., *Democracy in the Americas: Stopping the Pendulum*. New York: Holmes & Meier.

Inforpress Centroamericana (Guatemala City). 1991. *Central America Report*, 11 January.

Inter-Parliamentary Union. 1968–91. *Chronicle of Parliamentary Elections and Developments*. Geneva: International Centre for Parliamentary Documentation.

International Foundation for Electoral Systems. 1992–94. Unpublished foundation country data files.

Irvine, William P. 1984. "Additional Member Electoral Systems." In Arend Lijphart and Bernard Grofman, eds., *Choosing an Electoral System*. New York: Praeger.

Jacobson, Gary C. 1991. "The Persistence of Democratic House Majorities." In Gary W. Cox and Samuel Kernell, eds., *The Politics of Divided Government*. Boulder: Westview Press.

Jacobson, Gary C. 1990. *The Electoral Origins of Divided Government: Competition in U.S. House Elections, 1946–1988*. Boulder: Westview Press.

Jiménez, Edgar C., et al. 1988. *El Salvador: Guerra, Política y Paz (1979–1988)*. San Salvador: CINAS.

Jiménez Peña, Oscar. 1993. Interview (02/25, Buenos Aires, Argentina) with Jiménez Peña, UCeDe legislative assistant and expert on provincial-central relations.

Jones, Mark P. 1995. "A Guide to the Electoral Systems of the Americas." *Electoral Studies* 14:5–21.

Jones, Mark P. 1994. "Electoral Laws and the Survival of Presidential Democracies." Ph.D. dissertation, University of Michigan.

Jones, Mark P. 1993. "The Political Consequences of Electoral Laws in Latin America and the Caribbean." *Electoral Studies* 12:59–75.

Jornal do Brasil. 1989. 22 November.

Junta Central Electoral. 1990. *Elecciones Generales del 16 de Mayo*. Santo Domingo.

Kaase, Max. 1984. "Personalized Proportional Representation: The 'Model' of the West German Electoral System." In Arend Lijphart and Bernard Grofman, eds., *Choosing an Electoral System*. New York: Praeger.

Keesing's Record of World Events. 1992. 38:39234.

Kernell, Samuel. 1977. "Presidential Popularity and Negative Voting: An Alternative Explanation of the Midterm Congressional Decline of the President's Party." *American Political Science Review* 71:44–66.

Kline, Harvey F. 1992. "Conflict Resolution through Constitution Writing: The Colombian Constituent Assembly of 1991." Paper presented at the Annual Meeting of the Southern Political Science Association, Atlanta.

Kornblith, Miriam, and Daniel H. Levine. 1993. *Venezuela: The Life and Times of the Party System*. Kellogg Institute Working Paper no. 197. University of Notre Dame: Kellogg Institute.

Krennerich, Michael. 1993. "Nicaragua." In Dieter Nohlen, ed., *Enciclopedia Electoral Latinoamericana y Del Caribe*. San José: Instituto Interamericano de Derechos Humanos.

Laakso, Markku, and Rein Taagepera. 1979. "Effective Number of Parties: A Measure with Application to West Europe." *Comparative Political Studies* 12:3–27.

Lamounier, Bolívar. 1994. "Brazil: Toward Parliamentarism." In Juan J. Linz and Arturo Valenzuela, eds., *The Failure of Presidential Democracy*. Baltimore: Johns Hopkins University Press.

Lamounier, Bolívar. 1992. "Presidentialism and Parliamentarism in Brazil." in Arend Lijphart, ed., *Parliamentary Versus Presidential Government*. Oxford: Oxford University Press.

Lamounier, Bolívar. 1989. "Brazil: Inequality Against Democracy." In Larry Diamond, Juan J. Linz, and Seymour Martin Lipset, eds., *Democracy in Developing Countries: Latin America*. Boulder: Lynne Rienner.

Lamounier, Bolívar, and Judith Muszynski. 1993. "Brasil." In Dieter Nohlen, ed., *Enciclopedia Electoral Latinoamericana y Del Caribe*. San José: Instituto Interamericano de Derechos Humanos.

Laski, Harold J. 1940. *The American Presidency, an Interpretation*. New York: Harper & Brothers.

Latin American Studies Association. 1990. *Electoral Democracy under International Pressure: The Report of the Latin American Studies Association Commission to Observe the 1990 Nicaraguan Election*. Pittsburgh: LASA.

Latin American Weekly Report. 1984–1993.

Latin American Weekly Report. number 28, July 23, 1992.

Laverada, Antonio. 1991. *A Democracia nas Urnas. O Proceso Partidario Eleitoral Brasileiro*. Rio de Janeiro: Rio Fundo Editora.

Lehoucq, Fabrice Edouard. 1992. "Presidentialism, Electoral Laws and the Development of Political Stability in Costa Rica, 1882–1990." Paper presented at the International Congress of the Latin American Studies Association, Los Angeles.

Lewis-Beck, Michael S. 1980. *Applied Regression: An Introduction*. Newbury Park: Sage Publications.

Libreria Linardi y Risso. 1989. *Uruguay: Elecciones Nacionales, 26 de Noviembre de 1989*. Montevideo.

Light, Paul C. 1991. *The President's Agenda: Domestic Policy Choice from Kennedy to Reagan*. Baltimore: Johns Hopkins University Press.

Light, Paul C. 1982. *The President's Agenda: Domestic Policy Choice from Kennedy to Carter (with notes on Ronald Reagan)*. Baltimore: Johns Hopkins University Press.

Lijphart, Arend. 1994a. *Electoral Systems and Party Systems: A Study of Twenty-Seven Democracies, 1945–1990*. Oxford: Oxford University Press.

Lijphart, Arend. 1994b. "Presidentialism and Majoritarian Democracy: Theoretical Observations." In Juan J. Linz and Arturo Valenzuela, eds., *The Failure of Presidential Democracy*. Baltimore: Johns Hopkins University Press.

Lijphart, Arend. 1990a. "The Southern European Examples of Democratization: Six Lessons for Latin America." *Government and Opposition* 25:68–84.

Lijphart, Arend. 1990b. "The Political Consequences of Electoral Laws, 1945–85." *American Political Science Review* 80:481–96.

Lijphart, Arend. 1985. "The Field of Electoral Systems Research: A Critical Survey." *Electoral Studies* 4:3–14.

Lijphart, Arend. 1984. *Democracies: Patterns of Majoritarian and Consensus Government in Twenty-One Countries*. New Haven: Yale University Press.

Linz, Juan J. 1994. "Presidential or Parliamentary Democracy: Does It Make a Difference?" In Juan J. Linz and Arturo Valenzuela, eds., *The*

Failure of Presidential Democracy. Baltimore: Johns Hopkins University Press.

Linz, Juan J. 1992. "Democracy: Presidential or Parliamentary. Does It Make A Difference? " Unpublished Manuscript.

Linz, Juan J., et al. 1990. *Hacia una Democracia Moderna: La Opción Parlamentaria*. Santiago de Chile: Ediciones Universidad Católica de Chile.

Listín Diario (Santo Domingo). 1990. 12 June, 12.

Mackie, Thomas T., and Richard Rose. 1991. *The International Almanac of Electoral History*, 3rd ed. Washington, D.C.: Congressional Quarterly.

Mainwaring, Scott. 1994. "Brazil: Weak Parties, Feckless Democracy." In Scott Mainwaring and Timothy Scully, eds., *Building Democratic Institutions: Parties and Party Systems in Latin America*. Stanford: Stanford University Press.

Mainwaring, Scott. 1993. "Presidentialism, Multipartism, and Democracy: The Difficult Combination." *Comparative Political Studies* 26:198–228.

Mainwaring, Scott. 1992. "Brazilian Party Underdevelopment in Comparative Perspective." *Political Science Quarterly* 107:677–707.

Mainwaring, Scott. 1991. "Politicians, Parties, and Electoral Systems: Brazil in Comparative Perspective." *Comparative Politics* (October) 24:21–43.

Mainwaring, Scott. 1990. "Presidentialism in Latin America." *Latin American Research Review* 25:157–79.

Mann, Thomas E. 1993. "The Prospects for Ending Gridlock." In James L. Sundquist, ed., *Gridlock?: Prospects for Governance in the Clinton Years—and After*. Washington, D.C.: Brookings Institution.

Marín, Daniel, and Pedro Rotay. 1992. *Atlas Geografico de la República Argentina*. Buenos Aires: Editorial Betina.

Martz, John D. 1990. "Ecuador: The Fragility of Dependent Democracy." In Howard J. Wiarda and Harvey F. Kline, eds., *Latin American Politics and Development*, 3rd ed. Boulder: Westview Press.

Mayer, Lawrence C. 1980. "Party Systems and Cabinet Stability." In Peter H. Merkl, ed., *Western European Party Systems: Trends and Prospects*. New York: The Free Press.

Mayhew, David R. 1991. *Divided We Govern: Party Control, Lawmaking, and Investigations, 1946–1990*. New Haven: Yale University Press.

McClintock, Cynthia. 1994. "Presidents, Messiahs, and Constitutional Breakdowns in Peru." In Juan J. Linz and Arturo Valenzuela, eds., *The Failure of Presidential Democracy*. Baltimore: Johns Hopkins University Press.

McClintock, Cynthia. 1993. "Peru's Fujimori: A Caudillo Derails Democracy." *Current History* (March): 112–19.

McClintock, Cynthia. 1989. "Peru: Precarious Regimes, Authoritarian and

Democratic." In Larry Diamond, Juan J. Linz, and Seymour Martin Lipset, eds., *Democracy in Developing Countries: Latin America.* Boulder: Lynne Rienner.

McCubbins, Mathew D. 1991. "Government on Lay-Away: Federal Spending and Deficits under Divided Party Control." In Gary W. Cox and Samuel Kernell, eds., *The Politics of Divided Government.* Boulder: Westview Press.

McKay, David. 1994. "Review Article: Divided and Governed? Recent Research on Divided Government in the United States." *British Journal of Political Science* 24:517–34.

Medina, Rubens. 1992. Personal Communication with Medina, Chief of the Hispanic Law Division of the United States Library of Congress.

El Mercurio, Edición Internacional (Santiago de Chile). 1993. Week of December 9–15.

Mesa Gisbert, Carlos D. 1990. *Presidentes de Bolivia: Entre Urnas y Fusiles,* 2nd ed. La Paz: Editorial Gisbert.

Mezey, Michael L. 1991. "The Legislature, the Executive, and Public Policy: The Futile Quest for Congressional Power." In James A. Thurber, ed., *Divided Democracy: Cooperation and Conflict between the President and Congress.* Washington, D.C.: Congressional Quarterly.

Mezey, Michael L. 1989. *Congress, the President, and Public Policy.* Boulder: Westview Press.

Mijeski, Kenneth. 1977. "Costa Rica: The Shrinking of the Presidency." In Thomas Dibacco, ed., *Presidential Power in Latin American Politics.* New York: Praeger.

Millett, Richard L. 1993. "Is Latin American Democracy Sustainable?" *North-South Issues* 2 (no. 3): 1–6.

Ministerio del Interior de España. 1992. *Legislación Electoral de Iberoamérica.* Madrid: Ministerio del Interior.

Molinelli, N. Guillermo. 1994. "Como Funcionaría la Nueva Constitución." *La Ley* 24 (March):1–3.

Molinelli, N. Guillermo. 1993. Interview (02/16, Buenos Aires, Argentina) with Molinelli, professor at the Universidad de Buenos Aires.

Molinelli, N. Guillermo. 1992. "Diseños Institucionales, Legislaturas 'Fuertes' y Proceso de Nominación." *Contribuciones* 9:7–20.

Molinelli, N. Guillermo. 1991. *Presidentes y Congresos en Argentina: Mitos y Realidades.* Buenos Aires: Grupo Editor Latinoamericano.

Mustapic, Ana María, and Matteo Goretti. 1992. "Gobierno y Oposición en el Congreso: La Práctica de la Cohabitación Durante La Presidencia de Alfonsín (1983–1989)." *Desarrollo Económico* 32:251–69.

National Democratic Institute for International Affairs. 1991. *The 1990 Elections in Guatemala.* Washington, D.C.

National Republican Institute for International Affairs. 1992. *The 1991 Elections in El Salvador: Report on the Observer Delegation.* Washington, D.C.

Nino, Carlos Santiago. 1992. "Que Reforma Constitucional?" *Propuesta y Control* 21:2307–35.

Nino, Carlos Santiago. 1989. "Transition to Democracy, Corporatism and Constitutional Reform in Latin America." *University of Miami Law Review* 44:129–64.

Niou, Emerson M. S., and Peter C. Ordeshook. 1993. "Notes on Constitutional Change in the ROC." Paper presented at the "Conference on Democratic Institutions in East Asia," Duke University, Durham, North Carolina.

Nohlen, Dieter, Coordinator. 1993a. *Enciclopedia Electoral Latinoamericana y del Caribe.* San José, Costa Rica: Instituto Interamericano de Derechos Humanos.

Nohlen, Dieter. 1993b. "Chile." In Dieter Nohlen, ed., *Enciclopedia Electoral Latinoamericana y Del Caribe.* San José: Instituto Interamericano de Derechos Humanos.

Nohlen, Dieter. 1984. "Two Incompatible Principles of Representation: Issues and Alternatives." In Arend Lijphart and Bernard Grofman, eds., *Choosing an Electoral System.* New York: Praeger.

Oliveira, Luia M. Lippi. 1973. "Partidos Politicos Brasileiros: O Partido Social Democrático." Tese de Mestrado, Instituto Universitario de Pesquisas de Rio de Janeiro.

Ordeshook, Peter C., and Olga V. Shvetsova. 1994. "Ethnic Heterogeneity, District Magnitude, and the Number of Parties." *American Journal of Political Science* 38:100–23.

Osterling, Jorge P. 1989. *Democracy in Colombia: Clientalist Politics and Guerrilla Warfare.* New Brunswick: Transaction Publishers.

Palmer, David Scott. 1990. "Peru: Democratic Interlude, Authoritarian Heritage, Uncertain Future." In Howard J. Wiarda and Harvey F. Kline, eds., *Latin American Politics and Development*, 3rd ed. Boulder: Westview Press.

Palmer, David Scott. 1980. *Peru: The Authoritarian Tradition.* New York: Praeger.

Panizza, Francisco. 1993. "Democracy's Lost Treasure." *Latin American Research Review* 28:251–66.

Paxton, John, ed. 1986. *The Statesman's Year-Book: Statistical and Historical Annual of the World for the Year 1986–1987.* London: Macmillan Press.

Peirce, Neal R., and Lawrence D. Longley. 1981 *The People's President: The Electoral College in American History and the Direct Vote Alternative.* New Haven: Yale University Press.

Peterson, Paul E., and Jay P. Greene. 1994. "Why Executive-Legislative Conflict in the United States Is Dwindling." *British Journal of Political Science* 24:33–55.

Petrocik, John R. 1991. "Divided Government: Is It All in the Campaigns?" In Gary W. Cox and Samuel Kernell, eds., *The Politics of Divided Government.* Boulder: Westview Press.

Pontussi, Ennio Pedro. 1993. Interview (04/01, Salta, Argentina) with Pontussi, president of the Senate bloc of the *Partido Renovador de Salta* in the Salta provincial Senate (1989–93).

Powell, G. Bingham, Jr. 1982. *Contemporary Democracies: Participation, Stability, and Violence.* Cambridge, Mass.: Harvard University Press.

Power, Timothy J. 1991. "Politicized Democracy: Competition, Institutions, and 'Civic Fatigue' in Brazil." *Journal of Interamerican Studies and World Affairs* 33:75–112.

Puig, Alfredo Gustavo. 1993. Interview (04/02, Salta, Argentina) with Puig, Minister of Government of the province of Salta.

Rae, Douglas. 1967. *The Political Consequences of Electoral Laws.* New Haven: Yale University Press.

Ranney, Austin. 1954. *The Doctrine of Responsible Party Government.* Champaign: University of Illinois Press.

Registraduría Nacional del Estado Civil. 1991. *Estadísticas Electorales 1990: Asamblea Constitucional.* Bogota.

Registraduría Nacional del Estado Civil. 1990. *Estadísticas Electorales 1990.* Bogota.

Registraduría Nacional del Estado Civil. 1988. *Historia Electoral Colombiano.* Bogota.

Remmer, Karen L. 1991. "The Political Impact of Economic Crisis in Latin America." *American Political Science Review* 85:777–800.

Rial, Juan. 1986. *Elecciones de 1984: Sistema Electoral y Resultados.* San José: CAPEL.

Riggs, Fred W. 1988. "The Survival of Presidentialism in America: Paraconstitutional Practices." *International Political Science Review* 9:247–78.

Riker, William H. 1986. "Duverger's Law Revisited." In Bernard Grofman and Arend Lijphart, eds., *Electoral Laws and Their Political Consequences.* New York: Agathon Press.

Riker, William H. 1962. *The Theory of Political Coalitions.* New Haven: Yale University Press.

Riquelme, Marcial A. 1994. *Negotiating Democratic Corridors in Paraguay: The Report of the Latin American Studies Association Delegation to Observe the 1993 Paraguayan National Elections.* Pittsburgh: LASA.

Robinson, Donald L. 1989. *Government for the Third American Century.* Boulder: Westview Press.

Rock, David. 1987. *Argentina 1516–1987: From Spanish Colonization to Alfonsín*. Berkeley: University of California Press.

Rodkey, Gretchen. 1995. Unpublished Manuscript. Ann Arbor: University of Michigan.

Rodríguez Sañudo, Hugo. 1993. Interview (03/04, Buenos Aires, Argentina) with Rodríguez Sañudo, Deputy of the *Partido Justicialista* and president of the Chamber Constitutional Affairs Commission.

Romero Feris, José Antonio. 1993. Interview (03/15, Buenos Aires, Argentina) with Romero Feris, Argentine National Senator from the province of Corrientes (1987–95), governor of Corrientes 1983–87, member of the *Pacto Autonomista Liberal*.

Sabsay, Daniel Alberto. 1991. *El Ballotage: Su Aplicación en América Latina y la Gobernabilidad*. San José, Costa Rica: IIDH-CAPEL.

Salta, Constitución de la Provincia de. 1986. Salta: Honorable Convención Constituyente.

Santos, Wanderley Guilherme dos. 1986. *Sessenta e Quatro: Anatomia da Crise*. Sao Paulo: Vértice.

Sanz, Matías. 1993. Interview (04/01, Salta, Argentina) with Sanz, advisor to Salta Vice-Governor Ricardo Gomez Diez.

Sartori, Giovanni. 1976. *Parties and Party Systems: A Framework for Analysis*. New York: Cambridge University Press.

Schodt, David W. 1989. "Ecuador." In Abraham F. Lowenthal, ed., *Latin America and Caribbean Contemporary Record, Volume VI*. New York: Holmes & Meier.

Shafer, Bryan E. 1989. " 'Exceptionalism' in American Politics?" *Political Science and Politics* 22:589–94.

Shugart, Matthew S. 1988. "Duverger's Rule, District Magnitude, and Presidentialism." Ph.D dissertation, University of California, Irvine.

Shugart, Matthew Soberg and John M. Carey. 1992. *Presidents and Assemblies: Constitutional Design and Electoral Dynamics*. Cambridge: Cambridge University Press.

Shugart, Matthew Soberg, and Scott Mainwaring. 1995. "Conclusion: Varieties of Presidentialism." In Scott Mainwaring and Matthew Soberg Shugart, eds., *Presidentialism and Democracy in Latin America*. Forthcoming.

Shugart, Matthew Soberg, and Rein Taagepera. 1994. "Plurality Versus Majority Election of Presidents: A Proposal for a 'Double Complement Rule.' " *Comparative Political Studies* 27:323–48.

Skidmore, Thomas E. 1989. "The Future of Democracy: An Analytical Summary." In Robert A. Pastor, ed., *Democracy in the Americas: Stopping the Pendulum*. New York: Holmes & Meier.

Smith, William C. 1990. "Brazil." In James M. Malloy and Eduardo A.

Gamarra, eds., *Latin America and Caribbean Contemporary Record*, volume VII, 1987–1988. New York: Holmes & Meier.

Sorauf, Frank J. 1968. *Party Politics in America*. Boston: Little, Brown.

Stepan, Alfred, and Cindy Skach. 1993. "Constitutional Frameworks and Democratic Consolidation: Parliamentarism versus Presidentialism." *World Politics* 46 (October): 1–22.

Stewart, Charles H., III. 1991. "Lessons from the Post–Civil War Era." In Gary W. Cox and Samuel Kernell, eds., *The Politics of Divided Government*. Boulder: Westview Press.

Strom, Kaare. 1990. *Minority Government and Minority Rule*. Cambridge: Cambridge University Press.

Suárez, Waldino Cleto. 1982. "El Poder Ejecutivo en América Latina: Su Capacidad Operativa Bajo Regímenes Presidencialistas de Gobierno." *Revista de Estudios Políticos* (Nueva Epoca) 29:109–44.

Sundquist, James L. 1992. *Constitutional Reform and Effective Government*. Washington, D.C.: Brookings Institution.

Sundquist, James L. 1988. "Needed: A Political Theory for the New Era of Coalition Government in the United States." *Political Science Quarterly* 103:613–35.

Taagepera, Rein, and Matthew Soberg Shugart. 1989. *Seats and Votes: The Effects and Determinants of Electoral Systems*. New Haven: Yale University Press.

Taylor, Michael, and V. M. Herman. 1971. "Party Systems and Government Stability." *American Political Science Review* 65:28–37.

Thurber, James A. 1991a. "Representation, Accountability, and Efficiency in Divided Party Control of Government." *Political Science and Polticis* 24:653–57.

Thurber, James A. 1991b. "Introduction: The Roots of Divided Democracy." In James A. Thurber, ed., *Divided Democracy: Cooperation and Conflict between the President and Congress*. Washington, D.C.: Congressional Quarterly.

Torres y Torres Lara, Carlos. 1992. *Los Nudos del Poder: Una Experiencia Peruana de Gobierno*. Lima: Desarrollo y Paz

Tribunal Superior Eleitoral. 1964. *Dados Estatísticos: Eleições Federal, Estadual e Municipal Realizadas no Brasil a partir de 1945*. Volumes 1–4. Rio de Janeiro: Departamento de Imprensa Nacional

Tribunal Supremo de Elecciones. 1994. *Cómputo de Votos y Declatorias de Elección para Presidente, Vicepresidentes, Diputados a la Asamblea Legislativa, Regidores y Síndicos Municipales (1994)*. San José: TSE.

Tribunal Supremo de Elecciones. 1990. *Cómputo de Votos y Declatorias de Elección para Presidente, Vicepresidentes, Diputados a la Asamblea Legislativa, Regidores y Síndicos Municipales (1990)*. San José: TSE.

Tribunal Supremo de Elecciones. 1986. *Cómputo de Votos y Declatorias de Elección para Presidente, Vicepresidentes, Diputados a la Asamblea Legislativa, Regidores y Síndicos Municipales (1986).* San José: TSE.

Tribunal Supremo de Elecciones. 1982. *Cómputo de Votos y Declatorias de Elección para Presidente, Vicepresidentes, Diputados a la Asamblea Legislativa, Regidores y Síndicos Municipales (1982).* San José: TSE.

Tribunal Supremo de Elecciones. 1978. *Elecciones en Cifras: 1953, 1958, 1962, 1966, 1970, 1974, 1978.* San José: TSE.

Tribunal Supremo de Elecciones. 1978. *Cómputo de Votos y Declatorias de Elección para Presidente, Vicepresidentes, Diputados a la Asamblea Legislativa, Regidores y Síndicos Municipales (1978).* San José: TSE.

Tribunal Supremo de Elecciones. 1974. *Cómputo de Votos y Declatorias de Elección para Presidente, Vicepresidentes, Diputados a la Asamblea Legislativa, Regidores y Síndicos Municipales (1974).* San José: TSE.

Tribunal Supremo de Elecciones. 1970. *Cómputo de Votos y Declatorias de Elección para Presidente, Vicepresidentes, Diputados a la Asamblea Legislativa, Regidores y Síndicos Municipales (1970).* San José: TSE.

Tribunal Supremo de Elecciones. 1969. *Cómputo de Votos y Declatorias de Elección para Presidente, Vicepresidentes, Diputados a la Asamblea Legislativa, Regidores y Síndicos Municipales (1953–1966).* San José: TSE.

Tribunal Supremo Electoral. 1985. *Memoria de las Elecciones Celebradas en los Meses de Noviembre y Diciembre de 1985.* Antigua, Guatemala: Libreria Mafcuense.

Tuesta Soldevilla, Fernando. 1993. "Perú." In Dieter Nohlen, ed., *Enciclopedia Electoral Latinoamericana y Del Caribe.* San José: Instituto Interamericano de Derechos Humanos.

Tuesta Soldevilla, Fernando. 1987. *Perú Político en Cifras: Elite Política y Elecciones.* Lima: Fundación Friedrich Ebert.

Ulloa, Roberto. 1993. Interview (04/02, Salta, Argentina) with Ulloa, Governor of Salta and former deputy in the national chamber (1985–89) for the *Partido Renovador de Salta.*

United States House of Representatives, Committee on Foreign Affairs. 1982. *Report on Congressional Study Mission, November 28–30, 1981.* Washington, D.C.: U.S. Government Printing Office.

Urzúa Valenzuela, Germán. 1986. *Historia Política Electoral de Chile 1931–1973.* Santiago de Chile: Tarmacos.

Urzúa Valenzuela, Germán. 1968. *Los Partidos Políticos Chilenos.* Santiago de Chile: Editorial Jurídica de Chile.

Valenzuela, Arturo. 1993. "Latin America: Presidentialism in Crisis." *Journal of Democracy* 4 (October): 3–16.

Valenzuela, Arturo. 1990. "Partidos Políticos y Crisis Presidencial en Chile: Proposición para un Gobierno Parlamentario." In Juan J. Linz et al., *Hacia una Democracia Moderna: La Opción Parlamentaria*. Santiago, Chile: Ediciones Universidad Católica de Chile.

Valenzuela, Arturo. 1978. "The Breakdown of Democratic Regimes: Chile." In Juan J. Linz and Alfred Stepan, eds., *The Breakdown of Democratic Regimes*. Baltimore: Johns Hopkins University Press.

Vanossi, Jorge. 1993. Interview (02/25, Buenos Aires, Argentina) with Vanossi, *Unión Cívica Radical* Deputy (1983–93), President of the Chamber's Constitutional Affairs Committee (1983–87) and Vice President of the Committee (1991–93).

Veliz, Claudio. 1980. *The Centralist Tradition in Latin America*. Princeton: Princeton University Press.

Venturini, Angel R. 1989. *Estadísticas Electorales, 1917–1982*. Montevideo: EBO.

Vittar, Sergio Fabían. 1993. Interview (03/30, Salta, Argentina) with Vittar, pro-secretary of the Senate of the province of Salta and an advisor to Salta Vice-Governor Ricardo Gomez Diez, *Partido Renovador de Salta*.

Wattenberg, Martin P. 1991. "The Republican Presidential Advantage in the Age of Party Disunity." In Gary W. Cox and Samuel Kernell, eds., *The Politics of Divided Government*. Boulder: Westview Press.

Weekly Analysis of Ecuadoran Issues, volume 22, #20, May 25, 1992.

Wiarda, Howard J., ed. 1982. *Politics and Social Change in Latin America: The Distinct Tradition*, 2nd ed. Amherst: University of Massachusetts Press.

Wiarda, Howard J., and Harvey F. Kline, eds. 1990. *Latin American Politics and Development*, 3rd ed. Boulder: Westview Press.

Wilson, Woodrow. 1908. *Constitutional Government in the United States*. New York: Columbia University Press.

Index